Twelth Night, A Winter's Tale, and The Tempest

William Shakespeare

Table of Contents

Table of Contents

Twelth Night, A Winter's Tale, The Tempest

William Shakespeare

Kessinger Publishing reprints thousands of hard–to–find books!

Visit us at http://www.kessinger.net

Twelfth Night

Act 1, Scene 1

DUKE ORSINO's palace.

Enter DUKE ORSINO, CURIO, and other Lords; Musicians attending

DUKE ORSINO

> If music be the food of love, play on;
> Give me excess of it, that, surfeiting,
> The appetite may sicken, and so die.
> That strain again! it had a dying fall:
> O, it came o'er my ear like the sweet sound,
> That breathes upon a bank of violets,
> Stealing and giving odour! Enough; no more:
> 'Tis not so sweet now as it was before.
> O spirit of love! how quick and fresh art thou,
> That, notwithstanding thy capacity
> Receiveth as the sea, nought enters there,
> Of what validity and pitch soe'er,
> But falls into abatement and low price,
> Even in a minute: so full of shapes is fancy
> That it alone is high fantastical.

CURIO

> Will you go hunt, my lord?

DUKE ORSINO

> What, Curio?

CURIO

The hart.

DUKE ORSINO

Why, so I do, the noblest that I have:
O, when mine eyes did see Olivia first,
Methought she purged the air of pestilence!
That instant was I turn'd into a hart;
And my desires, like fell and cruel hounds,
E'er since pursue me.

Enter VALENTINE

How now! what news from her?

VALENTINE

So please my lord, I might not be admitted;
But from her handmaid do return this answer:
The element itself, till seven years' heat,
Shall not behold her face at ample view;
But, like a cloistress, she will veiled walk
And water once a day her chamber round
With eye–offending brine: all this to season
A brother's dead love, which she would keep fresh
And lasting in her sad remembrance.

DUKE ORSINO

O, she that hath a heart of that fine frame
To pay this debt of love but to a brother,

How will she love, when the rich golden shaft
Hath kill'd the flock of all affections else
That live in her; when liver, brain and heart,
These sovereign thrones, are all supplied, and fill'd
Her sweet perfections with one self king!
Away before me to sweet beds of flowers:
Love–thoughts lie rich when canopied with bowers.

Exeunt

Act 1, Scene 2

The sea–coast.

Enter VIOLA, a Captain, and Sailors

VIOLA

What country, friends, is this?

Captain

This is Illyria, lady.

VIOLA

And what should I do in Illyria?
My brother he is in Elysium.
Perchance he is not drown'd: what think you, sailors?

Captain

It is perchance that you yourself were saved.

Twelth Night, A Winter's Tale, The Tempest

VIOLA

O my poor brother! and so perchance may he be.

Captain

True, madam: and, to comfort you with chance,
Assure yourself, after our ship did split,
When you and those poor number saved with you
Hung on our driving boat, I saw your brother,
Most provident in peril, bind himself,
Courage and hope both teaching him the practise,
To a strong mast that lived upon the sea;
Where, like Arion on the dolphin's back,
I saw him hold acquaintance with the waves
So long as I could see.

VIOLA

For saying so, there's gold:
Mine own escape unfoldeth to my hope,
Whereto thy speech serves for authority,
The like of him. Know'st thou this country?

Captain

Ay, madam, well; for I was bred and born
Not three hours' travel from this very place.

VIOLA

Who governs here?

Captain

A noble duke, in nature as in name.

VIOLA

What is the name?

Captain

Orsino.

VIOLA

Orsino! I have heard my father name him:
He was a bachelor then.

Captain

And so is now, or was so very late;
For but a month ago I went from hence,
And then 'twas fresh in murmur,—as, you know,
What great ones do the less will prattle of,—
That he did seek the love of fair Olivia.

VIOLA

What's she?

Captain

A virtuous maid, the daughter of a count
That died some twelvemonth since, then leaving her
In the protection of his son, her brother,

6

Who shortly also died: for whose dear love,
They say, she hath abjured the company
And sight of men.

VIOLA

O that I served that lady
And might not be delivered to the world,
Till I had made mine own occasion mellow,
What my estate is!

Captain

That were hard to compass;
Because she will admit no kind of suit,
No, not the duke's.

VIOLA

There is a fair behavior in thee, captain;
And though that nature with a beauteous wall
Doth oft close in pollution, yet of thee
I will believe thou hast a mind that suits
With this thy fair and outward character.
I prithee, and I'll pay thee bounteously,
Conceal me what I am, and be my aid
For such disguise as haply shall become
The form of my intent. I'll serve this duke:
Thou shall present me as an eunuch to him:
It may be worth thy pains; for I can sing
And speak to him in many sorts of music
That will allow me very worth his service.
What else may hap to time I will commit;

7

Only shape thou thy silence to my wit.

Captain

Be you his eunuch, and your mute I'll be:
When my tongue blabs, then let mine eyes not see.

VIOLA

I thank thee: lead me on.

Exeunt

Act 1, Scene 3

OLIVIA'S house.

Enter SIR TOBY BELCH and MARIA

SIR TOBY BELCH

What a plague means my niece, to take the death of
her brother thus? I am sure care's an enemy to life.

MARIA

By my troth, Sir Toby, you must come in earlier o'
nights: your cousin, my lady, takes great
exceptions to your ill hours.

SIR TOBY BELCH

Why, let her except, before excepted.

MARIA

Ay, but you must confine yourself within the modest
limits of order.

SIR TOBY BELCH

Confine! I'll confine myself no finer than I am:
these clothes are good enough to drink in; and so be
these boots too: an they be not, let them hang
themselves in their own straps.

MARIA

That quaffing and drinking will undo you: I heard
my lady talk of it yesterday; and of a foolish
knight that you brought in one night here to be her wooer.

SIR TOBY BELCH

Who, Sir Andrew Aguecheek?

MARIA

Ay, he.

SIR TOBY BELCH

He's as tall a man as any's in Illyria.

MARIA

What's that to the purpose?

SIR TOBY BELCH

Why, he has three thousand ducats a year.

MARIA

Ay, but he'll have but a year in all these ducats:
he's a very fool and a prodigal.

SIR TOBY BELCH

Fie, that you'll say so! he plays o' the
viol–de–gamboys, and speaks three or four languages
word for word without book, and hath all the good
gifts of nature.

MARIA

He hath indeed, almost natural: for besides that
he's a fool, he's a great quarreller: and but that
he hath the gift of a coward to allay the gust he
hath in quarrelling, 'tis thought among the prudent
he would quickly have the gift of a grave.

SIR TOBY BELCH

By this hand, they are scoundrels and subtractors
that say so of him. Who are they?

MARIA

They that add, moreover, he's drunk nightly in your company.

SIR TOBY BELCH

> With drinking healths to my niece: I'll drink to
> her as long as there is a passage in my throat and
> drink in Illyria: he's a coward and a coystrill
> that will not drink to my niece till his brains turn
> o' the toe like a parish–top. What, wench!
> Castiliano vulgo! for here comes Sir Andrew Agueface.

Enter SIR ANDREW

SIR ANDREW

> Sir Toby Belch! how now, Sir Toby Belch!

SIR TOBY BELCH

> Sweet Sir Andrew!

SIR ANDREW

> Bless you, fair shrew.

MARIA

> And you too, sir.

SIR TOBY BELCH

> Accost, Sir Andrew, accost.

SIR ANDREW

What's that?

SIR TOBY BELCH

My niece's chambermaid.

SIR ANDREW *— Comedy Factor - Put down by a woman (Maria)*

Good Mistress Accost, I desire better acquaintance.

MARIA

My name is Mary, sir.

SIR ANDREW

Good Mistress Mary Accost,—

SIR TOBY BELCH

You mistake, knight; 'accost' is front her, board her, woo her, assail her.

SIR ANDREW

By my troth, I would not undertake her in this company. Is that the meaning of 'accost'?

MARIA

Fare you well, gentlemen.

SIR TOBY BELCH

An thou let part so, Sir Andrew, would thou mightst
never draw sword again.

SIR ANDREW

An you part so, mistress, I would I might never
draw sword again. Fair lady, do you think you have
fools in hand?

MARIA

Sir, I have not you by the hand.

SIR ANDREW

Marry, but you shall have; and here's my hand.

MARIA

Now, sir, 'thought is free:' I pray you, bring
your hand to the buttery–bar and let it drink.

SIR ANDREW

Wherefore, sweet–heart? what's your metaphor?

MARIA

It's dry, sir.

SIR ANDREW

Why, I think so: I am not such an ass but I can
keep my hand dry. But what's your jest?

MARIA

A dry jest, sir.

SIR ANDREW

Are you full of them?

MARIA

Ay, sir, I have them at my fingers' ends: marry,
now I let go your hand, I am barren.

Exit

SIR TOBY BELCH

O knight thou lackest a cup of canary: when did I
see thee so put down?   *Strong wine*

SIR ANDREW

Never in your life, I think; unless you see canary
put me down. Methinks sometimes I have no more wit
than a Christian or an ordinary man has: but I am a
great eater of beef and I believe that does harm to my wit.

SIR TOBY BELCH   — *Loves Maria*

No question.

SIR ANDREW

An I thought that, I'ld forswear it. I'll ride home to–morrow, Sir Toby.

SIR TOBY BELCH

Pourquoi, my dear knight?

SIR ANDREW

What is 'Pourquoi'? do or not do? I would I had bestowed that time in the tongues that I have in fencing, dancing and bear–baiting: O, had I but followed the arts!

SIR TOBY BELCH

Then hadst thou had an excellent head of hair.

SIR ANDREW

Why, would that have mended my hair?

SIR TOBY BELCH

Past question; for thou seest it will not curl by nature.

SIR ANDREW

But it becomes me well enough, does't not?

SIR TOBY BELCH

> Excellent; it hangs like flax on a distaff; and I
> hope to see a housewife take thee between her legs
> and spin it off.

SIR ANDREW

> Faith, I'll home to–morrow, Sir Toby: your niece
> will not be seen; or if she be, it's four to one
> she'll none of me: the count himself here hard by woos her.

SIR TOBY BELCH

> She'll none o' the count: she'll not match above
> her degree, neither in estate, years, nor wit; I
> have heard her swear't. Tut, there's life in't,
> man.

SIR ANDREW

> I'll stay a month longer. I am a fellow o' the
> strangest mind i' the world; I delight in masques
> and revels sometimes altogether.

SIR TOBY BELCH

> Art thou good at these kickshawses, knight?

SIR ANDREW

As any man in Illyria, whatsoever he be, under the
degree of my betters; and yet I will not compare
with an old man.

SIR TOBY BELCH

What is thy excellence in a galliard, knight?

SIR ANDREW

Faith, I can cut a caper.

SIR TOBY BELCH

And I can cut the mutton to't.

SIR ANDREW

And I think I have the back−trick simply as strong
as any man in Illyria.

SIR TOBY BELCH

Wherefore are these things hid? wherefore have
these gifts a curtain before 'em? are they like to
take dust, like Mistress Mall's picture? why dost
thou not go to church in a galliard and come home in
a coranto? My very walk should be a jig; I would not
so much as make water but in a sink−a−pace. What
dost thou mean? Is it a world to hide virtues in?
I did think, by the excellent constitution of thy
leg, it was formed under the star of a galliard.

SIR ANDREW

Ay, 'tis strong, and it does indifferent well in a
flame–coloured stock. Shall we set about some revels?

SIR TOBY BELCH

What shall we do clsc? wcre we not born under Taurus?

SIR ANDREW

Taurus! That's sides and heart.

SIR TOBY BELCH

No, sir; it is legs and thighs. Let me see the
caper; ha! higher: ha, ha! excellent!

Exeunt

Act 1, Scene 4

DUKE ORSINO's palace.

↗ now dressed AS a man

Enter VALENTINE and VIOLA in man's attire

VALENTINE

If the duke continue these favours towards you,
Cesario, you are like to be much advanced: he hath
known you but three days, and already you are no stranger.

18

VIOLA

You either fear his humour or my negligence, that
you call in question the continuance of his love:
is he inconstant, sir, in his favours?

VALENTINE

No, believe me.

VIOLA

I thank you. Here comes the count.

Enter DUKE ORSINO, CURIO, and Attendants

DUKE ORSINO

Who saw Cesario, ho?

VIOLA

On your attendance, my lord; here.

DUKE ORSINO

Stand you a while aloof, Cesario,
Thou know'st no less but all; I have unclasp'd
To thee the book even of my secret soul:
Therefore, good youth, address thy gait unto her;
Be not denied access, stand at her doors,
And tell them, there thy fixed foot shall grow
Till thou have audience.

VIOLA

Sure, my noble lord,
If she be so abandon'd to her sorrow
As it is spoke, she never will admit me.

DUKE ORSINO

Be clamorous and leap all civil bounds
Rather than make unprofited return.

VIOLA

Say I do speak with her, my lord, what then?

DUKE ORSINO

O, then unfold the passion of my love,
Surprise her with discourse of my dear faith:
It shall become thee well to act my woes;
She will attend it better in thy youth
Than in a nuncio's of more grave aspect.

VIOLA

I think not so, my lord.

DUKE ORSINO

Dear lad, believe it;
For they shall yet belie thy happy years,
That say thou art a man: Diana's lip
Is not more smooth and rubious; thy small pipe

Is as the maiden's organ, shrill and sound,
And all is semblative a woman's part.
I know thy constellation is right apt
For this affair. Some four or five attend him;
All, if you will; for I myself am best
When least in company. Prosper well in this,
And thou shalt live as freely as thy lord,
To call his fortunes thine.

VIOLA

I'll do my best
To woo your lady:

Aside

yet, a barful strife!
Whoe'er I woo, myself would be his wife.

Exeunt

Act 1, Scene 5

OLIVIA'S house.

Enter MARIA and Clown

MARIA

Nay, either tell me where thou hast been, or I will
not open my lips so wide as a bristle may enter in
way of thy excuse: my lady will hang thee for thy absence.

21

Clown — The computer of words / artist / using the power of words to bring down Malvolio.

Let her hang me: he that is well hanged in this
world needs to fear no colours.

MARIA

Make that good.

Clown

He shall see none to fear.

MARIA

A good lenten answer: I can tell thee where that
saying was born, of 'I fear no colours.'

Clown

Where, good Mistress Mary?

MARIA

In the wars; and that may you be bold to say in your foolery.

Clown

Well, God give them wisdom that have it; and those
that are fools, let them use their talents.

22

MARIA

> Yet you will be hanged for being so long absent; or,
> to be turned away, is not that as good as a hanging to you?

Clown

> Many a good hanging prevents a bad marriage; and,
> for turning away, let summer bear it out.

MARIA

> You are resolute, then?

Clown

> Not so, neither; but I am resolved on two points.

MARIA

> That if one break, the other will hold; or, if both
> break, your gaskins fall.

Clown

> Apt, in good faith; very apt. Well, go thy way; if
> Sir Toby would leave drinking, thou wert as witty a
> piece of Eve's flesh as any in Illyria.

MARIA

Peace, you rogue, no more o' that. Here comes my
lady: make your excuse wisely, you were best.

Exit

Clown

Wit, an't be thy will, put me into good fooling!
Those wits, that think they have thee, do very oft
prove fools; and I, that am sure I lack thee, may
pass for a wise man: for what says Quinapalus?
'Better a witty fool, than a foolish wit.'

Enter OLIVIA with MALVOLIO

God bless thee, lady!

OLIVIA

Take the fool away.

Clown

Do you not hear, fellows? Take away the lady.

OLIVIA

Go to, you're a dry fool; I'll no more of you:
besides, you grow dishonest.

Clown

Two faults, madonna, that drink and good counsel
will amend: for give the dry fool drink, then is
the fool not dry: bid the dishonest man mend
himself; if he mend, he is no longer dishonest; if
he cannot, let the botcher mend him. Any thing
that's mended is but patched: virtue that
transgresses is but patched with sin; and sin that
amends is but patched with virtue. If that this
simple syllogism will serve, so; if it will not,
what remedy? As there is no true cuckold but
calamity, so beauty's a flower. The lady bade take
away the fool; therefore, I say again, take her away.

OLIVIA

Sir, I bade them take away you.

Clown

Misprision in the highest degree! Lady, cucullus non
facit monachum; that's as much to say as I wear not
motley in my brain. Good madonna, give me leave to
prove you a fool.

(Latin) – known due to the Chruch etc

OLIVIA

Can you do it?

Clown

Dexterously, good madonna.

OLIVIA

25

Twelth Night, A Winter's Tale, The Tempest

Make your proof.

Clown

I must catechise you for it, madonna: good my mouse
of virtue, answer me.

OLIVIA

Well, sir, for want of other idleness, I'll bide your proof.

Clown

Good madonna, why mournest thou?

OLIVIA

Good fool, for my brother's death.

Clown

I think his soul is in hell, madonna.

OLIVIA

I know his soul is in heaven, fool.

Clown

The more fool, madonna, to mourn for your brother's
soul being in heaven. Take away the fool, gentlemen.

OLIVIA

What think you of this fool, Malvolio? doth he not mend?

MALVOLIO

Yes, and shall do till the pangs of death shake him:
infirmity, that decays the wise, doth ever make the
better fool.

Clown

God send you, sir, a speedy infirmity, for the
better increasing your folly! Sir Toby will be
sworn that I am no fox; but he will not pass his
word for two pence that you are no fool.

OLIVIA

How say you to that, Malvolio?

MALVOLIO

I marvel your ladyship takes delight in such a
barren rascal: I saw him put down the other day
with an ordinary fool that has no more brain
than a stone. Look you now, he's out of his guard
already; unless you laugh and minister occasion to
him, he is gagged. I protest, I take these wise men,
that crow so at these set kind of fools, no better
than the fools' zanies.

OLIVIA

Oh, you are sick of self-love, Malvolio, and taste
with a distempered appetite. To be generous,
guiltless and of free disposition, is to take those
things for bird-bolts that you deem cannon-bullets:
there is no slander in an allowed fool, though he do
nothing but rail; nor no railing in a known discreet
man, though he do nothing but reprove.

Clown

Now Mercury endue thee with leasing, for thou
speakest well of fools!

Re-enter MARIA

MARIA

Madam, there is at the gate a young gentleman much
desires to speak with you.

OLIVIA

From the Count Orsino, is it?

MARIA

I know not, madam: 'tis a fair young man, and well attended.

OLIVIA

Who of my people hold him in delay?

MARIA

Sir Toby, madam, your kinsman.

OLIVIA

Fetch him off, I pray you; he speaks nothing but madman: fie on him!

Exit MARIA

Go you, Malvolio: if it be a suit from the count, I am sick, or not at home; what you will, to dismiss it.

Exit MALVOLIO

Now you see, sir, how your fooling grows old, and people dislike it.

Clown

Thou hast spoke for us, madonna, as if thy eldest son should be a fool; whose skull Jove cram with brains! for,—here he comes,—one of thy kin has a most weak pia mater.

Enter SIR TOBY BELCH

OLIVIA

By mine honour, half drunk. What is he at the gate, cousin?

SIR TOBY BELCH

A gentleman.

OLIVIA

A gentleman! what gentleman?

SIR TOBY BELCH

'Tis a gentle man here—a plague o' these
pickle–herring! How now, sot!

Her uncle (cousin? affection term?)

Clown

Good Sir Toby!

OLIVIA

Cousin, cousin, how have you come so early by this lethargy?

SIR TOBY BELCH

Lechery! I defy lechery. There's one at the gate.

OLIVIA

Ay, marry, what is he?

SIR TOBY BELCH

Let him be the devil, an he will, I care not: give
me faith, say I. Well, it's all one.

Exit

30

OLIVIA

What's a drunken man like, fool?

Clown

Like a drowned man, a fool and a mad man: one
draught above heat makes him a fool; the second mads
him; and a third drowns him.

OLIVIA

Go thou and seek the crowner, and let him sit o' my
coz; for he's in the third degree of drink, he's
drowned: go, look after him.

Clown

, tern 4 My Lady

He is but mad yet, madonna; and the fool shall look
to the madman.

Exit

Re—enter MALVOLIO

MALVOLIO

Madam, yond young fellow swears he will speak with
you. I told him you were sick; he takes on him to
understand so much, and therefore comes to speak
with you. I told him you were asleep; he seems to
have a foreknowledge of that too, and therefore
comes to speak with you. What is to be said to him,

31

lady? he's fortified against any denial.

OLIVIA

Tell him he shall not speak with me.

MALVOLIO

Has been told so; and he says, he'll stand at your
door like a sheriff's post, and be the supporter to
a bench, but he'll speak with you.

OLIVIA

What kind o' man is he?

MALVOLIO

Why, of mankind.

OLIVIA

What manner of man?

MALVOLIO

Of very ill manner; he'll speak with you, will you or no.

OLIVIA

Of what personage and years is he?

MALVOLIO

Not yet old enough for a man, nor young enough for
a boy; as a squash is before 'tis a peascod, or a
cooling when 'tis almost an apple: 'tis with him
in standing water, between boy and man. He is very
well–favoured and he speaks very shrewishly; one
would think his mother's milk were scarce out of him.

OLIVIA

Let him approach: call in my gentlewoman.

MALVOLIO

Gentlewoman, my lady calls.

Exit

Re–enter MARIA

OLIVIA

Give me my veil: come, throw it o'er my face.
We'll once more hear Orsino's embassy.

Enter VIOLA, and Attendants

VIOLA

The honourable lady of the house, which is she?

OLIVIA

Speak to me; I shall answer for her.
Your will?

VIOLA

Most radiant, exquisite and unmatchable beauty,—I
pray you, tell me if this be the lady of the house,
for I never saw her: I would be loath to cast away
my speech, for besides that it is excellently well
penned, I have taken great pains to con it. Good
beauties, let me sustain no scorn; I am very
comptible, even to the least sinister usage.

OLIVIA

Whence came you, sir?

VIOLA

I can say little more than I have studied, and that
question's out of my part. Good gentle one, give me
modest assurance if you be the lady of the house,
that I may proceed in my speech.

OLIVIA

Are you a comedian?

VIOLA

No, my profound heart: and yet, by the very fangs
of malice I swear, I am not that I play. Are you
the lady of the house?

Twelfth Night, A Winter's Tale, The Tempest

OLIVIA

If I do not usurp myself, I am.

VIOLA

Most certain, if you are she, you do usurp
yourself; for what is yours to bestow is not yours
to reserve. But this is from my commission: I will
on with my speech in your praise, and then show you
the heart of my message.

OLIVIA

Come to what is important in't: I forgive you the praise.

VIOLA

Alas, I took great pains to study it, and 'tis poetical.

OLIVIA

It is the more like to be feigned: I pray you,
keep it in. I heard you were saucy at my gates,
and allowed your approach rather to wonder at you
than to hear you. If you be not mad, be gone; if
you have reason, be brief: 'tis not that time of
moon with me to make one in so skipping a dialogue.

MARIA

Will you hoist sail, sir? here lies your way.

VIOLA

35

But after Maria has left - Olivia becomes
a huge flirt. - Needing affection. She dosent want
to play her role - wants abit of fun

Twelth Night, A Winter's Tale, The Tempest

No, good swabber; I am to hull here a little
longer. Some mollification for your giant, sweet
lady. Tell me your mind: I am a messenger.

OLIVIA

Sure, you have some hideous matter to deliver, when
the courtesy of it is so fearful. Speak your office.

VIOLA

It alone concerns your ear. I bring no overture of
war, no taxation of homage: I hold the olive in my
hand; my words are as fun of peace as matter.

OLIVIA

Yet you began rudely. What are you? what would you?

VIOLA

The rudeness that hath appeared in me have I
learned from my entertainment. What I am, and what I
would, are as secret as maidenhead; to your ears,
divinity, to any other's, profanation.

OLIVIA

Give us the place alone: we will hear this divinity.

Exeunt MARIA and Attendants

36

Now, sir, what is your text?

VIOLA

Most sweet lady,—

OLIVIA

A comfortable doctrine, and much may be said of it.
Where lies your text?

VIOLA

In Orsino's bosom.

OLIVIA

In his bosom! In what chapter of his bosom?

VIOLA

To answer by the method, in the first of his heart.

OLIVIA

O, I have read it: it is heresy. Have you no more to say?

VIOLA

Good madam, let me see your face.

OLIVIA

Have you any commission from your lord to negotiate
with my face? You are now out of your text: but
we will draw the curtain and show you the picture.
Look you, sir, such a one I was this present: is't
not well done?

Unveiling

VIOLA

Excellently done, if God did all.

OLIVIA

'Tis in grain, sir; 'twill endure wind and weather.

VIOLA

'Tis beauty truly blent, whose red and white
Nature's own sweet and cunning hand laid on:
Lady, you are the cruell'st she alive,
If you will lead these graces to the grave
And leave the world no copy.— children

OLIVIA — Makes fun of herself too.

O, sir, I will not be so hard-hearted; I will give
out divers schedules of my beauty: it shall be
inventoried, and every particle and utensil
labelled to my will: as, item, two lips,
indifferent red; item, two grey eyes, with lids to
them; item, one neck, one chin, and so forth. Were
you sent hither to praise me?

Twelth Night, A Winter's Tale, The Tempest

VIOLA

I see you what you are, you are too proud;
But, if you were the devil, you are fair.
My lord and master loves you: O, such love
Could be but recompensed, though you were crown'd
The nonpareil of beauty!

OLIVIA

How does he love me?

VIOLA

With adorations, fertile tears,
With groans that thunder love, with sighs of fire.

OLIVIA

Your lord does know my mind; I cannot love him:
Yet I suppose him virtuous, know him noble,
Of great estate, of fresh and stainless youth;
In voices well divulged, free, learn'd and valiant;
And in dimension and the shape of nature
A gracious person: but yet I cannot love him;
He might have took his answer long ago.

VIOLA

If I did love you in my master's flame,
With such a suffering, such a deadly life,
In your denial I would find no sense;
I would not understand it.

OLIVIA

Why, what would you?

VIOLA

Make me a willow cabin at your gate,
And call upon my soul within the house;
Write loyal cantons of contemned love
And sing them loud even in the dead of night;
Halloo your name to the reverberate hills
And make the babbling gossip of the air
Cry out 'Olivia!' O, You should not rest
Between the elements of air and earth,
But you should pity me!

OLIVIA

You might do much.
What is your parentage?

VIOLA

Above my fortunes, yet my state is well:
I am a gentleman.

OLIVIA

Get you to your lord;
I cannot love him: let him send no more;
Unless, perchance, you come to me again,

To tell me how he takes it. Fare you well:
I thank you for your pains: spend this for me.

VIOLA

I am no fee'd post, lady; keep your purse:
My master, not myself, lacks recompense.
Love make his heart of flint that you shall love;
And let your fervor, like my master's, be
Placed in contempt! Farewell, fair cruelty.

Exit

OLIVIA - Fancys viola

'What is your parentage?'
'Above my fortunes, yet my state is well:
I am a gentleman.' I'll be sworn thou art;
Thy tongue, thy face, thy limbs, actions and spirit,
Do give thee five−fold blazon: not too fast:
soft, soft!
Unless the master were the man. How now!
Even so quickly may one catch the plague?
Methinks I feel this youth's perfections
With an invisible and subtle stealth
To creep in at mine eyes. Well, let it be.
What ho, Malvolio!

Re−enter MALVOLIO

MALVOLIO

Here, madam, at your service.

41

OLIVIA

Run after that same peevish messenger,
The county's man: he left this ring behind him,
Would I or not: tell him I'll none of it.
Desire him not to flatter with his lord,
Nor hold him up with hopes; I am not for him:
If that the youth will come this way to−morrow,
I'll give him reasons for't: hie thee, Malvolio.

MALVOLIO — Fancys olivia

Madam, I will.

Exit

OLIVIA

I do I know not what, and fear to find
Mine eye too great a flatterer for my mind.
Fate, show thy force: ourselves we do not owe;
What is decreed must be, and be this so.

Exit

Act 2, Scene 1

The sea−coast.

Enter ANTONIO and SEBASTIAN

ANTONIO

Will you stay no longer? nor will you not that I go with you?

SEBASTIAN

> By your patience, no. My stars shine darkly over
> me: the malignancy of my fate might perhaps
> distemper yours; therefore I shall crave of you your
> leave that I may bear my evils alone: it were a bad
> recompense for your love, to lay any of them on you.

SEBASTIAN

> No, sooth, sir: my determinate voyage is mere
> extravagancy. But I perceive in you so excellent a
> touch of modesty, that you will not extort from me
> what I am willing to keep in; therefore it charges
> me in manners the rather to express myself. You
> must know of me then, Antonio, my name is Sebastian,
> which I called Roderigo. My father was that
> Sebastian of Messaline, whom I know you have heard
> of. He left behind him myself and a sister, both
> born in an hour: if the heavens had been pleased,
> would we had so ended! but you, sir, altered that;
> for some hour before you took me from the breach of
> the sea was my sister drowned.

ANTONIO

Possiable love attraction

> Alas the day!

SEBASTIAN

43

A lady, sir, though it was said she much resembled
me, was yet of many accounted beautiful: but,
though I could not with such estimable wonder
overfar believe that, yet thus far I will boldly
publish her; she bore a mind that envy could not but
call fair. She is drowned already, sir, with salt
water, though I seem to drown her remembrance again with more.

ANTONIO

Pardon me, sir, your bad entertainment.

SEBASTIAN

O good Antonio, forgive me your trouble.

ANTONIO

If you will not murder me for my love, let me be
your servant.

SEBASTIAN

If you will not undo what you have done, that is,
kill him whom you have recovered, desire it not.
Fare ye well at once: my bosom is full of kindness,
and I am yet so near the manners of my mother, that
upon the least occasion more mine eyes will tell
tales of me. I am bound to the Count Orsino's court: farewell.

Exit

ANTONIO

The gentleness of all the gods go with thee!
I have many enemies in Orsino's court,
Else would I very shortly see thee there.
But, come what may, I do adore thee so,
That danger shall seem sport, and I will go.

Exit

Act 2, Scene 2

A street.

Enter VIOLA, MALVOLIO following

MALVOLIO

Were not you even now with the Countess Olivia?

VIOLA

Even now, sir; on a moderate pace I have since
arrived but hither.

MALVOLIO

She returns this ring to you, sir: you might have
saved me my pains, to have taken it away yourself.
She adds, moreover, that you should put your lord
into a desperate assurance she will none of him:
and one thing more, that you be never so hardy to
come again in his affairs, unless it be to report
your lord's taking of this. Receive it so.

VIOLA

She took the ring of me: I'll none of it.

MALVOLIO

Come, sir, you peevishly threw it to her; and her
will is, it should be so returned: if it be worth
stooping for, there it lies in your eye; if not, be
it his that finds it.

Exit

VIOLA

I left no ring with her: what means this lady?
Fortune forbid my outside have not charm'd her!
She made good view of me; indeed, so much,
That sure methought her eyes had lost her tongue,
For she did speak in starts distractedly.
She loves me, sure; the cunning of her passion
Invites me in this churlish messenger.
None of my lord's ring! why, he sent her none.
I am the man: if it be so, as 'tis,
Poor lady, she were better love a dream.
Disguise, I see, thou art a wickedness,
Wherein the pregnant enemy does much.
How easy is it for the proper−false
In women's waxen hearts to set their forms!
Alas, our frailty is the cause, not we!
For such as we are made of, such we be.
How will this fadge? my master loves her dearly;
And I, poor monster, fond as much on him;
And she, mistaken, seems to dote on me.
What will become of this? As I am man,

My state is desperate for my master's love;
As I am woman,—now alas the day!—
What thriftless sighs shall poor Olivia breathe!
O time! thou must untangle this, not I;
It is too hard a knot for me to untie!

Exit

Act 2, Scene 3

OLIVIA's house.

Enter SIR TOBY BELCH and SIR ANDREW

SIR TOBY BELCH

> Approach, Sir Andrew: not to be abed after
> midnight is to be up betimes; and 'diluculo
> surgere,' thou know'st,—

SIR ANDREW *— Ment to be woeing Oliva — Not really bothered*

> Nay, my troth, I know not: but I know, to be up
> late is to be up late.

SIR TOBY BELCH

> A false conclusion: I hate it as an unfilled can.
> To be up after midnight and to go to bed then, is
> early: so that to go to bed after midnight is to go
> to bed betimes. Does not our life consist of the
> four elements?

SIR ANDREW

Faith, so they say; but I think it rather consists
of eating and drinking.

SIR TOBY BELCH

Thou'rt a scholar; let us therefore eat and drink.
Marian, I say! a stoup of wine!

Enter Clown

SIR ANDREW

Here comes the fool, i' faith.

Clown

How now, my hearts! did you never see the picture
of 'we three'?

SIR TOBY BELCH

Welcome, ass. Now let's have a catch.

SIR ANDREW

By my troth, the fool has an excellent breast. I
had rather than forty shillings I had such a leg,
and so sweet a breath to sing, as the fool has. In
sooth, thou wast in very gracious fooling last

night, when thou spokest of Pigrogromitus, of the
Vapians passing the equinoctial of Queubus: 'twas
very good, i' faith. I sent thee sixpence for thy
leman: hadst it?

Clown

I did impeticos thy gratillity; for Malvolio's nose
is no whipstock: my lady has a white hand, and the
Myrmidons are no bottle−ale houses.

SIR ANDREW

Excellent! why, this is the best fooling, when all
is done. Now, a song.

SIR TOBY BELCH

Come on; there is sixpence for you: let's have a song.

SIR ANDREW

There's a testril of me too: if one knight give a—

Clown

Would you have a love−song, or a song of good life?

SIR TOBY BELCH

A love−song, a love−song.

SIR ANDREW

Ay, ay: I care not for good life.

Clown

[Sings]
O mistress mine, where are you roaming?
O, stay and hear; your true love's coming,
That can sing both high and low:
Trip no further, pretty sweeting;
Journeys end in lovers meeting,
Every wise man's son doth know.

SIR ANDREW

Excellent good, i' faith.

SIR TOBY BELCH

Good, good.

Clown

[Sings]
What is love? 'tis not hereafter;
Present mirth hath present laughter;
What's to come is still unsure:
In delay there lies no plenty;
Then come kiss me, sweet and twenty,
Youth's a stuff will not endure.

SIR ANDREW

A mellifluous voice, as I am true knight.

3>

SIR TOBY BELCH

A contagious breath.

SIR ANDREW

Very sweet and contagious, i' faith.

SIR TOBY BELCH

To hear by the nose, it is dulcet in contagion.
But shall we make the welkin dance indeed? shall we
rouse the night-owl in a catch that will draw three
souls out of one weaver? shall we do that?

SIR ANDREW

An you love me, let's do't: I am dog at a catch.

Clown

By'r lady, sir, and some dogs will catch well.

SIR ANDREW

Most certain. Let our catch be, 'Thou knave.'

Clown

'Hold thy peace, thou knave,' knight? I shall be
constrained in't to call thee knave, knight.

SIR ANDREW

'Tis not the first time I have constrained one to
call me knave. Begin, fool: it begins 'Hold thy peace.'

Clown

I shall never begin if I hold my peace.

SIR ANDREW

Good, i' faith. Come, begin.

Catch sung

Enter MARIA

MARIA

What a caterwauling do you keep here! If my lady
have not called up her steward Malvolio and bid him
turn you out of doors, never trust me.

SIR TOBY BELCH

My lady's a Cataian, we are politicians, Malvolio's
a Peg–a–Ramsey, and 'Three merry men be we.' Am not
I consanguineous? am I not of her blood?
Tillyvally. Lady!

Sings

'There dwelt a man in Babylon, lady, lady!'

Clown

Beshrew me, the knight's in admirable fooling.

SIR ANDREW

Ay, he does well enough if he be disposed, and so do
I too: he does it with a better grace, but I do it
more natural.

SIR TOBY BELCH

[Sings] 'O, the twelfth day of December,'—

MARIA

For the love o' God, peace!

Enter MALVOLIO

MALVOLIO

My masters, are you mad? or what are you? Have ye
no wit, manners, nor honesty, but to gabble like
tinkers at this time of night? Do ye make an
alehouse of my lady's house, that ye squeak out your
coziers' catches without any mitigation or remorse
of voice? Is there no respect of place, persons, nor
time in you?

SIR TOBY BELCH

We did keep time, sir, in our catches. Sneck up!

MALVOLIO

Sir Toby, I must be round with you. My lady bade me
tell you, that, though she harbours you as her
kinsman, she's nothing allied to your disorders. If
you can separate yourself and your misdemeanors, you
are welcome to the house; if not, an it would please
you to take leave of her, she is very willing to bid
you farewell.

SIR TOBY BELCH

'Farewell, dear heart, since I must needs be gone.'

MARIA

Nay, good Sir Toby.

Clown

'His eyes do show his days are almost done.'

MALVOLIO

Is't even so?

SIR TOBY BELCH

'But I will never die.'

Clown

Sir Toby, there you lie.

MALVOLIO

This is much credit to you.

SIR TOBY BELCH

'Shall I bid him go?'

Clown

'What an if you do?'

SIR TOBY BELCH

'Shall I bid him go, and spare not?'

Clown

'O no, no, no, no, you dare not.'

SIR TOBY BELCH

Out o' tune, sir: ye lie. Art any more than a
steward? Dost thou think, because thou art
virtuous, there shall be no more cakes and ale?

Clown

Yes, by Saint Anne, and ginger shall be hot i' the
mouth too.

SIR TOBY BELCH

Thou'rt i' the right. Go, sir, rub your chain with
crumbs. A stoup of wine, Maria!

MALVOLIO

Mistress Mary, if you prized my lady's favour at any
thing more than contempt, you would not give means
for this uncivil rule: she shall know of it, by this hand.

Exit

MARIA

Go shake your ears.

SIR ANDREW

'Twere as good a deed as to drink when a man's
a–hungry, to challenge him the field, and then to
break promise with him and make a fool of him.

SIR TOBY BELCH

Do't, knight: I'll write thee a challenge: or I'll
deliver thy indignation to him by word of mouth.

MARIA

Sweet Sir Toby, be patient for tonight: since the
youth of the count's was today with thy lady, she is
much out of quiet. For Monsieur Malvolio, let me
alone with him: if I do not gull him into a
nayword, and make him a common recreation, do not
think I have wit enough to lie straight in my bed:
I know I can do it.

SIR TOBY BELCH

Possess us, possess us; tell us something of him.

MARIA

Marry, sir, sometimes he is a kind of puritan.

SIR ANDREW

O, if I thought that I'ld beat him like a dog!

SIR TOBY BELCH

What, for being a puritan? thy exquisite reason,
dear knight?

SIR ANDREW

I have no exquisite reason for't, but I have reason
good enough.

MARIA

The devil a puritan that he is, or any thing
constantly, but a time-pleaser; an affectioned ass,
that cons state without book and utters it by great
swarths: the best persuaded of himself, so
crammed, as he thinks, with excellencies, that it is
his grounds of faith that all that look on him love
him; and on that vice in him will my revenge find
notable cause to work.

SIR TOBY BELCH

What wilt thou do?

MARIA

I will drop in his way some obscure epistles of
love; wherein, by the colour of his beard, the shape
of his leg, the manner of his gait, the expressure
of his eye, forehead, and complexion, he shall find
himself most feelingly personated. I can write very
like my lady your niece: on a forgotten matter we
can hardly make distinction of our hands.

SIR TOBY BELCH

Excellent! I smell a device.

SIR ANDREW

I have't in my nose too.

SIR TOBY BELCH

He shall think, by the letters that thou wilt drop,
that they come from my niece, and that she's in
love with him.

Trying to set up Oliva and Malvolio. Want him to think oliva loves him by a secret letter

MARIA

My purpose is, indeed, a horse of that colour.

SIR ANDREW

And your horse now would make him an ass.

MARIA

Ass, I doubt not.

SIR ANDREW

O, 'twill be admirable!

MARIA

Sport royal, I warrant you: I know my physic will
work with him. I will plant you two, and let the
fool make a third, where he shall find the letter:
observe his construction of it. For this night, to
bed, and dream on the event. Farewell.

Exit

SIR TOBY BELCH

Good night, Penthesilea.

SIR ANDREW

Before me, she's a good wench.

SIR TOBY BELCH

She's a beagle, true–bred, and one that adores me:
what o' that?

SIR ANDREW

I was adored once too.

SIR TOBY BELCH

Let's to bed, knight. Thou hadst need send for
more money.

SIR ANDREW

If I cannot recover your niece, I am a foul way out.

SIR TOBY BELCH

Send for money, knight: if thou hast her not i'
the end, call me cut.

SIR ANDREW

If I do not, never trust me, take it how you will.

SIR TOBY BELCH

Come, come, I'll go burn some sack; 'tis too late
to go to bed now: come, knight; come, knight.

Exeunt

Act 2, Scene 4

DUKE ORSINO's palace.

Enter DUKE ORSINO, VIOLA, CURIO, and others

DUKE ORSINO

Viola ←

Give me some music. Now, good morrow, friends.
Now, good (Cesario) but that piece of song,
That old and antique song we heard last night:
Methought it did relieve my passion much,
More than light airs and recollected terms
Of these most brisk and giddy–paced times:
Come, but one verse.

CURIO

He is not here, so please your lordship that should sing it.

DUKE ORSINO

Who was it?

CURIO

Feste, the jester, my lord; a fool that the lady
Olivia's father took much delight in. He is about the house.

DUKE ORSINO

Seek him out, and play the tune the while.

Exit CURIO. Music plays

Come hither, boy: if ever thou shalt love,
In the sweet pangs of it remember me;
For such as I am all true lovers are,
Unstaid and skittish in all motions else,
Save in the constant image of the creature

That is beloved. How dost thou like this tune?

VIOLA — Fancys Duke Orsino

It gives a very echo to the seat
Where Love is throned.

DUKE ORSINO

Thou dost speak masterly:
My life upon't, young though thou art, thine eye
Hath stay'd upon some favour that it loves:
Hath it not, boy?

VIOLA

A little, by your favour.

DUKE ORSINO

What kind of woman is't?

VIOLA

Of your complexion.

DUKE ORSINO

She is not worth thee, then. What years, i' faith?

VIOLA

About your years, my lord.

62

DUKE ORSINO

> Too old by heaven: let still the woman take
> An elder than herself: so wears she to him,
> So sways she level in her husband's heart:
> For, boy, however we do praise ourselves,
> Our fancies are more giddy and unfirm,
> More longing, wavering, sooner lost and worn,
> Than women's are.

VIOLA

> I think it well, my lord.

DUKE ORSINO

> Then let thy love be younger than thyself,
> Or thy affection cannot hold the bent;
> For women are as roses, whose fair flower
> Being once display'd, doth fall that very hour.

VIOLA

> And so they are: alas, that they are so;
> To die, even when they to perfection grow!

> *Re−enter CURIO and Clown*

DUKE ORSINO

> O, fellow, come, the song we had last night.
> Mark it, Cesario, it is old and plain;
> The spinsters and the knitters in the sun

And the free maids that weave their thread with bones
Do use to chant it: it is silly sooth,
And dallies with the innocence of love,
Like the old age.

Clown

Are you ready, sir?

DUKE ORSINO

Ay; prithee, sing.

Music

SONG.

Clown

Come away, come away, death,
And in sad cypress let me be laid;
Fly away, fly away breath;
I am slain by a fair cruel maid.
My shroud of white, stuck all with yew,
O, prepare it!
My part of death, no one so true
Did share it.
Not a flower, not a flower sweet
On my black coffin let there be strown;
Not a friend, not a friend greet
My poor corpse, where my bones shall be thrown:
A thousand thousand sighs to save,
Lay me, O, where
Sad true lover never find my grave,

To weep there!

DUKE ORSINO

There's for thy pains.

Clown

No pains, sir: I take pleasure in singing, sir.

DUKE ORSINO

I'll pay thy pleasure then.

Clown

Truly, sir, and pleasure will be paid, one time or another.

DUKE ORSINO

Give me now leave to leave thee.

Clown

Now, the melancholy god protect thee; and the
tailor make thy doublet of changeable taffeta, for
thy mind is a very opal. I would have men of such
constancy put to sea, that their business might be
every thing and their intent every where; for that's
it that always makes a good voyage of nothing. Farewell.

Exit

DUKE ORSINO

Let all the rest give place.

CURIO and Attendants retire

Once more, Cesario,
Get thee to yond same sovereign cruelty:
Tell her, my love, more noble than the world,
Prizes not quantity of dirty lands;
The parts that fortune hath bestow'd upon her,
Tell her, I hold as giddily as fortune;
But 'tis that miracle and queen of gems
That nature pranks her in attracts my soul.

VIOLA

But if she cannot love you, sir?

DUKE ORSINO

I cannot be so answer'd.

VIOLA

Sooth, but you must.
Say that some lady, as perhaps there is,
Hath for your love a great a pang of heart
As you have for Olivia: you cannot love her;
You tell her so; must she not then be answer'd?

DUKE ORSINO

There is no woman's sides
Can bide the beating of so strong a passion
As love doth give my heart; no woman's heart

66

So big, to hold so much; they lack retention
Alas, their love may be call'd appetite,
No motion of the liver, but the palate,
That suffer surfeit, cloyment and revolt;
But mine is all as hungry as the sea,
And can digest as much: make no compare
Between that love a woman can bear me
And that I owe Olivia.

VIOLA

Ay, but I know—

DUKE ORSINO

What dost thou know?

VIOLA

Too well what love women to men may owe:
In faith, they are as true of heart as we.
My father had a daughter loved a man,
As it might be, perhaps, were I a woman,
I should your lordship.

DUKE ORSINO

And what's her history?

VIOLA

A blank, my lord. She never told her love,
But let concealment, like a worm i' the bud,
Feed on her damask cheek: she pined in thought,

And with a green and yellow melancholy
She sat like patience on a monument,
Smiling at grief. Was not this love indeed?
We men may say more, swear more: but indeed
Our shows are more than will; for still we prove
Much in our vows, but little in our love.

DUKE ORSINO

But died thy sister of her love, my boy?

VIOLA

I am all the daughters of my father's house,
And all the brothers too: and yet I know not.
Sir, shall I to this lady?

DUKE ORSINO

Ay, that's the theme.
To her in haste; give her this jewel; say,
My love can give no place, bide no denay.

Exeunt

Act 2, Scene 5

OLIVIA's garden.

Enter SIR TOBY BELCH, SIR ANDREW, and FABIAN

SIR TOBY BELCH

Come thy ways, Signior Fabian.

FABIAN

Nay, I'll come: if I lose a scruple of this sport,
let me be boiled to death with melancholy.

SIR TOBY BELCH

Wouldst thou not be glad to have the niggardly
rascally sheep–biter come by some notable shame?

FABIAN

I would exult, man: you know, he brought me out o'
favour with my lady about a bear–baiting here.

SIR TOBY BELCH

To anger him we'll have the bear again; and we will
fool him black and blue: shall we not, Sir Andrew?

SIR ANDREW

An we do not, it is pity of our lives.

SIR TOBY BELCH

Here comes the little villain.

Enter MARIA

How now, my metal of India!

MARIA

Get ye all three into the box−tree: Malvolio's
coming down this walk: he has been yonder i' the
sun practising behavior to his own shadow this half
hour: observe him, for the love of mockery; for I
know this letter will make a contemplative idiot of
him. Close, in the name of jesting! Lie thou there,

Throws down a letter

for here comes the trout that must be caught with tickling.

Exit

Enter MALVOLIO

MALVOLIO — up himself — thinks Maria likes him

'Tis but fortune; all is fortune. Maria once told
me she did affect me: and I have heard herself come
thus near, that, should she fancy, it should be one
of my complexion. Besides, she uses me with a more
exalted respect than any one else that follows her.
What should I think on't?

SIR TOBY BELCH

Here's an overweening rogue!

FABIAN

O, peace! Contemplation makes a rare turkey−cock
of him: how he jets under his advanced plumes!

SIR ANDREW

'Slight, I could so beat the rogue!

SIR TOBY BELCH

Peace, I say.

MALVOLIO

To be Count Malvolio!

SIR TOBY BELCH

Ah, rogue!

SIR ANDREW

Pistol him, pistol him.

SIR TOBY BELCH

Peace, peace!

MALVOLIO

There is example for't; the lady of the Strachy
married the yeoman of the wardrobe.

SIR ANDREW

Fie on him, Jezebel!

FABIAN

O, peace! now he's deeply in: look how
imagination blows him.

MALVOLIO

Having been three months married to her, sitting in
my state,—

SIR TOBY BELCH

O, for a stone–bow, to hit him in the eye!

MALVOLIO

Calling my officers about me, in my branched velvet
gown; having come from a day–bed, where I have left
Olivia sleeping,—

SIR TOBY BELCH

Fire and brimstone!

FABIAN

O, peace, peace!

MALVOLIO

And then to have the humour of state; and after a
demure travel of regard, telling them I know my
place as I would they should do theirs, to for my
kinsman Toby,—

SIR TOBY BELCH

Bolts and shackles!

FABIAN

O peace, peace, peace! now, now.

MALVOLIO

Seven of my people, with an obedient start, make
out for him: I frown the while; and perchance wind
up watch, or play with my—some rich jewel. Toby
approaches; courtesies there to me,—

SIR TOBY BELCH

Shall this fellow live?

FABIAN

Though our silence be drawn from us with cars, yet peace.

MALVOLIO

I extend my hand to him thus, quenching my familiar
smile with an austere regard of control,—

SIR TOBY BELCH

And does not Toby take you a blow o' the lips then?

MALVOLIO

Saying, 'Cousin Toby, my fortunes having cast me on
your niece give me this prerogative of speech,'—

SIR TOBY BELCH

What, what?

MALVOLIO

'You must amend your drunkenness.'

SIR TOBY BELCH

Out, scab!

FABIAN

Nay, patience, or we break the sinews of our plot.

MALVOLIO

'Besides, you waste the treasure of your time with
a foolish knight,'—

SIR ANDREW

That's me, I warrant you.

MALVOLIO

'One Sir Andrew,'—

SIR ANDREW

I knew 'twas I; for many do call me fool.

MALVOLIO

What employment have we here?

Taking up the letter

FABIAN

Now is the woodcock near the gin.

SIR TOBY BELCH

O, peace! and the spirit of humour intimate reading
aloud to him!

MALVOLIO

By my life, this is my lady's hand these be her
very C's, her U's and her T's and thus makes she her
great P's. It is, in contempt of question, her hand.

SIR ANDREW

Her C's, her U's and her T's: why that?

MALVOLIO

[Reads] 'To the unknown beloved, this, and my good
wishes:'—her very phrases! By your leave, wax.
Soft! and the impressure her Lucrece, with which she
uses to seal: 'tis my lady. To whom should this be?

FABIAN

This wins him, liver and all.

MALVOLIO

[Reads]
Jove knows I love: But who?
Lips, do not move;
No man must know.
'No man must know.' What follows? the numbers
altered! 'No man must know:' if this should be
thee, Malvolio?

SIR TOBY BELCH

Marry, hang thee, brock!

MALVOLIO

[Reads]
I may command where I adore;
But silence, like a Lucrece knife,
With bloodless stroke my heart doth gore:
M, O, A, I, doth sway my life.

FABIAN

A fustian riddle!

SIR TOBY BELCH

Excellent wench, say I.

MALVOLIO

'M, O, A, I, doth sway my life.' Nay, but first, let
me see, let me see, let me see.

FABIAN

What dish o' poison has she dressed him!

SIR TOBY BELCH

And with what wing the staniel cheques at it!

MALVOLIO

'I may command where I adore.' Why, she may command
me: I serve her; she is my lady. Why, this is
evident to any formal capacity; there is no
obstruction in this: and the end,—what should
that alphabetical position portend? If I could make
that resemble something in me,—Softly! M, O, A,
I,—

SIR TOBY BELCH

O, ay, make up that: he is now at a cold scent.

FABIAN

Sowter will cry upon't for all this, though it be as
rank as a fox.

MALVOLIO

M,—Malvolio; M,—why, that begins my name.

FABIAN

Did not I say he would work it out? the cur is
excellent at faults.

MALVOLIO

M,—but then there is no consonancy in the sequel;
that suffers under probation A should follow but O does.

FABIAN

And O shall end, I hope.

SIR TOBY BELCH

Ay, or I'll cudgel him, and make him cry O!

MALVOLIO

And then I comes behind.

FABIAN

Ay, an you had any eye behind you, you might see
more detraction at your heels than fortunes before

you.

MALVOLIO

M, O, A, I; this simulation is not as the former: and
yet, to crush this a little, it would bow to me, for
every one of these letters are in my name. Soft!
here follows prose.

Reads

'If this fall into thy hand, revolve. In my stars I
am above thee; but be not afraid of greatness: some
are born great, some achieve greatness, and some
have greatness thrust upon 'em. Thy Fates open
their hands; let thy blood and spirit embrace them;
and, to inure thyself to what thou art like to be,
cast thy humble slough and appear fresh. Be
opposite with a kinsman, surly with servants; let
thy tongue tang arguments of state; put thyself into
the trick of singularity: she thus advises thee
that sighs for thee. Remember who commended thy
yellow stockings, and wished to see thee ever
cross−gartered: I say, remember. Go to, thou art
made, if thou desirest to be so; if not, let me see
thee a steward still, the fellow of servants, and
not worthy to touch Fortune's fingers. Farewell.
She that would alter services with thee,
THE FORTUNATE−UNHAPPY.'
Daylight and champaign discovers not more: this is
open. I will be proud, I will read politic authors,
I will baffle Sir Toby, I will wash off gross
acquaintance, I will be point−devise the very man.
I do not now fool myself, to let imagination jade

me; for every reason excites to this, that my lady
loves me. She did commend my yellow stockings of
late, she did praise my leg being cross–gartered;
and in this she manifests herself to my love, and
with a kind of injunction drives me to these habits
of her liking. I thank my stars I am happy. I will
be strange, stout, in yellow stockings, and
cross–gartered, even with the swiftness of putting
on. Jove and my stars be praised! Here is yet a
postscript.

Reads

'Thou canst not choose but know who I am. If thou
entertainest my love, let it appear in thy smiling;
thy smiles become thee well; therefore in my
presence still smile, dear my sweet, I prithee.'
Jove, I thank thee: I will smile; I will do
everything that thou wilt have me.

Exit

FABIAN

I will not give my part of this sport for a pension
of thousands to be paid from the Sophy.

SIR TOBY BELCH

I could marry this wench for this device.

SIR ANDREW

So could I too.

SIR TOBY BELCH

And ask no other dowry with her but such another jest.

SIR ANDREW

Nor I neither.

FABIAN

Here comes my noble gull–catcher.

Re–enter MARIA

SIR TOBY BELCH

Wilt thou set thy foot o' my neck?

SIR ANDREW

Or o' mine either?

SIR TOBY BELCH

Shall I play my freedom at traytrip, and become thy
bond–slave?

SIR ANDREW

I' faith, or I either?

SIR TOBY BELCH

Why, thou hast put him in such a dream, that when
the image of it leaves him he must run mad.

MARIA

Nay, but say true; does it work upon him?

SIR TOBY BELCH

Like aqua–vitae with a midwife.

MARIA

If you will then see the fruits of the sport, mark
his first approach before my lady: he will come to
her in yellow stockings, and 'tis a colour she
abhors, and cross–gartered, a fashion she detests;
and he will smile upon her, which will now be so
unsuitable to her disposition, being addicted to a
melancholy as she is, that it cannot but turn him
into a notable contempt. If you will see it, follow
me.

SIR TOBY BELCH

To the gates of Tartar, thou most excellent devil of wit!

SIR ANDREW

I'll make one too.

Exeunt

Act 3, Scene 1

OLIVIA's garden.

Enter VIOLA, and Clown with a tabour

VIOLA

Save thee, friend, and thy music: dost thou live by
thy tabour?

Clown

No, sir, I live by the church.

VIOLA

Art thou a churchman?

Clown

No such matter, sir: I do live by the church; for
I do live at my house, and my house doth stand by
the church.

VIOLA

So thou mayst say, the king lies by a beggar, if a
beggar dwell near him; or, the church stands by thy
tabour, if thy tabour stand by the church.

Clown

You have said, sir. To see this age! A sentence is
but a cheveril glove to a good wit: how quickly the
wrong side may be turned outward!

VIOLA

Nay, that's certain; they that dally nicely with
words may quickly make them wanton.

Clown

I would, therefore, my sister had had no name, sir.

VIOLA

Why, man?

Clown

Why, sir, her name's a word; and to dally with that
word might make my sister wanton. But indeed words
are very rascals since bonds disgraced them.

VIOLA

Thy reason, man?

Clown

Troth, sir, I can yield you none without words; and
words are grown so false, I am loath to prove
reason with them.

VIOLA

I warrant thou art a merry fellow and carest for nothing.

Clown

Not so, sir, I do care for something; but in my
conscience, sir, I do not care for you: if that be
to care for nothing, sir, I would it would make you invisible.

VIOLA

Art not thou the Lady Olivia's fool?

Clown

No, indeed, sir; the Lady Olivia has no folly: she
will keep no fool, sir, till she be married; and
fools are as like husbands as pilchards are to
herrings; the husband's the bigger: I am indeed not
her fool, but her corrupter of words.

VIOLA

I saw thee late at the Count Orsino's.

Clown

Foolery, sir, does walk about the orb like the sun,
it shines every where. I would be sorry, sir, but
the fool should be as oft with your master as with
my mistress: I think I saw your wisdom there.

VIOLA

Nay, an thou pass upon me, I'll no more with thee.
Hold, there's expenses for thee.

Clown

Now Jove, in his next commodity of hair, send thee a beard!

VIOLA

By my troth, I'll tell thee, I am almost sick for
one;

Aside

though I would not have it grow on my chin. Is thy
lady within?

Clown

Would not a pair of these have bred, sir?

VIOLA

Yes, being kept together and put to use.

Clown

I would play Lord Pandarus of Phrygia, sir, to bring
a Cressida to this Troilus.

86

VIOLA

I understand you, sir; 'tis well begged.

Clown

The matter, I hope, is not great, sir, begging but
a beggar: Cressida was a beggar. My lady is
within, sir. I will construe to them whence you
come; who you are and what you would are out of my
welkin, I might say 'element,' but the word is over–worn.

Exit

VIOLA

This fellow is wise enough to play the fool;
And to do that well craves a kind of wit:
He must observe their mood on whom he jests,
The quality of persons, and the time,
And, like the haggard, cheque at every feather
That comes before his eye. This is a practise
As full of labour as a wise man's art
For folly that he wisely shows is fit;
But wise men, folly–fall'n, quite taint their wit.

Enter SIR TOBY BELCH, and SIR ANDREW

SIR TOBY BELCH

Save you, gentleman.

VIOLA

And you, sir.

SIR ANDREW

Dieu vous garde, monsieur.

VIOLA

Et vous aussi; votre serviteur.

SIR ANDREW

I hope, sir, you are; and I am yours.

SIR TOBY BELCH

Will you encounter the house? my niece is desirous
you should enter, if your trade be to her.

VIOLA

I am bound to your niece, sir; I mean, she is the
list of my voyage.

SIR TOBY BELCH

Taste your legs, sir; put them to motion.

VIOLA

My legs do better understand me, sir, than I
understand what you mean by bidding me taste my legs.

SIR TOBY BELCH

I mean, to go, sir, to enter.

VIOLA

I will answer you with gait and entrance. But we
are prevented.

Enter OLIVIA and MARIA

Most excellent accomplished lady, the heavens rain
odours on you!

SIR ANDREW

That youth's a rare courtier: 'Rain odours;' well.

VIOLA

My matter hath no voice, to your own most pregnant
and vouchsafed ear.

SIR ANDREW

'Odours,' 'pregnant' and 'vouchsafed:' I'll get 'em
all three all ready.

OLIVIA

Let the garden door be shut, and leave me to my hearing.

Exeunt SIR TOBY BELCH, SIR ANDREW, and MARIA

Give me your hand, sir.

VIOLA

My duty, madam, and most humble service.

OLIVIA

What is your name?

VIOLA

Cesario is your servant's name, fair princess.

OLIVIA

My servant, sir! 'Twas never merry world
Since lowly feigning was call'd compliment:
You're servant to the Count Orsino, youth.

VIOLA

And he is yours, and his must needs be yours:
Your servant's servant is your servant, madam.

OLIVIA

For him, I think not on him: for his thoughts,
Would they were blanks, rather than fill'd with me!

VIOLA

Madam, I come to whet your gentle thoughts
On his behalf.

OLIVIA

O, by your leave, I pray you,
I bade you never speak again of him:
But, would you undertake another suit,
I had rather hear you to solicit that
Than music from the spheres.

VIOLA

Dear lady,—

OLIVIA

Give me leave, beseech you. I did send,
After the last enchantment you did here,
A ring in chase of you: so did I abuse
Myself, my servant and, I fear me, you:
Under your hard construction must I sit,
To force that on you, in a shameful cunning,
Which you knew none of yours: what might you think?
Have you not set mine honour at the stake
And baited it with all the unmuzzled thoughts
That tyrannous heart can think? To one of your receiving
Enough is shown: a cypress, not a bosom,
Hideth my heart. So, let me hear you speak.

VIOLA

I pity you.

OLIVIA

That's a degree to love.

VIOLA

No, not a grize; for 'tis a vulgar proof,
That very oft we pity enemies.

OLIVIA

Why, then, methinks 'tis time to smile again.
O, world, how apt the poor are to be proud!
If one should be a prey, how much the better
To fall before the lion than the wolf!

Clock strikes

The clock upbraids me with the waste of time.
Be not afraid, good youth, I will not have you:
And yet, when wit and youth is come to harvest,
Your were is alike to reap a proper man:
There lies your way, due west.

VIOLA

Then westward–ho! Grace and good disposition
Attend your ladyship!
You'll nothing, madam, to my lord by me?

Twelth Night, A Winter's Tale, The Tempest

OLIVIA

Stay:
I prithee, tell me what thou thinkest of me.

VIOLA

That you do think you are not what you are.

OLIVIA

If I think so, I think the same of you.

VIOLA

Then think you right: I am not what I am.

OLIVIA

I would you were as I would have you be!

VIOLA

Would it be better, madam, than I am?
I wish it might, for now I am your fool.

OLIVIA

O, what a deal of scorn looks beautiful
In the contempt and anger of his lip!
A murderous guilt shows not itself more soon
Than love that would seem hid: love's night is noon.
Cesario, by the roses of the spring,
By maidhood, honour, truth and every thing,

I love thee so, that, maugre all thy pride,
Nor wit nor reason can my passion hide.
Do not extort thy reasons from this clause,
For that I woo, thou therefore hast no cause,
But rather reason thus with reason fetter,
Love sought is good, but given unsought better.

VIOLA

By innocence I swear, and by my youth
I have one heart, one bosom and one truth,
And that no woman has; nor never none
Shall mistress be of it, save I alone.
And so adieu, good madam: never more
Will I my master's tears to you deplore.

OLIVIA

Yet come again; for thou perhaps mayst move
That heart, which now abhors, to like his love.

Exeunt

Act 3, Scene 2

OLIVIA's house.

Enter SIR TOBY BELCH, SIR ANDREW, and FABIAN

SIR ANDREW

No, faith, I'll not stay a jot longer.

94

SIR TOBY BELCH

Thy reason, dear venom, give thy reason.

FABIAN

You must needs yield your reason, Sir Andrew.

SIR ANDREW

Marry, I saw your niece do more favours to the
count's serving–man than ever she bestowed upon me;
I saw't i' the orchard.

SIR TOBY BELCH

Did she see thee the while, old boy? tell me that.

SIR ANDREW

As plain as I see you now.

FABIAN

This was a great argument of love in her toward you.

SIR ANDREW

'Slight, will you make an ass o' me?

FABIAN

I will prove it legitimate, sir, upon the oaths of
judgment and reason.

SIR TOBY BELCH

And they have been grand–jury–men since before Noah
was a sailor.

FABIAN

She did show favour to the youth in your sight only
to exasperate you, to awake your dormouse valour, to
put fire in your heart and brimstone in your liver.
You should then have accosted her; and with some
excellent jests, fire–new from the mint, you should
have banged the youth into dumbness. This was
looked for at your hand, and this was balked: the
double gilt of this opportunity you let time wash
off, and you are now sailed into the north of my
lady's opinion; where you will hang like an icicle
on a Dutchman's beard, unless you do redeem it by
some laudable attempt either of valour or policy.

SIR ANDREW

An't be any way, it must be with valour; for policy
I hate: I had as lief be a Brownist as a
politician.

SIR TOBY BELCH

Why, then, build me thy fortunes upon the basis of
valour. Challenge me the count's youth to fight
with him; hurt him in eleven places: my niece shall
take note of it; and assure thyself, there is no
love–broker in the world can more prevail in man's

96

commendation with woman than report of valour.

FABIAN

There is no way but this, Sir Andrew.

SIR ANDREW

Will either of you bear me a challenge to him?

SIR TOBY BELCH

Go, write it in a martial hand; be curst and brief;
it is no matter how witty, so it be eloquent and fun
of invention: taunt him with the licence of ink:
if thou thou'st him some thrice, it shall not be
amiss; and as many lies as will lie in thy sheet of
paper, although the sheet were big enough for the
bed of Ware in England, set 'em down: go, about it.
Let there be gall enough in thy ink, though thou
write with a goose–pen, no matter: about it.

SIR ANDREW

Where shall I find you?

SIR TOBY BELCH

We'll call thee at the cubiculo: go.

Exit SIR ANDREW

FABIAN

This is a dear manikin to you, Sir Toby.

SIR TOBY BELCH

I have been dear to him, lad, some two thousand
strong, or so.

FABIAN

We shall have a rare letter from him: but you'll
not deliver't?

SIR TOBY BELCH

Never trust me, then; and by all means stir on the
youth to an answer. I think oxen and wainropes
cannot hale them together. For Andrew, if he were
opened, and you find so much blood in his liver as
will clog the foot of a flea, I'll eat the rest of
the anatomy.

FABIAN

And his opposite, the youth, bears in his visage no
great presage of cruelty.

Enter MARIA

SIR TOBY BELCH

Look, where the youngest wren of nine comes.

MARIA

If you desire the spleen, and will laugh yourself
into stitches, follow me. Yond gull Malvolio is
turned heathen, a very renegado; for there is no
Christian, that means to be saved by believing
rightly, can ever believe such impossible passages
of grossness. He's in yellow stockings.

SIR TOBY BELCH

And cross–gartered?

MARIA

Most villanously; like a pedant that keeps a school
i' the church. I have dogged him, like his
murderer. He does obey every point of the letter
that I dropped to betray him: he does smile his
face into more lines than is in the new map with the
augmentation of the Indies: you have not seen such
a thing as 'tis. I can hardly forbear hurling things
at him. I know my lady will strike him: if she do,
he'll smile and take't for a great favour.

SIR TOBY BELCH

Come, bring us, bring us where he is.

Exeunt

Act 3, Scene 3

A street.

Enter SEBASTIAN and ANTONIO

SEBASTIAN

I would not by my will have troubled you;
But, since you make your pleasure of your pains,
I will no further chide you.

ANTONIO

I could not stay behind you: my desire,
More sharp than filed steel, did spur me forth;
And not all love to see you, though so much
As might have drawn one to a longer voyage,
But jealousy what might befall your travel,
Being skilless in these parts; which to a stranger,
Unguided and unfriended, often prove
Rough and unhospitable: my willing love,
The rather by these arguments of fear,
Set forth in your pursuit.

SEBASTIAN

My kind Antonio,
I can no other answer make but thanks,
And thanks; and ever [ ] oft good turns
Are shuffled off with such uncurrent pay:
But, were my worth as is my conscience firm,
You should find better dealing. What's to do?

Shall we go see the reliques of this town?

ANTONIO

To–morrow, sir: best first go see your lodging.

SEBASTIAN

I am not weary, and 'tis long to night:
I pray you, let us satisfy our eyes
With the memorials and the things of fame
That do renown this city.

ANTONIO

Would you'ld pardon me;
I do not without danger walk these streets:
Once, in a sea–fight, 'gainst the count his galleys
I did some service; of such note indeed,
That were I ta'en here it would scarce be answer'd.

SEBASTIAN

Belike you slew great number of his people.

ANTONIO

The offence is not of such a bloody nature;
Albeit the quality of the time and quarrel
Might well have given us bloody argument.
It might have since been answer'd in repaying
What we took from them; which, for traffic's sake,
Most of our city did: only myself stood out;

For which, if I be lapsed in this place,
I shall pay dear.

SEBASTIAN

Do not then walk too open.

ANTONIO

It doth not fit me. Hold, sir, here's my purse.
In the south suburbs, at the Elephant,
Is best to lodge: I will bespeak our diet,
Whiles you beguile the time and feed your knowledge
With viewing of the town: there shall you have me.

SEBASTIAN

Why I your purse?

ANTONIO

Haply your eye shall light upon some toy
You have desire to purchase; and your store,
I think, is not for idle markets, sir.

SEBASTIAN

I'll be your purse–bearer and leave you
For an hour.

ANTONIO

To the Elephant.

SEBASTIAN

I do remember.

Exeunt

Act 3, Scene 4

OLIVIA's garden.

Enter OLIVIA and MARIA

OLIVIA

> I have sent after him: he says he'll come;
> How shall I feast him? what bestow of him?
> For youth is bought more oft than begg'd or borrow'd.
> I speak too loud.
> Where is Malvolio? he is sad and civil,
> And suits well for a servant with my fortunes:
> Where is Malvolio?

MARIA

> He's coming, madam; but in very strange manner. He
> is, sure, possessed, madam.

OLIVIA

> Why, what's the matter? does he rave?

MARIA

No. madam, he does nothing but smile: your
ladyship were best to have some guard about you, if
he come; for, sure, the man is tainted in's wits.

OLIVIA

Go call him hither.

Exit MARIA

I am as mad as he,
If sad and merry madness equal be.

Re−enter MARIA, with MALVOLIO

How now, Malvolio!

MALVOLIO

Sweet lady, ho, ho.

OLIVIA

Smilest thou?
I sent for thee upon a sad occasion.

MALVOLIO

Sad, lady! I could be sad: this does make some
obstruction in the blood, this cross−gartering; but

what of that? if it please the eye of one, it is
with me as the very true sonnet is, 'Please one, and
please all.'

OLIVIA

Why, how dost thou, man? what is the matter with thee?

MALVOLIO

Not black in my mind, though yellow in my legs. It
did come to his hands, and commands shall be
executed: I think we do know the sweet Roman hand.

OLIVIA

Wilt thou go to bed, Malvolio?

MALVOLIO

To bed! ay, sweet–heart, and I'll come to thee.

OLIVIA

God comfort thee! Why dost thou smile so and kiss
thy hand so oft?

MARIA

How do you, Malvolio?

MALVOLIO

At your request! yes; nightingales answer daws.

MARIA

Why appear you with this ridiculous boldness before my lady?

MALVOLIO

'Be not afraid of greatness:' 'twas well writ.

OLIVIA

What meanest thou by that, Malvolio?

MALVOLIO

'Some are born great,'—

OLIVIA

Ha!

MALVOLIO

'Some achieve greatness,'—

OLIVIA

What sayest thou?

MALVOLIO

'And some have greatness thrust upon them.'

OLIVIA

Heaven restore thee!

MALVOLIO

'Remember who commended thy yellow stockings,'—

OLIVIA

Thy yellow stockings!

MALVOLIO

'And wished to see thee cross–gartered.'

OLIVIA

Cross–gartered!

MALVOLIO

'Go to thou art made, if thou desirest to be so;'—

OLIVIA

Am I made?

MALVOLIO

'If not, let me see thee a servant still.'

OLIVIA

Why, this is very midsummer madness.

Enter Servant

Servant

Madam, the young gentleman of the Count Orsino's is
returned: I could hardly entreat him back: he
attends your ladyship's pleasure.

OLIVIA

I'll come to him.

Exit Servant

Good Maria, let this fellow be looked to. Where's
my cousin Toby? Let some of my people have a special
care of him: I would not have him miscarry for the
half of my dowry.

Exeunt OLIVIA and MARIA

MALVOLIO

O, ho! do you come near me now? no worse man than
Sir Toby to look to me! This concurs directly with
the letter: she sends him on purpose, that I may
appear stubborn to him; for she incites me to that
in the letter. 'Cast thy humble slough,' says she;
'be opposite with a kinsman, surly with servants;
let thy tongue tang with arguments of state; put
thyself into the trick of singularity;' and
consequently sets down the manner how; as, a sad
face, a reverend carriage, a slow tongue, in the
habit of some sir of note, and so forth. I have
limed her; but it is Jove's doing, and Jove make me
thankful! And when she went away now, 'Let this

fellow be looked to:' fellow! not Malvolio, nor
after my degree, but fellow. Why, every thing
adheres together, that no dram of a scruple, no
scruple of a scruple, no obstacle, no incredulous
or unsafe circumstance—What can be said? Nothing
that can be can come between me and the full
prospect of my hopes. Well, Jove, not I, is the
doer of this, and he is to be thanked.

Re-enter MARIA, with SIR TOBY BELCH and FABIAN

SIR TOBY BELCH

Which way is he, in the name of sanctity? If all
the devils of hell be drawn in little, and Legion
himself possessed him, yet I'll speak to him.

FABIAN

Here he is, here he is. How is't with you, sir?
how is't with you, man?

MALVOLIO

Go off; I discard you: let me enjoy my private: go
off.

MARIA

Lo, how hollow the fiend speaks within him! did not
I tell you? Sir Toby, my lady prays you to have a
care of him.

MALVOLIO

Ah, ha! does she so?

SIR TOBY BELCH

Go to, go to; peace, peace; we must deal gently
with him: let me alone. How do you, Malvolio? how
is't with you? What, man! defy the devil:
consider, he's an enemy to mankind.

MALVOLIO

Do you know what you say?

MARIA

La you, an you speak ill of the devil, how he takes
it at heart! Pray God, he be not bewitched!

FABIAN

Carry his water to the wise woman.

MARIA

Marry, and it shall be done to—morrow morning, if I
live. My lady would not lose him for more than I'll say.

MALVOLIO

How now, mistress!

MARIA

O Lord!

SIR TOBY BELCH

Prithee, hold thy peace; this is not the way: do
you not see you move him? let me alone with him.

FABIAN

No way but gentleness; gently, gently: the fiend is
rough, and will not be roughly used.

SIR TOBY BELCH

Why, how now, my bawcock! how dost thou, chuck?

MALVOLIO

Sir!

SIR TOBY BELCH

Ay, Biddy, come with me. What, man! 'tis not for
gravity to play at cherry–pit with Satan: hang
him, foul collier!

MARIA

Get him to say his prayers, good Sir Toby, get him to pray.

MALVOLIO

My prayers, minx!

MARIA

No, I warrant you, he will not hear of godliness.

MALVOLIO

Go, hang yourselves all! you are idle shallow
things: I am not of your element: you shall know
more hereafter.

Exit

SIR TOBY BELCH

Is't possible?

FABIAN

If this were played upon a stage now, I could
condemn it as an improbable fiction.

SIR TOBY BELCH

His very genius hath taken the infection of the device, man.

MARIA

Nay, pursue him now, lest the device take air and taint.

FABIAN

Why, we shall make him mad indeed.

MARIA

The house will be the quieter.

SIR TOBY BELCH

Come, we'll have him in a dark room and bound. My
niece is already in the belief that he's mad: we
may carry it thus, for our pleasure and his penance,
till our very pastime, tired out of breath, prompt
us to have mercy on him: at which time we will
bring the device to the bar and crown thee for a
finder of madmen. But see, but see.

Enter SIR ANDREW

FABIAN

More matter for a May morning.

SIR ANDREW

Here's the challenge, read it: warrant there's
vinegar and pepper in't.

FABIAN

Is't so saucy?

SIR ANDREW

Ay, is't, I warrant him: do but read.

SIR TOBY BELCH

Give me.

Reads

'Youth, whatsoever thou art, thou art but a scurvy fellow.'

FABIAN

Good, and valiant.

SIR TOBY BELCH

[Reads] 'Wonder not, nor admire not in thy mind,
why I do call thee so, for I will show thee no reason for't.'

FABIAN

A good note; that keeps you from the blow of the law.

SIR TOBY BELCH

[Reads] 'Thou comest to the lady Olivia, and in my
sight she uses thee kindly: but thou liest in thy
throat; that is not the matter I challenge thee for.'

FABIAN

Very brief, and to exceeding good sense—less.

SIR TOBY BELCH

[Reads] 'I will waylay thee going home; where if it
be thy chance to kill me,'—

FABIAN

Good.

SIR TOBY BELCH

[Reads] 'Thou killest me like a rogue and a villain.'

FABIAN

Still you keep o' the windy side of the law: good.

SIR TOBY BELCH

[Reads] 'Fare thee well; and God have mercy upon
one of our souls! He may have mercy upon mine; but
my hope is better, and so look to thyself. Thy
friend, as thou usest him, and thy sworn enemy,
ANDREW AGUECHEEK.
If this letter move him not, his legs cannot:
I'll give't him.

Displaying his power by using evlated language — Thou clearly dosent understand the words he is using.

MARIA

You may have very fit occasion for't: he is now in
some commerce with my lady, and will by and by depart.

SIR TOBY BELCH

Go, Sir Andrew: scout me for him at the corner the
orchard like a bum–baily: so soon as ever thou seest
him, draw; and, as thou drawest swear horrible; for
it comes to pass oft that a terrible oath, with a
swaggering accent sharply twanged off, gives manhood
more approbation than ever proof itself would have
earned him. Away!

SIR ANDREW

Nay, let me alone for swearing.

Exit

SIR TOBY BELCH

Now will not I deliver his letter: for the behavior
of the young gentleman gives him out to be of good
capacity and breeding; his employment between his
lord and my niece confirms no less: therefore this
letter, being so excellently ignorant, will breed no
terror in the youth: he will find it comes from a
clodpole. But, sir, I will deliver his challenge by
word of mouth; set upon Aguecheek a notable report
of valour; and drive the gentleman, as I know his
youth will aptly receive it, into a most hideous
opinion of his rage, skill, fury and impetuosity.
This will so fright them both that they will kill
one another by the look, like cockatrices.

Re–enter OLIVIA, with VIOLA

FABIAN

Here he comes with your niece: give them way till
he take leave, and presently after him.

SIR TOBY BELCH

I will meditate the while upon some horrid message
for a challenge.

Exeunt SIR TOBY BELCH, FABIAN, and MARIA

OLIVIA

I have said too much unto a heart of stone
And laid mine honour too unchary out:
There's something in me that reproves my fault;
But such a headstrong potent fault it is,
That it but mocks reproof.

VIOLA

With the same 'havior that your passion bears
Goes on my master's grief.

OLIVIA

Here, wear this jewel for me, 'tis my picture;
Refuse it not; it hath no tongue to vex you;
And I beseech you come again to—morrow.
What shall you ask of me that I'll deny,
That honour saved may upon asking give?

VIOLA

Nothing but this; your true love for my master.

OLIVIA

How with mine honour may I give him that
Which I have given to you?

VIOLA

I will acquit you.

OLIVIA

Well, come again to–morrow: fare thee well:
A fiend like thee might bear my soul to hell.

Exit

Re–enter SIR TOBY BELCH and FABIAN

SIR TOBY BELCH

Gentleman, God save thee.

VIOLA

And you, sir.

SIR TOBY BELCH

That defence thou hast, betake thee to't: of what
nature the wrongs are thou hast done him, I know

118

not; but thy intercepter, full of despite, bloody as
the hunter, attends thee at the orchard–end:
dismount thy tuck, be yare in thy preparation, for
thy assailant is quick, skilful and deadly.

VIOLA

You mistake, sir; I am sure no man hath any quarrel
to me: my remembrance is very free and clear from
any image of offence done to any man.

SIR TOBY BELCH

You'll find it otherwise, I assure you: therefore,
if you hold your life at any price, betake you to
your guard; for your opposite hath in him what
youth, strength, skill and wrath can furnish man withal.

VIOLA

I pray you, sir, what is he?

SIR TOBY BELCH

He is knight, dubbed with unhatched rapier and on
carpet consideration; but he is a devil in private
brawl: souls and bodies hath he divorced three; and
his incensement at this moment is so implacable,
that satisfaction can be none but by pangs of death
and sepulchre. Hob, nob, is his word; give't or take't.

VIOLA

I will return again into the house and desire some
conduct of the lady. I am no fighter. I have heard
of some kind of men that put quarrels purposely on
others, to taste their valour: belike this is a man
of that quirk.

SIR TOBY BELCH

Sir, no; his indignation derives itself out of a
very competent injury: therefore, get you on and
give him his desire. Back you shall not to the
house, unless you undertake that with me which with
as much safety you might answer him: therefore, on,
or strip your sword stark naked; for meddle you
must, that's certain, or forswear to wear iron about you.

VIOLA

This is as uncivil as strange. I beseech you, do me
this courteous office, as to know of the knight what
my offence to him is: it is something of my
negligence, nothing of my purpose.

SIR TOBY BELCH

I will do so. Signior Fabian, stay you by this
gentleman till my return.

Exit

VIOLA

Pray you, sir, do you know of this matter?

FABIAN

I know the knight is incensed against you, even to a
mortal arbitrement; but nothing of the circumstance more.

VIOLA

I beseech you, what manner of man is he?

FABIAN

Nothing of that wonderful promise, to read him by
his form, as you are like to find him in the proof
of his valour. He is, indeed, sir, the most skilful,
bloody and fatal opposite that you could possibly
have found in any part of Illyria. Will you walk
towards him? I will make your peace with him if I
can.

VIOLA

I shall be much bound to you for't: I am one that
had rather go with sir priest than sir knight: I
care not who knows so much of my mettle.

Exeunt

Re−enter SIR TOBY BELCH, with SIR ANDREW

SIR TOBY BELCH

Why, man, he's a very devil; I have not seen such a
firago. I had a pass with him, rapier, scabbard and
all, and he gives me the stuck in with such a mortal
motion, that it is inevitable; and on the answer, he
pays you as surely as your feet hit the ground they
step on. They say he has been fencer to the Sophy.

SIR ANDREW

Pox on't, I'll not meddle with him.

SIR TOBY BELCH

Ay, but he will not now be pacified: Fabian can
scarce hold him yonder.

SIR ANDREW

Plague on't, an I thought he had been valiant and so
cunning in fence, I'ld have seen him damned ere I'ld
have challenged him. Let him let the matter slip,
and I'll give him my horse, grey Capilet.

SIR TOBY BELCH

I'll make the motion: stand here, make a good show
on't: this shall end without the perdition of souls.

Aside

Marry, I'll ride your horse as well as I ride you.

Re−enter FABIAN and VIOLA

To FABIAN

I have his horse to take up the quarrel:
I have persuaded him the youth's a devil.

FABIAN

He is as horribly conceited of him; and pants and
looks pale, as if a bear were at his heels.

SIR TOBY BELCH

[To VIOLA] There's no remedy, sir; he will fight
with you for's oath sake: marry, he hath better
bethought him of his quarrel, and he finds that now
scarce to be worth talking of: therefore draw, for
the supportance of his vow; he protests he will not hurt you.

VIOLA

[Aside] Pray God defend me! A little thing would
make me tell them how much I lack of a man.

FABIAN

Give ground, if you see him furious.

SIR TOBY BELCH

Come, Sir Andrew, there's no remedy; the gentleman
will, for his honour's sake, have one bout with you;
he cannot by the duello avoid it: but he has
promised me, as he is a gentleman and a soldier, he
will not hurt you. Come on; to't.

SIR ANDREW

Pray God, he keep his oath!

VIOLA

I do assure you, 'tis against my will.

They draw

Enter ANTONIO

ANTONIO

Put up your sword. If this young gentleman
Have done offence, I take the fault on me:
If you offend him, I for him defy you.

SIR TOBY BELCH

You, sir! why, what are you?

ANTONIO

One, sir, that for his love dares yet do more
Than you have heard him brag to you he will.

SIR TOBY BELCH

Nay, if you be an undertaker, I am for you.

They draw

Enter Officers

FABIAN

O good Sir Toby, hold! here come the officers.

SIR TOBY BELCH

I'll be with you anon.

VIOLA

Pray, sir, put your sword up, if you please.

SIR ANDREW

Marry, will I, sir; and, for that I promised you,
I'll be as good as my word: he will bear you easily
and reins well.

First Officer

This is the man; do thy office.

Second Officer

Antonio, I arrest thee at the suit of Count Orsino.

ANTONIO

You do mistake me, sir.

First Officer

No, sir, no jot; I know your favour well,
Though now you have no sea–cap on your head.
Take him away: he knows I know him well.

ANTONIO

I must obey.

To VIOLA

This comes with seeking you:
But there's no remedy; I shall answer it.
What will you do, now my necessity
Makes me to ask you for my purse? It grieves me
Much more for what I cannot do for you
Than what befalls myself. You stand amazed;
But be of comfort.

Second Officer

Come, sir, away.

ANTONIO

I must entreat of you some of that money.

VIOLA

What money, sir?
For the fair kindness you have show'd me here,

And, part, being prompted by your present trouble,
Out of my lean and low ability
I'll lend you something: my having is not much;
I'll make division of my present with you:
Hold, there's half my coffer.

ANTONIO

Will you deny me now?
Is't possible that my deserts to you
Can lack persuasion? Do not tempt my misery,
Lest that it make me so unsound a man
As to upbraid you with those kindnesses
That I have done for you.

VIOLA

I know of none;
Nor know I you by voice or any feature:
I hate ingratitude more in a man
Than lying, vainness, babbling, drunkenness,
Or any taint of vice whose strong corruption
Inhabits our frail blood.

ANTONIO

O heavens themselves!

Second Officer

Come, sir, I pray you, go.

ANTONIO

Let me speak a little. This youth that you see here
I snatch'd one half out of the jaws of death,
Relieved him with such sanctity of love,
And to his image, which methought did promise
Most venerable worth, did I devotion.

First Officer

What's that to us? The time goes by: away!

ANTONIO

But O how vile an idol proves this god
Thou hast, Sebastian, done good feature shame.
In nature there's no blemish but the mind;
None can be call'd deform'd but the unkind:
Virtue is beauty, but the beauteous evil
Are empty trunks o'erflourish'd by the devil.

First Officer

The man grows mad: away with him! Come, come, sir.

ANTONIO

Lead me on.

Exit with Officers

VIOLA

Methinks his words do from such passion fly,
That he believes himself: so do not I.
Prove true, imagination, O, prove true,

That I, dear brother, be now ta'en for you!

SIR TOBY BELCH

Come hither, knight; come hither, Fabian: we'll
whisper o'er a couplet or two of most sage saws.

VIOLA

He named Sebastian: I my brother know
Yet living in my glass; even such and so
In favour was my brother, and he went
Still in this fashion, colour, ornament,
For him I imitate: O, if it prove,
Tempests are kind and salt waves fresh in love.

Exit

SIR TOBY BELCH

A very dishonest paltry boy, and more a coward than
a hare: his dishonesty appears in leaving his
friend here in necessity and denying him; and for
his cowardship, ask Fabian.

FABIAN

A coward, a most devout coward, religious in it.

SIR ANDREW

'Slid, I'll after him again and beat him.

129

SIR TOBY BELCH

Do; cuff him soundly, but never draw thy sword.

SIR ANDREW

An I do not,—

FABIAN

Come, let's see the event.

SIR TOBY BELCH

I dare lay any money 'twill be nothing yet.

Exeunt

Act 4, Scene 1

Before OLIVIA's house.

Enter SEBASTIAN and Clown

Clown

Will you make me believe that I am not sent for you?

SEBASTIAN

Go to, go to, thou art a foolish fellow:
Let me be clear of thee.

Clown

Well held out, i' faith! No, I do not know you; nor
I am not sent to you by my lady, to bid you come
speak with her; nor your name is not Master Cesario;
nor this is not my nose neither. Nothing that is so is so.

SEBASTIAN

I prithee, vent thy folly somewhere else: Thou
know'st not me.

Clown

Vent my folly! he has heard that word of some
great man and now applies it to a fool. Vent my
folly! I am afraid this great lubber, the world,
will prove a cockney. I prithee now, ungird thy
strangeness and tell me what I shall vent to my
lady: shall I vent to her that thou art coming?

SEBASTIAN

I prithee, foolish Greek, depart from me: There's
money for thee: if you tarry longer, I shall give
worse payment.

Clown

By my troth, thou hast an open hand. These wise men
that give fools money get themselves a good
report—after fourteen years' purchase.

Enter SIR ANDREW, SIR TOBY BELCH, and FABIAN

SIR ANDREW

Now, sir, have I met you again? there's for you.

SEBASTIAN

Why, there's for thee, and there, and there. Are all
the people mad?

SIR TOBY BELCH

Hold, sir, or I'll throw your dagger o'er the house.

Clown

This will I tell my lady straight: I would not be
in some of your coats for two pence.

Exit

SIR TOBY BELCH

Come on, sir; hold.

SIR ANDREW

Nay, let him alone: I'll go another way to work
with him; I'll have an action of battery against
him, if there be any law in Illyria: though I
struck him first, yet it's no matter for that.

SEBASTIAN

Let go thy hand.

SIR TOBY BELCH

Come, sir, I will not let you go. Come, my young
soldier, put up your iron: you are well fleshed; come on.

SEBASTIAN

I will be free from thee. What wouldst thou now? If
thou darest tempt me further, draw thy sword.

SIR TOBY BELCH

What, what? Nay, then I must have an ounce or two
of this malapert blood from you.

Enter OLIVIA

OLIVIA

Hold, Toby; on thy life I charge thee, hold!

SIR TOBY BELCH

Madam!

OLIVIA

Will it be ever thus? Ungracious wretch,
Fit for the mountains and the barbarous caves,

133

Where manners ne'er were preach'd! out of my sight!
Be not offended, dear Cesario.
Rudesby, be gone!

Exeunt SIR TOBY BELCH, SIR ANDREW, and FABIAN

I prithee, gentle friend,
Let thy fair wisdom, not thy passion, sway
In this uncivil and thou unjust extent
Against thy peace. Go with me to my house,
And hear thou there how many fruitless pranks
This ruffian hath botch'd up, that thou thereby
Mayst smile at this: thou shalt not choose but go:
Do not deny. Beshrew his soul for me,
He started one poor heart of mine in thee.

SEBASTIAN

What relish is in this? how runs the stream?
Or I am mad, or else this is a dream:
Let fancy still my sense in Lethe steep;
If it be thus to dream, still let me sleep!

OLIVIA

Nay, come, I prithee; would thou'ldst be ruled by me!

SEBASTIAN

Madam, I will.

OLIVIA

O, say so, and so be!

Exeunt

Act 4, Scene 2

OLIVIA's house.

Enter MARIA and Clown

MARIA

Nay, I prithee, put on this gown and this beard;
make him believe thou art Sir Topas the curate: do
it quickly; I'll call Sir Toby the whilst.

Exit

Clown

Well, I'll put it on, and I will dissemble myself
in't; and I would I were the first that ever
dissembled in such a gown. I am not tall enough to
become the function well, nor lean enough to be
thought a good student; but to be said an honest man
and a good housekeeper goes as fairly as to say a
careful man and a great scholar. The competitors enter.

Enter SIR TOBY BELCH and MARIA

SIR TOBY BELCH

Jove bless thee, master Parson.

Clown

Bonos dies, Sir Toby: for, as the old hermit of
Prague, that never saw pen and ink, very wittily
said to a niece of King Gorboduc, 'That that is is;'
so I, being Master Parson, am Master Parson; for,
what is 'that' but 'that,' and 'is' but 'is'?

SIR TOBY BELCH

To him, Sir Topas.

Clown

What, ho, I say! peace in this prison!

SIR TOBY BELCH

The knave counterfeits well; a good knave.

MALVOLIO — Gets locked up because olvia thinks him mad

[*Within*] Who calls there?

Clown

Sir Topas the curate, who comes to visit Malvolio
the lunatic.

MALVOLIO

Sir Topas, Sir Topas, good Sir Topas, go to my lady.

Clown

Out, hyperbolical fiend! how vexest thou this man!
talkest thou nothing but of ladies?

SIR TOBY BELCH

Well said, Master Parson.

MALVOLIO

Sir Topas, never was man thus wronged: good Sir
Topas, do not think I am mad: they have laid me
here in hideous darkness.

Clown

Fie, thou dishonest Satan! I call thee by the most
modest terms; for I am one of those gentle ones
that will use the devil himself with courtesy:
sayest thou that house is dark?

MALVOLIO

As hell, Sir Topas.

Clown

Why it hath bay windows transparent as barricadoes,
and the clearstores toward the south north are as
lustrous as ebony; and yet complainest thou of
obstruction?

MALVOLIO

I am not mad, Sir Topas: I say to you, this house is dark.

Clown

Madman, thou errest: I say, there is no darkness
but ignorance; in which thou art more puzzled than
the Egyptians in their fog.

MALVOLIO

I say, this house is as dark as ignorance, though
ignorance were as dark as hell; and I say, there
was never man thus abused. I am no more mad than you
are: make the trial of it in any constant question.

Clown

What is the opinion of Pythagoras concerning wild fowl?

MALVOLIO

That the soul of our grandam might haply inhabit a bird.

Clown

What thinkest thou of his opinion?

MALVOLIO

I think nobly of the soul, and no way approve his opinion.

Clown

Fare thee well. Remain thou still in darkness:
thou shalt hold the opinion of Pythagoras ere I will
allow of thy wits, and fear to kill a woodcock, lest
thou dispossess the soul of thy grandam. Fare thee well.

MALVOLIO

Sir Topas, Sir Topas!

SIR TOBY BELCH

My most exquisite Sir Topas!

Clown

Nay, I am for all waters.

MARIA

Thou mightst have done this without thy beard and
gown: he sees thee not.

SIR TOBY BELCH

To him in thine own voice, and bring me word how
thou findest him: I would we were well rid of this
knavery. If he may be conveniently delivered, I
would he were, for I am now so far in offence with
my niece that I cannot pursue with any safety this
sport to the upshot. Come by and by to my chamber.

Exeunt SIR TOBY BELCH and MARIA

Clown — *Coupter - truth becomes lies and lies become truth.*

[Singing]
'Hey, Robin, jolly Robin,
Tell me how thy lady does.'

MALVOLIO

Fool!

Change in class and power using language to mess with his mind, controlling what they think. Being told that he is mad / taught to be mad!

Clown

'My lady is unkind, perdy.'

MALVOLIO

Fool!

Clown

'Alas, why is she so?'

MALVOLIO

Fool, I say!

Clown

'She loves another'—Who calls, ha?

MALVOLIO

Good fool, as ever thou wilt deserve well at my
hand, help me to a candle, and pen, ink and paper:
as I am a gentleman, I will live to be thankful to

140

thee for't.

Clown

Master Malvolio?

MALVOLIO

Ay, good fool.

Clown

Alas, sir, how fell you besides your five wits?

MALVOLIO

Fool, there was never a man so notoriously abused: I
am as well in my wits, fool, as thou art.

Clown

But as well? then you are mad indeed, if you be no
better in your wits than a fool.

MALVOLIO

They have here propertied me; keep me in darkness,
send ministers to me, asses, and do all they can to
face me out of my wits.

Clown

Advise you what you say; the minister is here.
Malvolio, Malvolio, thy wits the heavens restore!
endeavour thyself to sleep, and leave thy vain
bibble babble.

MALVOLIO

Sir Topas!

Clown

Maintain no words with him, good fellow. Who, I,
sir? not I, sir. God be wi' you, good Sir Topas.
Merry, amen. I will, sir, I will.

MALVOLIO

Fool, fool, fool, I say!

Clown

Alas, sir, be patient. What say you sir? I am
shent for speaking to you.

MALVOLIO

Good fool, help me to some light and some paper: I
tell thee, I am as well in my wits as any man in Illyria.

Clown

Well–a–day that you were, sir

MALVOLIO

By this hand, I am. Good fool, some ink, paper and
light; and convey what I will set down to my lady:
it shall advantage thee more than ever the bearing
of letter did.

Clown

I will help you to't. But tell me true, are you
not mad indeed? or do you but counterfeit?

MALVOLIO

Believe me, I am not; I tell thee true.

Clown

Nay, I'll ne'er believe a madman till I see his
brains. I will fetch you light and paper and ink.

MALVOLIO

Fool, I'll requite it in the highest degree: I
prithee, be gone.

Clown

[Singing]
I am gone, sir,
And anon, sir,
I'll be with you again,

In a trice,
Like to the old Vice,
Your need to sustain;
Who, with dagger of lath,
In his rage and his wrath,
Cries, ah, ha! to the devil:
Like a mad lad,
Pare thy nails, dad;
Adieu, good man devil.

Exit

Act 4, Scene 3

OLIVIA's garden.

Enter SEBASTIAN

SEBASTIAN

This is the air; that is the glorious sun;
This pearl she gave me, I do feel't and see't;
And though 'tis wonder that enwraps me thus,
Yet 'tis not madness. Where's Antonio, then?
I could not find him at the Elephant:
Yet there he was; and there I found this credit,
That he did range the town to seek me out.
His counsel now might do me golden service;
For though my soul disputes well with my sense,
That this may be some error, but no madness,
Yet doth this accident and flood of fortune
So far exceed all instance, all discourse,
That I am ready to distrust mine eyes
And wrangle with my reason that persuades me

To any other trust but that I am mad
Or else the lady's mad; yet, if 'twere so,
She could not sway her house, command her followers,
Take and give back affairs and their dispatch
With such a smooth, discreet and stable bearing
As I perceive she does: there's something in't
That is deceiveable. But here the lady comes.

Enter OLIVIA and Priest

OLIVIA

Blame not this haste of mine. If you mean well,
Now go with me and with this holy man
Into the chantry by: there, before him,
And underneath that consecrated roof,
Plight me the full assurance of your faith;
That my most jealous and too doubtful soul
May live at peace. He shall conceal it
Whiles you are willing it shall come to note,
What time we will our celebration keep
According to my birth. What do you say?

SEBASTIAN

I'll follow this good man, and go with you;
And, having sworn truth, ever will be true.

OLIVIA

Then lead the way, good father; and heavens so shine,
That they may fairly note this act of mine!

145

Exeunt

Act 5, Scene 1

Before OLIVIA's house.

Enter Clown and FABIAN

FABIAN

Now, as thou lovest me, let me see his letter.

Clown

Good Master Fabian, grant me another request.

FABIAN

Any thing.

Clown

Do not desire to see this letter.

FABIAN

This is, to give a dog, and in recompense desire my dog again.

Enter DUKE ORSINO, VIOLA, CURIO, and Lords

DUKE ORSINO

Belong you to the Lady Olivia, friends?

Clown

Ay, sir; we are some of her trappings.

DUKE ORSINO

I know thee well; how dost thou, my good fellow?

Clown

Truly, sir, the better for my foes and the worse
for my friends.

DUKE ORSINO

Just the contrary; the better for thy friends.

Clown

No, sir, the worse.

DUKE ORSINO

How can that be?

Clown

Marry, sir, they praise me and make an ass of me;
now my foes tell me plainly I am an ass: so that by
my foes, sir I profit in the knowledge of myself,
and by my friends, I am abused: so that,
conclusions to be as kisses, if your four negatives
make your two affirmatives why then, the worse for
my friends and the better for my foes.

DUKE ORSINO

Why, this is excellent.

Clown

By my troth, sir, no; though it please you to be
one of my friends.

DUKE ORSINO

Thou shalt not be the worse for me: there's gold.

Clown

But that it would be double–dealing, sir, I would
you could make it another.

DUKE ORSINO

O, you give me ill counsel.

Clown

Put your grace in your pocket, sir, for this once,
and let your flesh and blood obey it.

DUKE ORSINO

Well, I will be so much a sinner, to be a
double–dealer: there's another.

Clown

Primo, secundo, tertio, is a good play; and the old
saying is, the third pays for all: the triplex,
sir, is a good tripping measure; or the bells of
Saint Bennet, sir, may put you in mind; one, two, three.

DUKE ORSINO

You can fool no more money out of me at this throw:
if you will let your lady know I am here to speak
with her, and bring her along with you, it may awake
my bounty further.

Clown

Marry, sir, lullaby to your bounty till I come
again. I go, sir; but I would not have you to think
that my desire of having is the sin of covetousness:
but, as you say, sir, let your bounty take a nap, I
will awake it anon.

Exit

VIOLA

Here comes the man, sir, that did rescue me.

Enter ANTONIO and Officers

DUKE ORSINO

That face of his I do remember well;
Yet, when I saw it last, it was besmear'd
As black as Vulcan in the smoke of war:
A bawbling vessel was he captain of,
For shallow draught and bulk unprizable;
With which such scathful grapple did he make
With the most noble bottom of our fleet,
That very envy and the tongue of loss
Cried fame and honour on him. What's the matter?

First Officer

Orsino, this is that Antonio
That took the Phoenix and her fraught from Candy;
And this is he that did the Tiger board,
When your young nephew Titus lost his leg:
Here in the streets, desperate of shame and state,
In private brabble did we apprehend him.

VIOLA

He did me kindness, sir, drew on my side;
But in conclusion put strange speech upon me:
I know not what 'twas but distraction.

DUKE ORSINO

Notable pirate! thou salt−water thief!
What foolish boldness brought thee to their mercies,
Whom thou, in terms so bloody and so dear,
Hast made thine enemies?

ANTONIO – Mistakes Vida For Sebastian

Orsino, noble sir,
Be pleased that I shake off these names you give me:
Antonio never yet was thief or pirate,
Though I confess, on base and ground enough,
Orsino's enemy. A witchcraft drew me hither:
That most ingrateful boy there by your side,
From the rude sea's enraged and foamy mouth
Did I redeem; a wreck past hope he was:
His life I gave him and did thereto add
My love, without retention or restraint,
All his in dedication; for his sake
Did I expose myself, pure for his love,
Into the danger of this adverse town;
Drew to defend him when he was beset:
Where being apprehended, his false cunning,
Not meaning to partake with me in danger,
Taught him to face me out of his acquaintance,
And grew a twenty years removed thing
While one would wink; denied me mine own purse,
Which I had recommended to his use
Not half an hour before.

VIOLA

How can this be?

DUKE ORSINO

When came he to this town?

ANTONIO

To–day, my lord; and for three months before,
No interim, not a minute's vacancy,
Both day and night did we keep company.

Enter OLIVIA and Attendants

DUKE ORSINO

Here comes the countess: now heaven walks on earth.
But for thee, fellow; fellow, thy words are madness:
Three months this youth hath tended upon me;
But more of that anon. Take him aside.

OLIVIA

What would my lord, but that he may not have,
Wherein Olivia may seem serviceable?
Cesario, you do not keep promise with me.

VIOLA

Madam!

DUKE ORSINO

Gracious Olivia,—

OLIVIA

What do you say, Cesario? Good my lord,—

VIOLA

My lord would speak; my duty hushes me.

OLIVIA

If it be aught to the old tune, my lord,
It is as fat and fulsome to mine ear
As howling after music.

DUKE ORSINO

Still so cruel?

OLIVIA

Still so constant, lord.

DUKE ORSINO

What, to perverseness? you uncivil lady,
To whose ingrate and unauspicious altars
My soul the faithfull'st offerings hath breathed out
That e'er devotion tender'd! What shall I do?

OLIVIA

Even what it please my lord, that shall become him.

DUKE ORSINO

Why should I not, had I the heart to do it,
Like to the Egyptian thief at point of death,
Kill what I love?—a savage jealousy
That sometimes savours nobly. But hear me this:
Since you to non−regardance cast my faith,

And that I partly know the instrument
That screws me from my true place in your favour,
Live you the marble–breasted tyrant still;
But this your minion, whom I know you love,
And whom, by heaven I swear, I tender dearly,
Him will I tear out of that cruel eye,
Where he sits crowned in his master's spite.
Come, boy, with me; my thoughts are ripe in mischief:
I'll sacrifice the lamb that I do love,
To spite a raven's heart within a dove.

VIOLA

And I, most jocund, apt and willingly,
To do you rest, a thousand deaths would die.

OLIVIA

Where goes Cesario?

VIOLA

After him I love
More than I love these eyes, more than my life,
More, by all mores, than e'er I shall love wife.
If I do feign, you witnesses above
Punish my life for tainting of my love!

OLIVIA

Ay me, detested! how am I beguiled!

VIOLA

Who does beguile you? who does do you wrong?

OLIVIA

Hast thou forgot thyself? is it so long?
Call forth the holy father.

DUKE ORSINO

Come, away!

OLIVIA

Whither, my lord? Cesario, husband, stay.

DUKE ORSINO

Husband!

OLIVIA

Ay, husband: can he that deny?

DUKE ORSINO

Her husband, sirrah!

VIOLA

No, my lord, not I.

OLIVIA

Alas, it is the baseness of thy fear
That makes thee strangle thy propriety:

Fear not, Cesario; take thy fortunes up;
Be that thou know'st thou art, and then thou art
As great as that thou fear'st.

Enter Priest

O, welcome, father!
Father, I charge thee, by thy reverence,
Here to unfold, though lately we intended
To keep in darkness what occasion now
Reveals before 'tis ripe, what thou dost know
Hath newly pass'd between this youth and me.

Priest

A contract of eternal bond of love,
Confirm'd by mutual joinder of your hands,
Attested by the holy close of lips,
Strengthen'd by interchangement of your rings;
And all the ceremony of this compact
Seal'd in my function, by my testimony:
Since when, my watch hath told me, toward my grave
I have travell'd but two hours.

DUKE ORSINO

O thou dissembling cub! what wilt thou be
When time hath sow'd a grizzle on thy case?
Or will not else thy craft so quickly grow,
That thine own trip shall be thine overthrow?
Farewell, and take her; but direct thy feet
Where thou and I henceforth may never meet.

VIOLA

My lord, I do protest—

OLIVIA

O, do not swear!
Hold little faith, though thou hast too much fear.

Enter SIR ANDREW

SIR ANDREW

For the love of God, a surgeon! Send one presently
to Sir Toby.

OLIVIA

What's the matter?

SIR ANDREW

He has broke my head across and has given Sir Toby
a bloody coxcomb too: for the love of God, your
help! I had rather than forty pound I were at home.

OLIVIA

Who has done this, Sir Andrew?

SIR ANDREW

The count's gentleman, one Cesario: we took him for
a coward, but he's the very devil incardinate.

DUKE ORSINO

My gentleman, Cesario?

SIR ANDREW

'Od's lifelings, here he is! You broke my head for
nothing; and that that I did, I was set on to do't
by Sir Toby.

VIOLA

Why do you speak to me? I never hurt you:
You drew your sword upon me without cause;
But I bespoke you fair, and hurt you not.

SIR ANDREW

If a bloody coxcomb be a hurt, you have hurt me: I
think you set nothing by a bloody coxcomb.

Enter SIR TOBY BELCH and Clown

Here comes Sir Toby halting; you shall hear more:
but if he had not been in drink, he would have
tickled you othergates than he did.

DUKE ORSINO

How now, gentleman! how is't with you?

SIR TOBY BELCH

That's all one: has hurt me, and there's the end
on't. Sot, didst see Dick surgeon, sot?

Clown

O, he's drunk, Sir Toby, an hour agone; his eyes
were set at eight i' the morning.

SIR TOBY BELCH

Then he's a rogue, and a passy measures panyn: I
hate a drunken rogue.

OLIVIA

Away with him! Who hath made this havoc with them?

SIR ANDREW

I'll help you, Sir Toby, because well be dressed together.

SIR TOBY BELCH

Will you help? an ass–head and a coxcomb and a
knave, a thin–faced knave, a gull!

OLIVIA

Get him to bed, and let his hurt be look'd to.

Exeunt Clown, FABIAN, SIR TOBY BELCH, and SIR ANDREW

Enter SEBASTIAN - All is releved to the characters

SEBASTIAN

> I am sorry, madam, I have hurt your kinsman:
> But, had it been the brother of my blood,
> I must have done no less with wit and safety.
> You throw a strange regard upon me, and by that
> I do perceive it hath offended you:
> Pardon me, sweet one, even for the vows
> We made each other but so late ago.

DUKE ORSINO

> One face, one voice, one habit, and two persons,
> A natural perspective, that is and is not!

SEBASTIAN

> Antonio, O my dear Antonio!
> How have the hours rack'd and tortured me,
> Since I have lost thee!

ANTONIO

> Sebastian are you?

SEBASTIAN

160

Fear'st thou that, Antonio?

ANTONIO

How have you made division of yourself?
An apple, cleft in two, is not more twin
Than these two creatures. Which is Sebastian?

OLIVIA

Most wonderful!

SEBASTIAN

Do I stand there? I never had a brother;
Nor can there be that deity in my nature,
Of here and every where. I had a sister,
Whom the blind waves and surges have devour'd.
Of charity, what kin are you to me?
What countryman? what name? what parentage?

VIOLA

Of Messaline: Sebastian was my father;
Such a Sebastian was my brother too,
So went he suited to his watery tomb:
If spirits can assume both form and suit
You come to fright us.

SEBASTIAN

A spirit I am indeed;
But am in that dimension grossly clad

Which from the womb I did participate.
Were you a woman, as the rest goes even,
I should my tears let fall upon your cheek,
And say 'Thrice–welcome, drowned Viola!'

VIOLA

My father had a mole upon his brow.

SEBASTIAN

And so had mine.

VIOLA

And died that day when Viola from her birth
Had number'd thirteen years.

SEBASTIAN

O, that record is lively in my soul!
He finished indeed his mortal act
That day that made my sister thirteen years.

VIOLA

If nothing lets to make us happy both
But this my masculine usurp'd attire,
Do not embrace me till each circumstance
Of place, time, fortune, do cohere and jump
That I am Viola: which to confirm,
I'll bring you to a captain in this town,
Where lie my maiden weeds; by whose gentle help

I was preserved to serve this noble count.
All the occurrence of my fortune since
Hath been between this lady and this lord.

SEBASTIAN

[To OLIVIA] So comes it, lady, you have been mistook:
But nature to her bias drew in that.
You would have been contracted to a maid;
Nor are you therein, by my life, deceived,
You are betroth'd both to a maid and man.

DUKE ORSINO - expects viola as a woman, now
wanted to kill her earlier.

Be not amazed; right noble is his blood.
If this be so, as yet the glass seems true,
I shall have share in this most happy wreck.

To VIOLA

Boy, thou hast said to me a thousand times
Thou never shouldst love woman like to me.

VIOLA

And all those sayings will I overswear;
And those swearings keep as true in soul
As doth that orbed continent the fire
That severs day from night.

DUKE ORSINO

163

Give me thy hand;
And let me see thee in thy woman's weeds.

VIOLA

The captain that did bring me first on shore
Hath my maid's garments: he upon some action
Is now in durance, at Malvolio's suit,
A gentleman, and follower of my lady's.

OLIVIA

He shall enlarge him: fetch Malvolio hither:
And yet, alas, now I remember me,
They say, poor gentleman, he's much distract.

Re−enter Clown with a letter, and FABIAN

A most extracting frenzy of mine own
From my remembrance clearly banish'd his.
How does he, sirrah?

Clown

Truly, madam, he holds Belzebub at the staves's end as
well as a man in his case may do: has here writ a
letter to you; I should have given't you to−day
morning, but as a madman's epistles are no gospels,
so it skills not much when they are delivered.

OLIVIA

Open't, and read it.

Clown

Look then to be well edified when the fool delivers
the madman.

Reads

'By the Lord, madam,'—

OLIVIA

How now! art thou mad?

Clown

No, madam, I do but read madness: an your ladyship
will have it as it ought to be, you must allow Vox.

OLIVIA

Prithee, read i' thy right wits.

Clown

So I do, madonna; but to read his right wits is to
read thus: therefore perpend, my princess, and give ear.

OLIVIA

Read it you, sirrah.

To FABIAN

FABIAN

[Reads] 'By the Lord, madam, you wrong me, and the
world shall know it: though you have put me into
darkness and given your drunken cousin rule over
me, yet have I the benefit of my senses as well as
your ladyship. I have your own letter that induced
me to the semblance I put on; with the which I doubt
not but to do myself much right, or you much shame.
Think of me as you please. I leave my duty a little
unthought of and speak out of my injury.
THE MADLY–USED MALVOLIO.'

OLIVIA

Did he write this?

Clown

Ay, madam.

DUKE ORSINO

This savours not much of distraction.

OLIVIA

See him deliver'd, Fabian; bring him hither.

Exit FABIAN

My lord so please you, these things further
thought on,

To think me as well a sister as a wife,
One day shall crown the alliance on't, so please you,
Here at my house and at my proper cost.

DUKE ORSINO

*Future
marriage/
now together*

Madam, I am most apt to embrace your offer.

To VIOLA

Your master quits you; and for your service done him,
So much against the mettle of your sex,
So far beneath your soft and tender breeding,
And since you call'd me master for so long,
Here is my hand: you shall from this time be
Your master's mistress.

OLIVIA

A sister! you are she.

Re—enter FABIAN, with MALVOLIO

DUKE ORSINO

Is this the madman?

OLIVIA

Ay, my lord, this same.
How now, Malvolio!

MALVOLIO

Madam, you have done me wrong,
Notorious wrong.

OLIVIA

Have I, Malvolio? no.

MALVOLIO

Lady, you have. Pray you, peruse that letter.
You must not now deny it is your hand:
Write from it, if you can, in hand or phrase;
Or say 'tis not your seal, nor your invention:
You can say none of this: well, grant it then
And tell me, in the modesty of honour,
Why you have given me such clear lights of favour,
Bade me come smiling and cross-garter'd to you,
To put on yellow stockings and to frown
Upon Sir Toby and the lighter people;
And, acting this in an obedient hope,
Why have you suffer'd me to be imprison'd,
Kept in a dark house, visited by the priest,
And made the most notorious geck and gull
That e'er invention play'd on? tell me why.

OLIVIA — relises her mistake — that she was set up
by Maria etc

Alas, Malvolio, this is not my writing,
Though, I confess, much like the character
But out of question 'tis Maria's hand.
And now I do bethink me, it was she
First told me thou wast mad; then camest in smiling,
And in such forms which here were presupposed
Upon thee in the letter. Prithee, be content:

168

This practise hath most shrewdly pass'd upon thee;
But when we know the grounds and authors of it,
Thou shalt be both the plaintiff and the judge
Of thine own cause.

FABIAN

Good madam, hear me speak,
And let no quarrel nor no brawl to come
Taint the condition of this present hour,
Which I have wonder'd at. In hope it shall not,
Most freely I confess, myself and Toby
Set this device against Malvolio here,
Upon some stubborn and uncourteous parts
We had conceived against him: Maria writ
The letter at Sir Toby's great importance;
In recompense whereof he hath married her.
How with a sportful malice it was follow'd,
May rather pluck on laughter than revenge;
If that the injuries be justly weigh'd
That have on both sides pass'd.

OLIVIA

Alas, poor fool, how have they baffled thee!

Clown

Why, 'some are born great, some achieve greatness,
and some have greatness thrown upon them.' I was
one, sir, in this interlude; one Sir Topas, sir; but
that's all one. 'By the Lord, fool, I am not mad.'
But do you remember? 'Madam, why laugh you at such
a barren rascal? an you smile not, he's gagged:'

and thus the whirligig of time brings in his revenges.

MALVOLIO

I'll be revenged on the whole pack of you.

Exit

OLIVIA

He hath been most notoriously abused.

DUKE ORSINO

Pursue him and entreat him to a peace:
He hath not told us of the captain yet:
When that is known and golden time convents,
A solemn combination shall be made
Of our dear souls. Meantime, sweet sister,
We will not part from hence. Cesario, come;
For so you shall be, while you are a man;
But when in other habits you are seen,   stablising / Fixing things
Orsino's mistress and his fancy's queen.

Exeunt all, except Clown

Clown (Feste)

[Sings]
When that I was and a little tiny boy,
With hey, ho, the wind and the rain,
A foolish thing was but a toy,
For the rain it raineth every day.

170

But when I came to man's estate,
With hey, ho, 'Gainst knaves and thieves men shut their gate,
For the rain,
But when I came, alas! to wive,
With hey, ho, By swaggering could I never thrive,
For the rain,
But when I came unto my beds,
With hey, ho, With toss−pots still had drunken heads,
For the rain,
A great while ago the world begun,
With hey, ho, But that's all one, our play is done,
And we'll strive to please you every day.

Pleasure against darkness

Exit

↑

Narrative of a young boy growing up into a man - A drunken person. A dark song to end with - drunkens / becoming a man placed against the comdey

171

A Winter's Tale

Act 1, Scene 1

— Sets the Sence. That both kyngs have known each other for years and Praise for the child (BOY).

Antechamber in LEONTES' palace.

Enter CAMILLO and ARCHIDAMUS

ARCHIDAMUS

> If you shall chance, Camillo, to visit Bohemia, on
> the like occasion whereon my services are now on
> foot, you shall see, as I have said, great
> difference betwixt our Bohemia and your Sicilia.

CAMILLO

> I think, this coming summer, the King of Sicilia
> means to pay Bohemia the visitation which he justly owes him.

ARCHIDAMUS

> Wherein our entertainment shall shame us we will be
> justified in our loves; for indeed—

CAMILLO

> Beseech you,—

ARCHIDAMUS

Verily, I speak it in the freedom of my knowledge:
we cannot with such magnificence—in so rare—I know
not what to say. We will give you sleepy drinks,
that your senses, unintelligent of our insufficience,
may, though they cannot praise us, as little accuse
us.

CAMILLO

You pay a great deal too dear for what's given freely.

ARCHIDAMUS

Believe me, I speak as my understanding instructs me
and as mine honesty puts it to utterance.

CAMILLO

Sicilia cannot show himself over–kind to Bohemia.
They were trained together in their childhoods; and
there rooted betwixt them then such an affection,
which cannot choose but branch now. Since their
more mature dignities and royal necessities made
separation of their society, their encounters,
though not personal, have been royally attorneyed
with interchange of gifts, letters, loving
embassies; that they have seemed to be together,
though absent, shook hands, as over a vast, and
embraced, as it were, from the ends of opposed
winds. The heavens continue their loves!

ARCHIDAMUS

I think there is not in the world either malice or
matter to alter it. You have an unspeakable
comfort of your young prince Mamillius: it is a
gentleman of the greatest promise that ever came
into my note.

CAMILLO

I very well agree with you in the hopes of him: it
is a gallant child; one that indeed physics the
subject, makes old hearts fresh: they that went on
crutches ere he was born desire yet their life to
see him a man.

ARCHIDAMUS

Would they else be content to die?

CAMILLO

Yes; if there were no other excuse why they should
desire to live.

ARCHIDAMUS

If the king had no son, they would desire to live
on crutches till he had one.

Exeunt

Act 1, Scene 2

A room of state in the same.

Enter LEONTES, HERMIONE, MAMILLIUS, POLIXENES, CAMILLO, and Attendants

POLIXENES

>Nine changes of the watery star hath been
>The shepherd's note since we have left our throne
>Without a burthen: time as long again
>Would be find up, my brother, with our thanks;
>And yet we should, for perpetuity,
>Go hence in debt: and therefore, like a cipher,
>Yet standing in rich place, I multiply
>With one 'We thank you' many thousands moe
>That go before it.

LEONTES

>Stay your thanks a while;
>And pay them when you part.

POLIXENES

>Sir, that's to–morrow.
>I am question'd by my fears, of what may chance
>Or breed upon our absence; that may blow
>No sneaping winds at home, to make us say
>'This is put forth too truly:' besides, I have stay'd
>To tire your royalty.

Twelth Night, A Winter's Tale, The Tempest

LEONTES

We are tougher, brother,
Than you can put us to't.

POLIXENES

No longer stay.

LEONTES — Sence of Jelousy towards his wife. because she can make him stay but he cant. They had to grow up, childhood left behind.

One seven–night longer.

POLIXENES

Very sooth, to–morrow.

LEONTES

We'll part the time between's then; and in that
I'll no gainsaying.

POLIXENES

Press me not, beseech you, so.
There is no tongue that moves, none, none i' the world,
So soon as yours could win me: so it should now,
Were there necessity in your request, although
'Twere needful I denied it. My affairs
Do even drag me homeward: which to hinder
Were in your love a whip to me; my stay
To you a charge and trouble: to save both,
Farewell, our brother.

Twelth Night, A Winter's Tale, The Tempest

LEONTES

Tongue–tied, our queen?
speak you.

HERMIONE

I had thought, sir, to have held my peace until
You have drawn oaths from him not to stay. You, sir,
Charge him too coldly. Tell him, you are sure
All in Bohemia's well; this satisfaction
The by–gone day proclaim'd: say this to him,
He's beat from his best ward.

LEONTES

Well said, Hermione.

HERMIONE - uses words and agruments to
make him stay e.g The two kings
Freindship

To tell, he longs to see his son, were strong:
But let him say so then, and let him go;
But let him swear so, and he shall not stay,
We'll thwack him hence with distaffs.
Yet of your royal presence I'll adventure
The borrow of a week. When at Bohemia
You take my lord, I'll give him my commission
To let him there a month behind the gest
Prefix'd for's parting: yet, good deed, Leontes,
I love thee not a jar o' the clock behind
What lady–she her lord. You'll stay?

POLIXENES

No, madam.

HERMIONE

Nay, but you will?

POLIXENES

I may not, verily.

HERMIONE

Verily!
You put me off with limber vows; but I,
Though you would seek to unsphere the
stars with oaths,
Should yet say 'Sir, no going.' Verily,
You shall not go: a lady's 'Verily' 's
As potent as a lord's. Will you go yet?
Force me to keep you as a prisoner,
Not like a guest; so you shall pay your fees
When you depart, and save your thanks. How say you?
My prisoner? or my guest? by your dread 'Verily,'
One of them you shall be.

POLIXENES

Your guest, then, madam:
To be your prisoner should import offending;
Which is for me less easy to commit
Than you to punish.

HERMIONE

Not your gaoler, then,
But your kind hostess. Come, I'll question you
Of my lord's tricks and yours when you were boys:
You were pretty lordings then?

POLIXENES

We were, fair queen,
Two lads that thought there was no more behind
But such a day to—morrow as to—day,
And to be boy eternal.

HERMIONE

Was not my lord
The verier wag o' the two?

POLIXENES

We were as twinn'd lambs that did frisk i' the sun,
And bleat the one at the other: what we changed
Was innocence for innocence; we knew not
The doctrine of ill—doing, nor dream'd
That any did. Had we pursued that life,
And our weak spirits ne'er been higher rear'd
With stronger blood, we should have answer'd heaven
Boldly 'not guilty;' the imposition clear'd
Hereditary ours.

HERMIONE

By this we gather
You have tripp'd since.

POLIXENES

O my most sacred lady!
Temptations have since then been born to's; for
In those unfledged days was my wife a girl;
Your precious self had then not cross'd the eyes
Of my young play–fellow.

HERMIONE

Grace to boot!
Of this make no conclusion, lest you say
Your queen and I are devils: yet go on;
The offences we have made you do we'll answer,
If you first sinn'd with us and that with us
You did continue fault and that you slipp'd not
With any but with us.

LEONTES

Is he won yet?

HERMIONE

He'll stay my lord.

LEONTES

At my request he would not.
Hermione, my dearest, thou never spokest

To better purpose.

HERMIONE

Never?

LEONTES

Never, but once.

HERMIONE

What! have I twice said well? when was't before?
I prithee tell me; cram's with praise, and make's
As fat as tame things: one good deed dying tongueless
Slaughters a thousand waiting upon that.
Our praises are our wages: you may ride's
With one soft kiss a thousand furlongs ere
With spur we beat an acre. But to the goal:
My last good deed was to entreat his stay:
What was my first? it has an elder sister,
Or I mistake you: O, would her name were Grace!
But once before I spoke to the purpose: when?
Nay, let me have't; I long.

LEONTES

Why, that was when
Three crabbed months had sour'd themselves to death,
Ere I could make thee open thy white hand
And clap thyself my love: then didst thou utter
'I am yours for ever.'

HERMIONE

'Tis grace indeed.
Why, lo you now, I have spoke to the purpose twice:
The one for ever earn'd a royal husband;
The other for some while a friend.

LEONTES *[Aside]*

Too hot, too hot!
To mingle friendship far is mingling bloods.
I have tremor cordis on me: my heart dances;
But not for joy; not joy. This entertainment
May a free face put on, derive a liberty
From heartiness, from bounty, fertile bosom,
And well become the agent; 't may, I grant;
But to be paddling palms and pinching fingers,
As now they are, and making practised smiles,
As in a looking–glass, and then to sigh, as 'twere
The mort o' the deer; O, that is entertainment
My bosom likes not, nor my brows! Mamillius,
Art thou my boy?

MAMILLIUS

Ay, my good lord.

LEONTES

I' fecks!
Why, that's my bawcock. What, hast
smutch'd thy nose?
They say it is a copy out of mine. Come, captain,
We must be neat; not neat, but cleanly, captain:

And yet the steer, the heifer and the calf
Are all call'd neat.—Still virginalling
Upon his palm!—How now, you wanton calf!
Art thou my calf?

MAMILLIUS

Yes, if you will, my lord.

LEONTES

Thou want'st a rough pash and the shoots that I have,
To be full like me: yet they say we are
Almost as like as eggs; women say so,
That will say anything but were they false
As o'er–dyed blacks, as wind, as waters, false
As dice are to be wish'd by one that fixes
No bourn 'twixt his and mine, yet were it true
To say this boy were like me. Come, sir page,
Look on me with your welkin eye: sweet villain!
Most dear'st! my collop! Can thy dam?—may't be?—
Affection! thy intention stabs the centre:
Thou dost make possible things not so held,
Communicatest with dreams;—how can this be?—
With what's unreal thou coactive art,
And fellow'st nothing: then 'tis very credent
Thou mayst co–join with something; and thou dost,
And that beyond commission, and I find it,
And that to the infection of my brains
And hardening of my brows.

POLIXENES

What means Sicilia?

HERMIONE

He something seems unsettled.

POLIXENES

How, my lord!
What cheer? how is't with you, best brother?

HERMIONE

You look as if you held a brow of much distraction
Are you moved, my lord?

LEONTES

No, in good earnest.
How sometimes nature will betray its folly,
Its tenderness, and make itself a pastime
To harder bosoms! Looking on the lines
Of my boy's face, methoughts I did recoil
Twenty–three years, and saw myself unbreech'd,
In my green velvet coat, my dagger muzzled,
Lest it should bite its master, and so prove,
As ornaments oft do, too dangerous:
How like, methought, I then was to this kernel,
This squash, this gentleman. Mine honest friend,
Will you take eggs for money?

MAMILLIUS

No, my lord, I'll fight.

Twelth Night, A Winter's Tale, The Tempest

LEONTES

> You will! why, happy man be's dole! My brother,
> Are you so fond of your young prince as we
> Do seem to be of ours?

POLIXENES

> If at home, sir,
> He's all my exercise, my mirth, my matter,
> Now my sworn friend and then mine enemy,
> My parasite, my soldier, statesman, all:
> He makes a July's day short as December,
> And with his varying childness cures in me
> Thoughts that would thick my blood.

LEONTES

> So stands this squire
> Officed with me: we two will walk, my lord,
> And leave you to your graver steps. Hermione,
> How thou lovest us, show in our brother's welcome;
> Let what is dear in Sicily be cheap:
> Next to thyself and my young rover, he's
> Apparent to my heart.

HERMIONE

> If you would seek us,
> We are yours i' the garden: shall's attend you there?

LEONTES

To your own bents dispose you: you'll be found,
Be you beneath the sky.

Aside

I am angling now,
Though you perceive me not how I give line.
Go to, go to!
How she holds up the neb, the bill to him!
And arms her with the boldness of a wife
To her allowing husband!

Exeunt POLIXENES, HERMIONE, and Attendants

Gone already!
Inch−thick, knee−deep, o'er head and
ears a fork'd one!
Go, play, boy, play: thy mother plays, and I
Play too, but so disgraced a part, whose issue
Will hiss me to my grave: contempt and clamour
Will be my knell. Go, play, boy, play.
There have been,
Or I am much deceived, cuckolds ere now;
And many a man there is, even at this present,
Now while I speak this, holds his wife by the arm,
That little thinks she has been sluiced in's absence
And his pond fish'd by his next neighbour, by
Sir Smile, his neighbour: nay, there's comfort in't
Whiles other men have gates and those gates open'd,
As mine, against their will. Should all despair
That have revolted wives, the tenth of mankind
Would hang themselves. Physic for't there is none;
It is a bawdy planet, that will strike
Where 'tis predominant; and 'tis powerful, think it,

From east, west, north and south: be it concluded,
No barricado for a belly; know't;
It will let in and out the enemy
With bag and baggage: many thousand on's
Have the disease, and feel't not. How now, boy!

MAMILLIUS

I am like you, they say.

LEONTES

Why that's some comfort. What, Camillo there?

CAMILLO

Ay, my good lord.

LEONTES

Go play, Mamillius; thou'rt an honest man.

Exit MAMILLIUS

Camillo, this great sir will yet stay longer.

CAMILLO

You had much ado to make his anchor hold:
When you cast out, it still came home.

LEONTES

Didst note it?

CAMILLO

He would not stay at your petitions: made
His business more material.

LEONTES

Didst perceive it?

Aside

They're here with me already, whispering, rounding
'Sicilia is a so–forth:' 'tis far gone,
When I shall gust it last. How came't, Camillo,
That he did stay?

CAMILLO

At the good queen's entreaty.

LEONTES

At the queen's be't: 'good' should be pertinent
But, so it is, it is not. Was this taken
By any understanding pate but thine?
For thy conceit is soaking, will draw in
More than the common blocks: not noted, is't,
But of the finer natures? by some severals
Of head–piece extraordinary? lower messes
Perchance are to this business purblind? say.

CAMILLO

Business, my lord! I think most understand
Bohemia stays here longer.

LEONTES

Ha!

CAMILLO

Stays here longer.

LEONTES

Ay, but why?

CAMILLO

To satisfy your highness and the entreaties
Of our most gracious mistress.

LEONTES

Satisfy!
The entreaties of your mistress! satisfy!
Let that suffice. I have trusted thee, Camillo,
With all the nearest things to my heart, as well
My chamber–councils, wherein, priest–like, thou
Hast cleansed my bosom, I from thee departed
Thy penitent reform'd: but we have been
Deceived in thy integrity, deceived
In that which seems so.

CAMILLO

Be it forbid, my lord!

LEONTES

Con finding about
the wide fere

To bide upon't, thou art not honest, or,
If thou inclinest that way, thou art a coward,
Which hoxes honesty behind, restraining
From course required; or else thou must be counted
A servant grafted in my serious trust
And therein negligent; or else a fool
That seest a game play'd home, the rich stake drawn,
And takest it all for jest.

CAMILLO

My gracious lord,
I may be negligent, foolish and fearful;
In every one of these no man is free,
But that his negligence, his folly, fear,
Among the infinite doings of the world,
Sometime puts forth. In your affairs, my lord,
If ever I were wilful–negligent,
It was my folly; if industriously
I play'd the fool, it was my negligence,
Not weighing well the end; if ever fearful
To do a thing, where I the issue doubted,
Where of the execution did cry out
Against the non–performance, 'twas a fear
Which oft infects the wisest: these, my lord,
Are such allow'd infirmities that honesty
Is never free of. But, beseech your grace,
Be plainer with me; let me know my trespass
By its own visage: if I then deny it,

190

'Tis none of mine.

LEONTES — Thinks his wife is cheating

    Ha' not you seen, Camillo,—
    But that's past doubt, you have, or your eye–glass
    Is thicker than a cuckold's horn,—or heard,—
    For to a vision so apparent rumour
    Cannot be mute,—or thought,—for cogitation
    Resides not in that man that does not think,—
    My wife is slippery? If thou wilt confess,
    Or else be impudently negative,
    To have nor eyes nor ears nor thought, then say
    My wife's a hobby–horse, deserves a name
    As rank as any flax–wench that puts to
    Before her troth–plight: say't and justify't.

CAMILLO

    I would not be a stander–by to hear
    My sovereign mistress clouded so, without
    My present vengeance taken: 'shrew my heart,
    You never spoke what did become you less
    Than this; which to reiterate were sin
    As deep as that, though true.

LEONTES

    Is whispering nothing?
    Is leaning cheek to cheek? is meeting noses?
    Kissing with inside lip? stopping the career
    Of laughing with a sigh?—a note infallible
    Of breaking honesty—horsing foot on foot?

Skulking in corners? wishing clocks more swift?
Hours, minutes? noon, midnight? and all eyes
Blind with the pin and web but theirs, theirs only,
That would unseen be wicked? is this nothing?
Why, then the world and all that's in't is nothing;
The covering sky is nothing; Bohemia nothing;
My wife is nothing; nor nothing have these nothings,
If this be nothing.

CAMILLO

Good my lord, be cured
Of this diseased opinion, and betimes;
For 'tis most dangerous.

LEONTES

Say it be, 'tis true.

CAMILLO

No, no, my lord.

LEONTES

It is; you lie, you lie:
I say thou liest, Camillo, and I hate thee,
Pronounce thee a gross lout, a mindless slave,
Or else a hovering temporizer, that
Canst with thine eyes at once see good and evil,
Inclining to them both: were my wife's liver
Infected as her life, she would not live
The running of one glass.

192

CAMILLO — Finds it hard that his
wife would cheat

Who does infect her?

LEONTES

Why, he that wears her like a medal, hanging
About his neck, Bohemia: who, if I
Had servants true about me, that bare eyes
To see alike mine honour as their profits,
Their own particular thrifts, they would do that
Which should undo more doing: ay, and thou,
His cupbearer,—whom I from meaner form
Have benched and reared to worship, who mayst see
Plainly as heaven sees earth and earth sees heaven,
How I am galled,—mightst bespice a cup,
To give mine enemy a lasting wink;
Which draught to me were cordial.

CAMILLO

Sir, my lord,
I could do this, and that with no rash potion,
But with a lingering dram that should not work
Maliciously like poison: but I cannot
Believe this crack to be in my dread mistress,
So sovereignly being honourable.
I have loved thee,—

LEONTES

Make that thy question, and go rot!
Dost think I am so muddy, so unsettled,
To appoint myself in this vexation, sully

193

The purity and whiteness of my sheets,
Which to preserve is sleep, which being spotted
Is goads, thorns, nettles, tails of wasps,
Give scandal to the blood o' the prince my son,
Who I do think is mine and love as mine,
Without ripe moving to't? Would I do this?
Could man so blench?

CAMILLO But Starts to belive him - Shut her up. Plots his Murder - Is Just to

I must believe you, sir:
I do; and will fetch off Bohemia for't;
Provided that, when he's removed, your highness
Will take again your queen as yours at first,
Even for your son's sake; and thereby for sealing
The injury of tongues in courts and kingdoms
Known and allied to yours.

LEONTES

Thou dost advise me
Even so as I mine own course have set down:
I'll give no blemish to her honour, none.

CAMILLO

My lord,
Go then; and with a countenance as clear
As friendship wears at feasts, keep with Bohemia
And with your queen. I am his cupbearer:
If from me he have wholesome beverage,
Account me not your servant.

194

Twelth Night, A Winter's Tale, The Tempest

LEONTES

This is all:
Do't and thou hast the one half of my heart;
Do't not, thou split'st thine own.

CAMILLO

I'll do't, my lord.

LEONTES

I will seem friendly, as thou hast advised me.

Exit

CAMILLO

O miserable lady! But, for me,
What case stand I in? I must be the poisoner
Of good Polixenes; and my ground to do't
Is the obedience to a master, one
Who in rebellion with himself will have
All that are his so too. To do this deed,
Promotion follows. If I could find example
Of thousands that had struck anointed kings
And flourish'd after, I'ld not do't; but since
Nor brass nor stone nor parchment bears not one,
Let villany itself forswear't. I must
Forsake the court: to do't, or no, is certain
To me a break–neck. Happy star, reign now!
Here comes Bohemia.

Re–enter POLIXENES

195

POLIXENES

This is strange: methinks
My favour here begins to warp. Not speak?
Good day, Camillo.

CAMILLO

Hail, most royal sir!

POLIXENES

What is the news i' the court?

CAMILLO

None rare, my lord.

POLIXENES

The king hath on him such a countenance
As he had lost some province and a region
Loved as he loves himself: even now I met him
With customary compliment; when he,
Wafting his eyes to the contrary and falling
A lip of much contempt, speeds from me and
So leaves me to consider what is breeding
That changeth thus his manners.

CAMILLO

I dare not know, my lord.

POLIXENES

How! dare not! do not. Do you know, and dare not?
Be intelligent to me: 'tis thereabouts;
For, to yourself, what you do know, you must.
And cannot say, you dare not. Good Camillo,
Your changed complexions are to me a mirror
Which shows me mine changed too; for I must be
A party in this alteration, finding
Myself thus alter'd with 't.

CAMILLO

There is a sickness
Which puts some of us in distemper, but
I cannot name the disease; and it is caught
Of you that yet are well.

POLIXENES — questioning Camillo because he
noticed Leontes is acting strange
but won't say.

How! caught of me!
Make me not sighted like the basilisk:
I have look'd on thousands, who have sped the better
By my regard, but kill'd none so. Camillo,—
As you are certainly a gentleman, thereto
Clerk–like experienced, which no less adorns
Our gentry than our parents' noble names,
In whose success we are gentle,—I beseech you,
If you know aught which does behove my knowledge
Thereof to be inform'd, imprison't not
In ignorant concealment.

CAMILLO

I may not answer.

POLIXENES

A sickness caught of me, and yet I well!
I must be answer'd. Dost thou hear, Camillo,
I conjure thee, by all the parts of man
Which honour does acknowledge, whereof the least
Is not this suit of mine, that thou declare
What incidency thou dost guess of harm
Is creeping toward me; how far off, how near;
Which way to be prevented, if to be;
If not, how best to bear it.

CAMILLO

Sir, I will tell you;
Since I am charged in honour and by him
That I think honourable: therefore mark my counsel,
Which must be even as swiftly follow'd as
I mean to utter it, or both yourself and me
Cry lost, and so good night!

POLIXENES

On, good Camillo.

CAMILLO

I am appointed him to murder you.

POLIXENES

By whom, Camillo?

CAMILLO

By the king.

POLIXENES

For what?

CAMILLO – But hen he tells all.

He thinks, nay, with all confidence he swears,
As he had seen't or been an instrument
To vice you to't, that you have touch'd his queen
Forbiddenly.

POLIXENES

O, then my best blood turn
To an infected jelly and my name
Be yoked with his that did betray the Best!
Turn then my freshest reputation to
A savour that may strike the dullest nostril
Where I arrive, and my approach be shunn'd,
Nay, hated too, worse than the great'st infection
That e'er was heard or read!

CAMILLO

Swear his thought over
By each particular star in heaven and
By all their influences, you may as well
Forbid the sea for to obey the moon
As or by oath remove or counsel shake
The fabric of his folly, whose foundation
Is piled upon his faith and will continue
The standing of his body.

199

POLIXENES

How should this grow?

CAMILLO

I know not: but I am sure 'tis safer to
Avoid what's grown than question how 'tis born.
If therefore you dare trust my honesty,
That lies enclosed in this trunk which you
Shall bear along impawn'd, away to—night!
Your followers I will whisper to the business,
And will by twos and threes at several posterns
Clear them o' the city. For myself, I'll put
My fortunes to your service, which are here
By this discovery lost. Be not uncertain;
For, by the honour of my parents, I
Have utter'd truth: which if you seek to prove,
I dare not stand by; nor shall you be safer
Than one condemn'd by the king's own mouth, thereon
His execution sworn.

POLIXENES

I do believe thee:
I saw his heart in 's face. Give me thy hand:
Be pilot to me and thy places shall
Still neighbour mine. My ships are ready and
My people did expect my hence departure
Two days ago. This jealousy
Is for a precious creature: as she's rare,
Must it be great, and as his person's mighty,
Must it be violent, and as he does conceive

He is dishonour'd by a man which ever
Profess'd to him, why, his revenges must
In that be made more bitter. Fear o'ershades me:
Good expedition be my friend, and comfort
The gracious queen, part of his theme, but nothing
Of his ill-ta'en suspicion! Come, Camillo;
I will respect thee as a father if
Thou bear'st my life off hence: let us avoid.

CAMILLO

It is in mine authority to command
The keys of all the posterns: please your highness
To take the urgent hour. Come, sir, away.

Exeunt

Act 2, Scene 1

A room in LEONTES' palace.

Enter HERMIONE, MAMILLIUS, and Ladies

HERMIONE

Take the boy to you: he so troubles me,
'Tis past enduring.

First Lady

Come, my gracious lord,
Shall I be your playfellow?

MAMILLIUS

No, I'll none of you.

First Lady

Why, my sweet lord?

MAMILLIUS

You'll kiss me hard and speak to me as if
I were a baby still. I love you better.

Second Lady

And why so, my lord?

MAMILLIUS

Not for because
Your brows are blacker; yet black brows, they say,
Become some women best, so that there be not
Too much hair there, but in a semicircle
Or a half–moon made with a pen.

Second Lady

Who taught you this?

MAMILLIUS

I learnt it out of women's faces. Pray now
What colour are your eyebrows?

First Lady

Blue, my lord.

MAMILLIUS

Nay, that's a mock: I have seen a lady's nose
That has been blue, but not her eyebrows.

First Lady

Hark ye;
The queen your mother rounds apace: we shall
Present our services to a fine new prince
One of these days; and then you'ld wanton with us,
If we would have you.

Second Lady

She is spread of late
Into a goodly bulk: good time encounter her!

HERMIONE

What wisdom stirs amongst you? Come, sir, now
I am for you again: pray you, sit by us,
And tell 's a tale.

MAMILLIUS

Merry or sad shall't be?

HERMIONE

As merry as you will.

MAMILLIUS

A sad tale's best for winter: I have one
Of sprites and goblins.

HERMIONE

Let's have that, good sir.
Come on, sit down: come on, and do your best
To fright me with your sprites; you're powerful at it.

MAMILLIUS

There was a man—

HERMIONE

Nay, come, sit down; then on.

MAMILLIUS

Dwelt by a churchyard: I will tell it softly;
Yond crickets shall not hear it.

HERMIONE

Come on, then,
And give't me in mine ear.

Enter LEONTES, with ANTIGONUS, Lords and others

LEONTES

Was he met there? his train? Camillo with him?

First Lord

Behind the tuft of pines I met them; never
Saw I men scour so on their way: I eyed them
Even to their ships.

LEONTES

How blest am I
In my just censure, in my true opinion!
Alack, for lesser knowledge! how accursed
In being so blest! There may be in the cup
A spider steep'd, and one may drink, depart,
And yet partake no venom, for his knowledge
Is not infected: but if one present
The abhorr'd ingredient to his eye, make known
How he hath drunk, he cracks his gorge, his sides,
With violent hefts. I have drunk,
and seen the spider.
Camillo was his help in this, his pander:
There is a plot against my life, my crown;
All's true that is mistrusted: that false villain
Whom I employ'd was pre–employ'd by him:
He has discover'd my design, and I
Remain a pinch'd thing; yea, a very trick

For them to play at will. How came the posterns
So easily open?

First Lord

By his great authority;
Which often hath no less prevail'd than so
On your command.

LEONTES

I know't too well.
Give me the boy: I am glad you did not nurse him:
Though he does bear some signs of me, yet you
Have too much blood in him.

HERMIONE

What is this? sport?

LEONTES — Confronts hermione about the cheating -
she dines all

Bear the boy hence; he shall not come about her;
Away with him! and let her sport herself
With that she's big with; for 'tis Polixenes
Has made thee swell thus.

HERMIONE

But I'ld say he had not,
And I'll be sworn you would believe my saying,
Howe'er you lean to the nayward.

206

LEONTES

> You, my lords,
> Look on her, mark her well; be but about
> To say 'she is a goodly lady,' and
> The justice of your bearts will thereto add
> 'Tis pity she's not honest, honourable:'
> Praise her but for this her without–door form,
> Which on my faith deserves high speech, and straight
> The shrug, the hum or ha, these petty brands
> That calumny doth use—O, I am out—
> That mercy does, for calumny will sear
> Virtue itself: these shrugs, these hums and ha's,
> When you have said 'she's goodly,' come between
> Ere you can say 'she's honest:' but be 't known,
> From him that has most cause to grieve it should be,
> She's an adulteress.

HERMIONE

> Should a villain say so,
> The most replenish'd villain in the world,
> He were as much more villain: you, my lord,
> Do but mistake.

LEONTES — dishonour hermione, everything.

> You have mistook, my lady,
> Polixenes for Leontes: O thou thing!
> Which I'll not call a creature of thy place,
> Lest barbarism, making me the precedent,
> Should a like language use to all degrees

207

And mannerly distinguishment leave out
Betwixt the prince and beggar: I have said
She's an adulteress; I have said with whom:
More, she's a traitor and Camillo is
A federary with her, and one that knows
What she should shame to know herself
But with her most vile principal, that she's
A bed–swerver, even as bad as those
That vulgars give bold'st titles, ay, and privy
To this their late escape.

HERMIONE

No, by my life.
Privy to none of this. How will this grieve you,
When you shall come to clearer knowledge, that
You thus have publish'd me! Gentle my lord,
You scarce can right me throughly then to say
You did mistake.

LEONTES   - Puts her In Jail

No; if I mistake
In those foundations which I build upon,
The centre is not big enough to bear
A school–boy's top. Away with her! to prison!
He who shall speak for her is afar off guilty
But that he speaks.

HERMIONE

There's some ill planet reigns:
I must be patient till the heavens look

With an aspect more favourable. Good my lords,
I am not prone to weeping, as our sex
Commonly are; the want of which vain dew
Perchance shall dry your pities: but I have
That honourable grief lodged here which burns
Worse than tears drown: beseech you all, my lords,
With thoughts so qualified as your charities
Shall best instruct you, measure me; and so
The king's will be perform'd!

LEONTES

Shall I be heard?

HERMIONE

Who is't that goes with me? Beseech your highness,
My women may be with me; for you see
My plight requires it. Do not weep, good fools;
There is no cause: when you shall know your mistress
Has deserved prison, then abound in tears
As I come out: this action I now go on
Is for my better grace. Adieu, my lord:
I never wish'd to see you sorry; now
I trust I shall. My women, come; you have leave.

LEONTES

Go, do our bidding; hence!

Exit HERMIONE, guarded; with Ladies

First Lord

Beseech your highness, call the queen again.

ANTIGONUS — Suggest him to rethink — his wife is completely innocent

Be certain what you do, sir, lest your justice
Prove violence; in the which three great ones suffer,
Yourself, your queen, your son.

First Lord

For her, my lord,
I dare my life lay down and will do't, sir,
Please you to accept it, that the queen is spotless
I' the eyes of heaven and to you; I mean,
In this which you accuse her.

ANTIGONUS

If it prove
She's otherwise, I'll keep my stables where
I lodge my wife; I'll go in couples with her;
Than when I feel and see her no farther trust her;
For every inch of woman in the world,
Ay, every dram of woman's flesh is false, If she be.

LEONTES

Hold your peaces.

First Lord

Good my lord,—

ANTIGONUS

> It is for you we speak, not for ourselves:
> You are abused and by some putter–on
> That will be damn'd for't; would I knew the villain,
> I would land–damn him. Be she honour–flaw'd,
> I have three daughters; the eldest is eleven
> The second and the third, nine, and some five;
> If this prove true, they'll pay for't:
> by mine honour,
> I'll geld 'em all; fourteen they shall not see,
> To bring false generations: they are co–heirs;
> And I had rather glib myself than they
> Should not produce fair issue.

LEONTES

> Cease; no more.
> You smell this business with a sense as cold
> As is a dead man's nose: but I do see't and feel't
> As you feel doing thus; and see withal
> The instruments that feel.

ANTIGONUS – A Priest

> If it be so,
> We need no grave to bury honesty:
> There's not a grain of it the face to sweeten
> Of the whole dungy earth.

LEONTES

> What! lack I credit?

First Lord

> I had rather you did lack than I, my lord,
> Upon this ground; and more it would content me
> To have her honour true than your suspicion,
> Be blamed for't how you might.

LEONTES

> Why, what need we
> Commune with you of this, but rather follow
> Our forceful instigation? Our prerogative
> Calls not your counsels, but our natural goodness
> Imparts this; which if you, or stupefied
> Or seeming so in skill, cannot or will not
> Relish a truth like us, inform yourselves
> We need no more of your advice: the matter,
> The loss, the gain, the ordering on't, is all
> Properly ours.

ANTIGONUS

> And I wish, my liege,
> You had only in your silent judgment tried it,
> Without more overture.

LEONTES

> How could that be?
> Either thou art most ignorant by age,
> Or thou wert born a fool. Camillo's flight,
> Added to their familiarity,
> Which was as gross as ever touch'd conjecture,

That lack'd sight only, nought for approbation
But only seeing, all other circumstances
Made up to the deed, doth push on this proceeding:
Yet, for a greater confirmation,
For in an act of this importance 'twere
Most piteous to be wild, I have dispatch'd in post
To sacred Delphos, to Apollo's temple,
Cleomenes and Dion, whom you know
Of stuff'd sufficiency: now from the oracle
They will bring all; whose spiritual counsel had,
Shall stop or spur me. Have I done well?

First Lord

Well done, my lord.

LEONTES

Though I am satisfied and need no more
Than what I know, yet shall the oracle
Give rest to the minds of others, such as he
Whose ignorant credulity will not
Come up to the truth. So have we thought it good
From our free person she should be confined,
Lest that the treachery of the two fled hence
Be left her to perform. Come, follow us;
We are to speak in public; for this business
Will raise us all.

ANTIGONUS

[Aside]
To laughter, as I take it,
If the good truth were known.

Exeunt

Act 2, Scene 2

A prison.

Enter PAULINA, a Gentleman, and Attendants

PAULINA

> The keeper of the prison, call to him;
> let him have knowledge who I am.

Exit Gentleman

> Good lady,
> No court in Europe is too good for thee;
> What dost thou then in prison?

Re-enter Gentleman, with the Gaoler

> Now, good sir,
> You know me, do you not?

Gaoler

> For a worthy lady
> And one whom much I honour.

PAULINA

Pray you then,
Conduct me to the queen.

Gaoler

I may not, madam:
To the contrary I have express commandment.

PAULINA

Here's ado,
To lock up honesty and honour from
The access of gentle visitors!
Is't lawful, pray you,
To see her women? any of them? Emilia?

Gaoler

So please you, madam,
To put apart these your attendants, I
Shall bring Emilia forth.

PAULINA

I pray now, call her.
Withdraw yourselves.

Exeunt Gentleman and Attendants

Gaoler

And, madam,
I must be present at your conference.

PAULINA

Well, be't so, prithee.

Exit Gaoler

Here's such ado to make no stain a stain
As passes colouring.

Re−enter Gaoler, with EMILIA

Dear gentlewoman,
How fares our gracious lady?

EMILIA — Hermione gives birth early − a girl

As well as one so great and so forlorn
May hold together: on her frights and griefs,
Which never tender lady hath born greater,
She is something before her time deliver'd.

PAULINA

A boy?

EMILIA

A daughter, and a goodly babe,
Lusty and like to live: the queen receives
Much comfort in't; says 'My poor prisoner,
I am innocent as you.'

PAULINA

I dare be sworn
These dangerous unsafe lunes i' the king,
beshrew them!
He must be told on't, and he shall: the office
Becomes a woman best; I'll take't upon me:
If I prove honey–mouth'd let my tongue blister
And never to my red–look'd anger be
The trumpet any more. Pray you, Emilia,
Commend my best obedience to the queen:
If she dares trust me with her little babe,
I'll show't the king and undertake to be
Her advocate to the loud'st. We do not know
How he may soften at the sight o' the child:
The silence often of pure innocence
Persuades when speaking fails.

EMILIA — Mfddlwige

Most worthy madam,
Your honour and your goodness is so evident
That your free undertaking cannot miss
A thriving issue: there is no lady living
So meet for this great errand. Please your ladyship
To visit the next room, I'll presently
Acquaint the queen of your most noble offer;
Who but to–day hammer'd of this design,
But durst not tempt a minister of honour,

217

Lest she should be denied.

PAULINA

Tell her, Emilia.
I'll use that tongue I have: if wit flow from't
As boldness from my bosom, let 't not be doubted
I shall do good.

EMILIA

Now be you blest for it!
I'll to the queen: please you,
come something nearer.

Gaoler

Madam, if't please the queen to send the babe,
I know not what I shall incur to pass it,
Having no warrant.

PAULINA

You need not fear it, sir:
This child was prisoner to the womb and is
By law and process of great nature thence
Freed and enfranchised, not a party to
The anger of the king nor guilty of,
If any be, the trespass of the queen.

Gaoler

I do believe it.

PAULINA

Do not you fear: upon mine honour,
I will stand betwixt you and danger.

Exeunt

Act 2, Scene 3

A room in LEONTES' palace.

Enter LEONTES, ANTIGONUS, Lords, and Servants

LEONTES - going slightly mad

Nor night nor day no rest: it is but weakness
To bear the matter thus; mere weakness. If
The cause were not in being,—part o' the cause,
She the adulteress; for the harlot king
Is quite beyond mine arm, out of the blank
And level of my brain, plot–proof; but she
I can hook to me: say that she were gone,
Given to the fire, a moiety of my rest
Might come to me again. Who's there?

First Servant

My lord?

LEONTES

219

How does the boy?

First Servant

He took good rest to–night;
'Tis hoped his sickness is discharged.

LEONTES

To see his nobleness!
Conceiving the dishonour of his mother,
He straight declined, droop'd, took it deeply,
Fasten'd and fix'd the shame on't in himself,
Threw off his spirit, his appetite, his sleep,
And downright languish'd. Leave me solely: go,
See how he fares.

Exit Servant

Fie, fie! no thought of him:
The thought of my revenges that way
Recoil upon me: in himself too mighty,
And in his parties, his alliance; let him be
Until a time may serve: for present vengeance,
Take it on her. Camillo and Polixenes
Laugh at me, make their pastime at my sorrow:
They should not laugh if I could reach them, nor
Shall she within my power.

Enter PAULINA, with a child

First Lord

You must not enter.

PAULINA

Nay, rather, good my lords, be second to me:
Fear you his tyrannous passion more, alas,
Than the queen's life? a gracious innocent soul,
More free than he is jealous.

ANTIGONUS

That's enough.

Second Servant

Madam, he hath not slept tonight; commanded
None should come at him.

PAULINA

Not so hot, good sir:
I come to bring him sleep. 'Tis such as you,
That creep like shadows by him and do sigh
At each his needless heavings, such as you
Nourish the cause of his awaking: I
Do come with words as medicinal as true,
Honest as either, to purge him of that humour
That presses him from sleep.

LEONTES

What noise there, ho?

PAULINA

No noise, my lord; but needful conference
About some gossips for your highness.

LEONTES

How!
Away with that audacious lady! Antigonus,
I charged thee that she should not come about me:
I knew she would.

ANTIGONUS

I told her so, my lord,
On your displeasure's peril and on mine,
She should not visit you.

LEONTES

What, canst not rule her?

PAULINA

From all dishonesty he can: in this,
Unless he take the course that you have done,
Commit me for committing honour, trust it,
He shall not rule me.

ANTIGONUS

La you now, you hear:
When she will take the rein I let her run;
But she'll not stumble.

PAULINA

Good my liege, I come;
And, I beseech you, hear me, who profess
Myself your loyal servant, your physician,
Your most obedient counsellor, yet that dare
Less appear so in comforting your evils,
Than such as most seem yours: I say, I come
From your good queen.

LEONTES

Good queen! — Jealously made him mad >
Playing / twisting his
mind

PAULINA

Good queen, my lord,
Good queen; I say good queen;
And would by combat make her good, so were I
A man, the worst about you.

LEONTES

Force her hence.

PAULINA

Let him that makes but trifles of his eyes
First hand me: on mine own accord I'll off;

But first I'll do my errand. The good queen,
For she is good, hath brought you forth a daughter;
Here 'tis; commends it to your blessing.

Laying down the child

LEONTES

Out!
A mankind witch! Hence with her, out o' door:
A most intelligencing bawd!

PAULINA

Not so:
I am as ignorant in that as you
In so entitling me, and no less honest
Than you are mad; which is enough, I'll warrant,
As this world goes, to pass for honest.

LEONTES - will not listen to anyone - belives his daughter is not his

Traitors!
Will you not push her out? Give her the bastard.
Thou dotard! thou art woman-tired, unroosted
By thy dame Partlet here. Take up the bastard;
Take't up, I say; give't to thy crone.

PAULINA

For ever
Unvenerable be thy hands, if thou

224

Takest up the princess by that forced baseness
Which he has put upon't!

LEONTES

He dreads his wife.

PAULINA

So I would you did; then 'twere past all doubt
You'ld call your children yours.

LEONTES

A nest of traitors!

ANTIGONUS

I am none, by this good light.

PAULINA

Nor I, nor any
But one that's here, and that's himself, for he
The sacred honour of himself, his queen's,
His hopeful son's, his babe's, betrays to slander,
Whose sting is sharper than the sword's;
and will not—
For, as the case now stands, it is a curse
He cannot be compell'd to't—once remove
The root of his opinion, which is rotten
As ever oak or stone was sound.

LEONTES

A callat
Of boundless tongue, who late hath beat her husband
And now baits me! This brat is none of mine;
It is the issue of Polixenes:
Hence with it, and together with the dam
Commit them to the fire!

PAULINA

It is yours;
And, might we lay the old proverb to your charge,
So like you, 'tis the worse. Behold, my lords,
Although the print be little, the whole matter
And copy of the father, eye, nose, lip,
The trick of's frown, his forehead, nay, the valley,
The pretty dimples of his chin and cheek,
His smiles,
The very mould and frame of hand, nail, finger:
And thou, good goddess Nature, which hast made it
So like to him that got it, if thou hast
The ordering of the mind too, 'mongst all colours
No yellow in't, lest she suspect, as he does,
Her children not her husband's!

LEONTES

A gross hag
And, lozel, thou art worthy to be hang'd,
That wilt not stay her tongue.

ANTIGONUS

Hang all the husbands
That cannot do that feat, you'll leave yourself
Hardly one subject.

LEONTES

Once more, take her hence.

PAULINA

A most unworthy and unnatural lord
Can do no more.

LEONTES

I'll ha' thee burnt.

PAULINA

I care not:
It is an heretic that makes the fire,
Not she which burns in't. I'll not call you tyrant;
But this most cruel usage of your queen,
Not able to produce more accusation
Than your own weak–hinged fancy, something savours
Of tyranny and will ignoble make you,
Yea, scandalous to the world.

LEONTES

On your allegiance,
Out of the chamber with her! Were I a tyrant,
Where were her life? she durst not call me so,

If she did know me one. Away with her!

PAULINA

I pray you, do not push me; I'll be gone.
Look to your babe, my lord; 'tis yours:
Jove send her
A better guiding spirit! What needs these hands?
You, that are thus so tender o'er his follies,
Will never do him good, not one of you.
So, so: farewell; we are gone.

Exit

LEONTES — Belives that antigous is a traiter, help-
ing his wife. Wants to burn the child

Thou, traitor, hast set on thy wife to this.
My child? away with't! Even thou, that hast
A heart so tender o'er it, take it hence
And see it instantly consumed with fire;
Even thou and none but thou. Take it up straight:
Within this hour bring me word 'tis done,
And by good testimony, or I'll seize thy life,
With what thou else call'st thine. If thou refuse
And wilt encounter with my wrath, say so;
The bastard brains with these my proper hands
Shall I dash out. Go, take it to the fire;
For thou set'st on thy wife.

ANTIGONUS

I did not, sir:
These lords, my noble fellows, if they please,

Can clear me in't.

Lords

> We can: my royal liege,
> He is not guilty of her coming hither.

LEONTES

> You're liars all.

First Lord

> Beseech your highness, give us better credit:
> We have always truly served you, and beseech you
> So to esteem of us, and on our knees we beg,
> As recompense of our dear services
> Past and to come, that you do change this purpose,
> Which being so horrible, so bloody, must
> Lead on to some foul issue: we all kneel.

LEONTES

> I am a feather for each wind that blows:
> Shall I live on to see this bastard kneel
> And call me father? better burn it now
> Than curse it then. But be it; let it live.
> It shall not neither. You, sir, come you hither;
> You that have been so tenderly officious
> With Lady Margery, your midwife there,
> To save this bastard's life,—for 'tis a bastard,
> So sure as this beard's grey,
> —what will you adventure

To save this brat's life?

ANTIGONUS *— tries to save the child*

> Any thing, my lord,
> That my ability may undergo
> And nobleness impose: at least thus much:
> I'll pawn the little blood which I have left
> To save the innocent: any thing possible.

LEONTES

> It shall be possible. Swear by this sword
> Thou wilt perform my bidding.

ANTIGONUS

> I will, my lord.

LEONTES *— now wants to get rid of the child, out of the kingdom*

> Mark and perform it, see'st thou! for the fail
> Of any point in't shall not only be
> Death to thyself but to thy lewd–tongued wife,
> Whom for this time we pardon. We enjoin thee,
> As thou art liege–man to us, that thou carry
> This female bastard hence and that thou bear it
> To some remote and desert place quite out
> Of our dominions, and that there thou leave it,
> Without more mercy, to its own protection
> And favour of the climate. As by strange fortune
> It came to us, I do in justice charge thee,
> On thy soul's peril and thy body's torture,

230

That thou commend it strangely to some place
Where chance may nurse or end it. Take it up.

ANTIGONUS

I swear to do this, though a present death
Had been more merciful. Come on, poor babe:
Some powerful spirit instruct the kites and ravens
To be thy nurses! Wolves and bears, they say
Casting their savageness aside have done
Like offices of pity. Sir, be prosperous
In more than this deed does require! And blessing
Against this cruelty fight on thy side,
Poor thing, condemn'd to loss!

Exit with the child

LEONTES

No, I'll not rear
Another's issue.

Enter a Servant

Servant

Please your highness, posts
From those you sent to the oracle are come
An hour since: Cleomenes and Dion,
Being well arrived from Delphos, are both landed,
Hasting to the court.

First Lord

> So please you, sir, their speed
> Hath been beyond account.

LEONTES

> Twenty–three days
> They have been absent: 'tis good speed; foretells
> The great Apollo suddenly will have
> The truth of this appear. Prepare you, lords;
> Summon a session, that we may arraign
> Our most disloyal lady, for, as she hath
> Been publicly accused, so shall she have
> A just and open trial. While she lives
> My heart will be a burthen to me. Leave me,
> And think upon my bidding.

> *Exeunt*

Act 3, Scene 1

A sea–port in Sicilia.

> *Enter CLEOMENES and DION*

CLEOMENES

> The climate's delicate, the air most sweet,
> Fertile the isle, the temple much surpassing
> The common praise it bears.

DION

> I shall report,
> For most it caught me, the celestial habits,
> Methinks I so should term them, and the reverence
> Of the grave wearers. O, the sacrifice!
> How ceremonious, solemn and unearthly
> It was i' the offering!

CLEOMENES

> But of all, the burst
> And the ear–deafening voice o' the oracle,
> Kin to Jove's thunder, so surprised my sense.
> That I was nothing.

DION

> If the event o' the journey
> Prove as successful to the queen,—O be't so!—
> As it hath been to us rare, pleasant, speedy,
> The time is worth the use on't.

CLEOMENES

> Great Apollo
> Turn all to the best! These proclamations,
> So forcing faults upon Hermione,
> I little like.

DION

The violent carriage of it
Will clear or end the business: when the oracle,
Thus by Apollo's great divine seal'd up,
Shall the contents discover, something rare
Even then will rush to knowledge. Go: fresh horses!
And gracious be the issue!

Exeunt

Act 3, Scene 2

A court of Justice.

Enter LEONTES, Lords, and Officers

LEONTES

This sessions, to our great grief we pronounce,
Even pushes 'gainst our heart: the party tried
The daughter of a king, our wife, and one
Of us too much beloved. Let us be clear'd
Of being tyrannous, since we so openly
Proceed in justice, which shall have due course,
Even to the guilt or the purgation.
Produce the prisoner.

Officer

It is his highness' pleasure that the queen
Appear in person here in court. Silence!

Enter HERMIONE guarded; PAULINA and Ladies attending

234

LEONTES

Read the indictment.

Officer

[Reads] Hermione, queen to the worthy
Leontes, king of Sicilia, thou art here accused and
arraigned of high treason, in committing adultery
with Polixenes, king of Bohemia, and conspiring
with Camillo to take away the life of our sovereign
lord the king, thy royal husband: the pretence
whereof being by circumstances partly laid open,
thou, Hermione, contrary to the faith and allegiance
of a true subject, didst counsel and aid them, for
their better safety, to fly away by night.

HERMIONE

Since what I am to say must be but that
Which contradicts my accusation and
The testimony on my part no other
But what comes from myself, it shall scarce boot me
To say 'not guilty:' mine integrity
Being counted falsehood, shall, as I express it,
Be so received. But thus: if powers divine
Behold our human actions, as they do,
I doubt not then but innocence shall make
False accusation blush and tyranny
Tremble at patience. You, my lord, best know,
Who least will seem to do so, my past life
Hath been as continent, as chaste, as true,
As I am now unhappy; which is more
Than history can pattern, though devised
And play'd to take spectators. For behold me

A fellow of the royal bed, which owe
A moiety of the throne a great king's daughter,
The mother to a hopeful prince, here standing
To prate and talk for life and honour 'fore
Who please to come and hear. For life, I prize it
As I weigh grief, which I would spare: for honour,
'Tis a derivative from me to mine,
And only that I stand for. I appeal
To your own conscience, sir, before Polixenes
Came to your court, how I was in your grace,
How merited to be so; since he came,
With what encounter so uncurrent I
Have strain'd to appear thus: if one jot beyond
The bound of honour, or in act or will
That way inclining, harden'd be the hearts
Of all that hear me, and my near'st of kin
Cry fie upon my grave!

LEONTES

I ne'er heard yet
That any of these bolder vices wanted
Less impudence to gainsay what they did
Than to perform it first.

HERMIONE

That's true enough;
Through 'tis a saying, sir, not due to me.

LEONTES

You will not own it.

HERMIONE

More than mistress of
Which comes to me in name of fault, I must not
At all acknowledge. For Polixenes,
With whom I am accused, I do confess
I loved him as in honour he required,
With such a kind of love as might become
A lady like me, with a love even such,
So and no other, as yourself commanded:
Which not to have done I think had been in me
Both disobedience and ingratitude
To you and toward your friend, whose love had spoke,
Even since it could speak, from an infant, freely
That it was yours. Now, for conspiracy,
I know not how it tastes; though it be dish'd
For me to try how: all I know of it
Is that Camillo was an honest man;
And why he left your court, the gods themselves,
Wotting no more than I, are ignorant.

LEONTES

You knew of his departure, as you know
What you have underta'en to do in's absence.

HERMIONE

Sir,
You speak a language that I understand not:
My life stands in the level of your dreams,
Which I'll lay down.

LEONTES

Your actions are my dreams;
You had a bastard by Polixenes,
And I but dream'd it. As you were past all shame,—
Those of your fact are so—so past all truth:
Which to deny concerns more than avails; for as
Thy brat hath been cast out, like to itself,
No father owning it,—which is, indeed,
More criminal in thee than it,—so thou
Shalt feel our justice, in whose easiest passage
Look for no less than death. – Sentences her to death

HERMIONE

Sir, spare your threats:
The bug which you would fright me with I seek.
To me can life be no commodity:
The crown and comfort of my life, your favour,
I do give lost; for I do feel it gone,
But know not how it went. My second joy
And first–fruits of my body, from his presence
I am barr'd, like one infectious. My third comfort
Starr'd most unluckily, is from my breast,
The innocent milk in its most innocent mouth,
Haled out to murder: myself on every post
Proclaimed a strumpet: with immodest hatred
The child–bed privilege denied, which 'longs
To women of all fashion; lastly, hurried
Here to this place, i' the open air, before
I have got strength of limit. Now, my liege,
Tell me what blessings I have here alive,
That I should fear to die? Therefore proceed.
But yet hear this: mistake me not; no life,
I prize it not a straw, but for mine honour,

238

Which I would free, if I shall be condemn'd
Upon surmises, all proofs sleeping else
But what your jealousies awake, I tell you
'Tis rigor and not law. Your honours all,
I do refer me to the oracle:
Apollo be my judge!

First Lord

This your request
Is altogether just: therefore bring forth,
And in Apollos name, his oracle.

Exeunt certain Officers

HERMIONE

The Emperor of Russia was my father:
O that he were alive, and here beholding
His daughter's trial! that he did but see
The flatness of my misery, yet with eyes
Of pity, not revenge!

Re−enter Officers, with CLEOMENES and DION

Officer

You here shall swear upon this sword of justice,
That you, Cleomenes and Dion, have
Been both at Delphos, and from thence have brought
The seal'd−up oracle, by the hand deliver'd
Of great Apollo's priest; and that, since then,
You have not dared to break the holy seal

Nor read the secrets in't.

CLEOMENES

> |
> | All this we swear.

DION

> |

LEONTES

> Break up the seals and read.

Officer [Reads]

> Hermione is chaste;
> Polixenes blameless; Camillo a true subject; Leontes
> a jealous tyrant; his innocent babe truly begotten;
> and the king shall live without an heir, if that
> which is lost be not found.

Lords

> Now blessed be the great Apollo!

HERMIONE

> Praised!

LEONTES

Hast thou read truth?

Officer

Ay, my lord; even so
As it is here set down.

LEONTES

There is no truth at all i' the oracle:
The sessions shall proceed: this is mere falsehood.

Enter Servant

Servant

My lord the king, the king!

LEONTES

What is the business?

Servant

O sir, I shall be hated to report it!
The prince your son, with mere conceit and fear
Of the queen's speed, is gone.

LEONTES

How! gone!

Servant - The Prince - Their son has dead!

241

Is dead.

LEONTES

> Apollo's angry; and the heavens themselves
> Do strike at my injustice.

> *HERMIONE swoons*

How now there!

PAULINA

> This news is mortal to the queen: look down
> And see what death is doing.

LEONTES

> Take her hence:
> Her heart is but o'ercharged; she will recover:
> I have too much believed mine own suspicion:
> Beseech you, tenderly apply to her
> Some remedies for life.

> *Exeunt PAULINA and Ladies, with HERMIONE*

Apollo, pardon — realised he was wrong — his
My great profaneness 'gainst thine oracle! sons death is apollo punishements.
I'll reconcile me to Polixenes,
New woo my queen, recall the good Camillo,
Whom I proclaim a man of truth, of mercy;
For, being transported by my jealousies

To bloody thoughts and to revenge, I chose
Camillo for the minister to poison
My friend Polixenes: which had been done,
But that the good mind of Camillo tardied
My swift command, though I with death and with
Reward did threaten and encourage him,
Not doing 't and being done: he, most humane
And fill'd with honour, to my kingly guest
Unclasp'd my practise, quit his fortunes here,
Which you knew great, and to the hazard
Of all encertainties himself commended,
No richer than his honour: how he glisters
Thorough my rust! and how his pity
Does my deeds make the blacker!

Re–enter PAULINA

PAULINA

    Woe the while!
    O, cut my lace, lest my heart, cracking it,
    Break too.

First Lord

    What fit is this, good lady?

PAULINA

    What studied torments, tyrant, hast for me?
    What wheels? racks? fires? what flaying? boiling?
    In leads or oils? what old or newer torture
    Must I receive, whose every word deserves
    To taste of thy most worst? Thy tyranny

Together working with thy jealousies,
Fancies too weak for boys, too green and idle
For girls of nine, O, think what they have done
And then run mad indeed, stark mad! for all
Thy by–gone fooleries were but spices of it.
That thou betray'dst Polixenes,'twas nothing;
That did but show thee, of a fool, inconstant
And damnable ingrateful: nor was't much,
Thou wouldst have poison'd good Camillo's honour,
To have him kill a king: poor trespasses,
More monstrous standing by: whereof I reckon
The casting forth to crows thy baby–daughter
To be or none or little; though a devil
Would have shed water out of fire ere done't:
Nor is't directly laid to thee, the death
Of the young prince, whose honourable thoughts,
Thoughts high for one so tender, cleft the heart
That could conceive a gross and foolish sire
Blemish'd his gracious dam: this is not, no,
Laid to thy answer: but the last,—O lords,
When I have said, cry 'woe!' the queen, the queen,
The sweet'st, dear'st creature's dead, *= his wife – the queen*
and vengeance for't *is now dead*
Not dropp'd down yet.

First Lord

The higher powers forbid!

PAULINA

I say she's dead; I'll swear't. If word nor oath
Prevail not, go and see: if you can bring
Tincture or lustre in her lip, her eye,
Heat outwardly or breath within, I'll serve you

244

As I would do the gods. But, O thou tyrant!
Do not repent these things, for they are heavier
Than all thy woes can stir; therefore betake thee
To nothing but despair. A thousand knees
Ten thousand years together, naked, fasting,
Upon a barren mountain and still winter
In storm perpetual, could not move the gods
To look that way thou wert.

LEONTES

Go on, go on
Thou canst not speak too much; I have deserved
All tongues to talk their bitterest.

First Lord

Say no more:
Howe'er the business goes, you have made fault
I' the boldness of your speech.

PAULINA

I am sorry for't:
All faults I make, when I shall come to know them,
I do repent. Alas! I have show'd too much
The rashness of a woman: he is touch'd
To the noble heart. What's gone and what's past help
Should be past grief: do not receive affliction
At my petition; I beseech you, rather
Let me be punish'd, that have minded you
Of what you should forget. Now, good my liege
Sir, royal sir, forgive a foolish woman:

The love I bore your queen—lo, fool again!—
I'll speak of her no more, nor of your children;
I'll not remember you of my own lord,
Who is lost too: take your patience to you,
And I'll say nothing.

LEONTES

Thou didst speak but well
When most the truth; which I receive much better
Than to be pitied of thee. Prithee, bring me
To the dead bodies of my queen and son:
One grave shall be for both: upon them shall
The causes of their death appear, unto
Our shame perpetual. Once a day I'll visit
The chapel where they lie, and tears shed there
Shall be my recreation: so long as nature
Will bear up with this exercise, so long
I daily vow to use it. Come and lead me
Unto these sorrows.

Exeunt

> Moving to a new place

^ Sicilica

Bohemia

Act 3, Scene 3

Bohemia. A desert country near the sea.

Enter ANTIGONUS with a Child, and a Mariner

ANTIGONUS

Thou art perfect then, our ship hath touch'd upon
The deserts of Bohemia?

246

Mariner

Ay, my lord: and fear
We have landed in ill time: the skies look grimly
And threaten present blusters. In my conscience,
The heavens with that we have in hand are angry
And frown upon 's.

ANTIGONUS

Their sacred wills be done! Go, get aboard;
Look to thy bark: I'll not be long before
I call upon thee.

Mariner

Make your best haste, and go not
Too far i' the land: 'tis like to be loud weather;
Besides, this place is famous for the creatures
Of prey that keep upon't.

ANTIGONUS

Go thou away:
I'll follow instantly.

Mariner

I am glad at heart
To be so rid o' the business.

Exit

ANTIGONUS

Come, poor babe:
I have heard, but not believed,
the spirits o' the dead
May walk again: if such thing be, thy mother
Appear'd to me last night, for ne'er was dream
So like a waking. To me comes a creature,
Sometimes her head on one side, some another;
I never saw a vessel of like sorrow,
So fill'd and so becoming: in pure white robes,
Like very sanctity, she did approach
My cabin where I lay; thrice bow'd before me,
And gasping to begin some speech, her eyes
Became two spouts: the fury spent, anon
Did this break–from her: 'Good Antigonus,
Since fate, against thy better disposition,
Hath made thy person for the thrower–out
Of my poor babe, according to thine oath,
Places remote enough are in Bohemia,
There weep and leave it crying; and, for the babe
Is counted lost for ever, Perdita, - childs name
I prithee, call't. For this ungentle business
Put on thee by my lord, thou ne'er shalt see
Thy wife Paulina more.' And so, with shrieks
She melted into air. Affrighted much,
I did in time collect myself and thought
This was so and no slumber. Dreams are toys:
Yet for this once, yea, superstitiously,
I will be squared by this. I do believe
Hermione hath suffer'd death, and that
Apollo would, this being indeed the issue

Of King Polixenes, it should here be laid,
Either for life or death, upon the earth
Of its right father. Blossom, speed thee well!
There lie, and there thy character: there these;
Which may, if fortune please, both breed thee, pretty,
And still rest thine. The storm begins; poor wretch,
That for thy mother's fault art thus exposed
To loss and what may follow! Weep I cannot,
But my heart bleeds; and most accursed am I
To be by oath enjoin'd to this. Farewell!
The day frowns more and more: thou'rt like to have
A lullaby too rough: I never saw
The heavens so dim by day. A savage clamour!
Well may I get aboard! This is the chase:
I am gone for ever.

Exit, pursued by a bear

Enter a Shepherd

Shepherd

I would there were no age between sixteen and
three−and−twenty, or that youth would sleep out the
rest; for there is nothing in the between but
getting wenches with child, wronging the ancientry,
stealing, fighting—Hark you now! Would any but
these boiled brains of nineteen and two−and−twenty
hunt this weather? They have scared away two of my
best sheep, which I fear the wolf will sooner find
than the master: if any where I have them, 'tis by
the seaside, browsing of ivy. Good luck, an't be thy
will what have we here! Mercy on 's, a barne a very
pretty barne! A boy or a child, I wonder? A
pretty one; a very pretty one: sure, some 'scape:

though I am not bookish, yet I can read
waiting–gentlewoman in the 'scape. This has been
some stair–work, some trunk–work, some
behind–door–work: they were warmer that got this
than the poor thing is here. I'll take it up for
pity: yet I'll tarry till my son come; he hallooed
but even now. Whoa, ho, hoa!

Enter Clown

Clown

Hilloa, loa!

Shepherd

What, art so near? If thou'lt see a thing to talk
on when thou art dead and rotten, come hither. What
ailest thou, man?

Clown

I have seen two such sights, by sea and by land!
but I am not to say it is a sea, for it is now the
sky: betwixt the firmament and it you cannot thrust
a bodkin's point.

Shepherd

Why, boy, how is it?

Clown

I would you did but see how it chafes, how it rages,
how it takes up the shore! but that's not the
point. O, the most piteous cry of the poor souls!
sometimes to see 'em, and not to see 'em; now the
ship boring the moon with her main–mast, and anon
swallowed with yest and froth, as you'ld thrust a
cork into a hogshead. And then for the
land–service, to see how the bear tore out his
shoulder–bone; how he cried to me for help and said
his name was Antigonus, a nobleman. But to make an
end of the ship, to see how the sea flap–dragoned
it: but, first, how the poor souls roared, and the
sea mocked them; and how the poor gentleman roared
and the bear mocked him, both roaring louder than
the sea or weather.

Shepherd

Name of mercy, when was this, boy?

Clown

Now, now: I have not winked since I saw these
sights: the men are not yet cold under water, nor
the bear half dined on the gentleman: he's at it
now.

Shepherd

Would I had been by, to have helped the old man!

Clown

I would you had been by the ship side, to have
helped her: there your charity would have lacked footing.

Shepherd

Heavy matters! heavy matters! but look thee here,
boy. Now bless thyself: thou mettest with things
dying, I with things newborn. Here's a sight for
thee; look thee, a bearing–cloth for a squire's
child! look thee here; take up, take up, boy;
open't. So, let's see: it was told me I should be
rich by the fairies. This is some changeling:
open't. What's within, boy?

Clown

You're a made old man: if the sins of your youth
are forgiven you, you're well to live. Gold! all gold!

Shepherd

This is fairy gold, boy, and 'twill prove so: up
with't, keep it close: home, home, the next way.
We are lucky, boy; and to be so still requires
nothing but secrecy. Let my sheep go: come, good
boy, the next way home.

Clown

Go you the next way with your findings. I'll go see
if the bear be gone from the gentleman and how much
he hath eaten: they are never curst but when they

are hungry: if there be any of him left, I'll bury
it.

Shepherd

That's a good deed. If thou mayest discern by that
which is left of him what he is, fetch me to the
sight of him.

Clown

Marry, will I; and you shall help to put him i' the ground.

Shepherd

'Tis a lucky day, boy, and we'll do good deeds on't.

Exeunt

Enter Time, the Chorus

Time

I, that please some, try all, both joy and terror
Of good and bad, that makes and unfolds error,
Now take upon me, in the name of Time,
To use my wings. Impute it not a crime
To me or my swift passage, that I slide
O'er sixteen years and leave the growth untried
Of that wide gap, since it is in my power
To o'erthrow law and in one self–born hour
To plant and o'erwhelm custom. Let me pass
The same I am, ere ancient'st order was
Or what is now received: I witness to

The times that brought them in; so shall I do
To the freshest things now reigning and make stale
The glistering of this present, as my tale
Now seems to it. Your patience this allowing,
I turn my glass and give my scene such growing
As you had slept between: Leontes leaving,
The effects of his fond jealousies so grieving
That he shuts up himself, imagine me,
Gentle spectators, that I now may be
In fair Bohemia, and remember well,
I mentioned a son o' the king's, which Florizel
I now name to you; and with speed so pace
To speak of Perdita, now grown in grace
Equal with wondering: what of her ensues
I list not prophecy; but let Time's news
Be known when 'tis brought forth.
A shepherd's daughter,
And what to her adheres, which follows after,
Is the argument of Time. Of this allow,
If ever you have spent time worse ere now;
If never, yet that Time himself doth say
He wishes earnestly you never may.

Exit

Act 3, Scene 1

A sea-port in Sicilia.

Enter CLEOMENES and DION

CLEOMENES

The climate's delicate, the air most sweet,
Fertile the isle, the temple much surpassing
The common praise it bears.

DION

I shall report,
For most it caught me, the celestial habits,
Methinks I so should term them, and the reverence
Of the grave wearers. O, the sacrifice!
How ceremonious, solemn and unearthly
It was i' the offering!

CLEOMENES

But of all, the burst
And the ear–deafening voice o' the oracle,
Kin to Jove's thunder, so surprised my sense.
That I was nothing.

DION

If the event o' the journey
Prove as successful to the queen,—O be't so!—
As it hath been to us rare, pleasant, speedy,
The time is worth the use on't.

CLEOMENES

Great Apollo
Turn all to the best! These proclamations,
So forcing faults upon Hermione,

I little like.

DION

The violent carriage of it
Will clear or end the business: when the oracle,
Thus by Apollo's great divine seal'd up,
Shall the contents discover, something rare
Even then will rush to knowledge. Go: fresh horses!
And gracious be the issue!

Exeunt

Act 4, Scene 2

Bohemia. The palace of POLIXENES.

Enter POLIXENES and CAMILLO

POLIXENES

I pray thee, good Camillo, be no more importunate:
'tis a sickness denying thee any thing; a death to
grant this.

CAMILLO

It is fifteen years since I saw my country: though
I have for the most part been aired abroad, I
desire to lay my bones there. Besides, the penitent
king, my master, hath sent for me; to whose feeling
sorrows I might be some allay, or I o'erween to

think so, which is another spur to my departure.

POLIXENES — His son Fancies ~~his~~ daughter *[handwritten: Leontes]*

As thou lovest me, Camillo, wipe not out the rest of
thy services by leaving me now: the need I have of
thee thine own goodness hath made; better not to
have had thee than thus to want thee: thou, having
made me businesses which none without thee can
sufficiently manage, must either stay to execute
them thyself or take away with thee the very
services thou hast done; which if I have not enough
considered, as too much I cannot, to be more
thankful to thee shall be my study, and my profit
therein the heaping friendships. Of that fatal
country, Sicilia, prithee speak no more; whose very
naming punishes me with the remembrance of that
penitent, as thou callest him, and reconciled king,
my brother; whose loss of his most precious queen
and children are even now to be afresh lamented.
Say to me, when sawest thou the Prince Florizel, my
son? Kings are no less unhappy, their issue not
being gracious, than they are in losing them when
they have approved their virtues.

CAMILLO

Sir, it is three days since I saw the prince. What
his happier affairs may be, are to me unknown: but I
have missingly noted, he is of late much retired
from court and is less frequent to his princely
exercises than formerly he hath appeared.

POLIXENES

I have considered so much, Camillo, and with some
care; so far that I have eyes under my service which
look upon his removedness; from whom I have this
intelligence, that he is seldom from the house of a
most homely shepherd; a man, they say, that from
very nothing, and beyond the imagination of his
neighbours, is grown into an unspeakable estate.

CAMILLO

I have heard, sir, of such a man, who hath a
daughter of most rare note: the report of her is
extended more than can be thought to begin from such a cottage.

POLIXENES

That's likewise part of my intelligence; but, I
fear, the angle that plucks our son thither. Thou
shalt accompany us to the place; where we will, not
appearing what we are, have some question with the
shepherd; from whose simplicity I think it not
uneasy to get the cause of my son's resort thither.
Prithee, be my present partner in this business, and
lay aside the thoughts of Sicilia.

CAMILLO

I willingly obey your command.

POLIXENES

My best Camillo! We must disguise ourselves.

Exeunt

Act 4, Scene 3

A road near the Shepherd's cottage.

Enter AUTOLYCUS, singing

AUTOLYCUS

> When daffodils begin to peer,
> With heigh! the doxy over the dale,
> Why, then comes in the sweet o' the year;
> For the red blood reigns in the winter's pale.
>
> The white sheet bleaching on the hedge,
> With heigh! the sweet birds, O, how they sing!
> Doth set my pugging tooth on edge;
> For a quart of ale is a dish for a king.
>
> The lark, that tirra–lyra chants,
> With heigh! with heigh! the thrush and the jay,
> Are summer songs for me and my aunts,
> While we lie tumbling in the hay.
>
> I have served Prince Florizel and in my time
> wore three–pile; but now I am out of service:
>
> But shall I go mourn for that, my dear?
> The pale moon shines by night:
> And when I wander here and there,
> I then do most go right.

If tinkers may have leave to live,
And bear the sow–skin budget,
Then my account I well may, give,
And in the stocks avouch it.

My traffic is sheets; when the kite builds, look to
lesser linen. My father named me Autolycus; who
being, as I am, littered under Mercury, was likewise
a snapper–up of unconsidered trifles. With die and
drab I purchased this caparison, and my revenue is
the silly cheat. Gallows and knock are too powerful
on the highway: beating and hanging are terrors to
me: for the life to come, I sleep out the thought
of it. A prize! a prize!

Enter Clown

Clown

Let me see: every 'leven wether tods; every tod
yields pound and odd shilling; fifteen hundred
shorn. what comes the wool to?

AUTOLYCUS

[Aside]
If the springe hold, the cock's mine.

Clown

I cannot do't without counters. Let me see; what am
I to buy for our sheep–shearing feast? Three pound
of sugar, five pound of currants, rice,—what will

this sister of mine do with rice? But my father
hath made her mistress of the feast, and she lays it
on. She hath made me four and twenty nose–gays for
the shearers, three–man–song–men all, and very good
ones; but they are most of them means and bases; but
one puritan amongst them, and he sings psalms to
horn–pipes. I must have saffron to colour the warden
pies; mace; dates?—none, that's out of my note;
nutmegs, seven; a race or two of ginger, but that I
may beg; four pound of prunes, and as many of
raisins o' the sun.

AUTOLYCUS

O that ever I was born!

Grovelling on the ground

Clown

I' the name of me—

AUTOLYCUS

O, help me, help me! pluck but off these rags; and
then, death, death!

Clown

Alack, poor soul! thou hast need of more rags to lay
on thee, rather than have these off.

AUTOLYCUS

O sir, the loathsomeness of them offends me more
than the stripes I have received, which are mighty
ones and millions.

Clown

Alas, poor man! a million of beating may come to a
great matter.

AUTOLYCUS

I am robbed, sir, and beaten; my money and apparel
ta'en from me, and these detestable things put upon
me.

Clown

What, by a horseman, or a footman?

AUTOLYCUS

A footman, sweet sir, a footman.

Clown

Indeed, he should be a footman by the garments he
has left with thee: if this be a horseman's coat,
it hath seen very hot service. Lend me thy hand,
I'll help thee: come, lend me thy hand.

AUTOLYCUS

O, good sir, tenderly, O!

Clown

Alas, poor soul!

AUTOLYCUS

O, good sir, softly, good sir! I fear, sir, my
shoulder–blade is out.

Clown

How now! canst stand?

AUTOLYCUS

[Picking his pocket]
Softly, dear sir; good sir, softly. You ha' done me
a charitable office.

Clown

Dost lack any money? I have a little money for thee.

AUTOLYCUS

No, good sweet sir; no, I beseech you, sir: I have
a kinsman not past three quarters of a mile hence,
unto whom I was going; I shall there have money, or
any thing I want: offer me no money, I pray you;
that kills my heart.

263

Clown

What manner of fellow was he that robbed you?

AUTOLYCUS

A fellow, sir, that I have known to go about with
troll–my–dames; I knew him once a servant of the
prince: I cannot tell, good sir, for which of his
virtues it was, but he was certainly whipped out of the court.

Clown

His vices, you would say; there's no virtue whipped
out of the court: they cherish it to make it stay
there; and yet it will no more but abide.

AUTOLYCUS

Vices, I would say, sir. I know this man well: he
hath been since an ape–bearer; then a
process–server, a bailiff; then he compassed a
motion of the Prodigal Son, and married a tinker's
wife within a mile where my land and living lies;
and, having flown over many knavish professions, he
settled only in rogue: some call him Autolycus.

Clown

Out upon him! prig, for my life, prig: he haunts
wakes, fairs and bear–baitings.

AUTOLYCUS

> Very true, sir; he, sir, he; that's the rogue that
> put me into this apparel.

Clown

> Not a more cowardly rogue in all Bohemia: if you had
> but looked big and spit at him, he'ld have run.

AUTOLYCUS

> I must confess to you, sir, I am no fighter: I am
> false of heart that way; and that he knew, I warrant
> him.

Clown

> How do you now?

AUTOLYCUS

> Sweet sir, much better than I was; I can stand and
> walk: I will even take my leave of you, and pace
> softly towards my kinsman's.

Clown

> Shall I bring thee on the way?

AUTOLYCUS

No, good–faced sir; no, sweet sir.

Clown

Then fare thee well: I must go buy spices for our
sheep–shearing.

AUTOLYCUS

Prosper you, sweet sir!

Exit Clown

Your purse is not hot enough to purchase your spice.
I'll be with you at your sheep–shearing too: if I
make not this cheat bring out another and the
shearers prove sheep, let me be unrolled and my name
put in the book of virtue!

Sings

Jog on, jog on, the foot–path way,
And merrily hent the stile–a:
A merry heart goes all the day,
Your sad tires in a mile–a.

Exit

Act 4, Scene 4

The Shepherd's cottage.

Enter FLORIZEL and PERDITA

FLORIZEL

These your unusual weeds to each part of you
Do give a life: no shepherdess, but Flora
Peering in April's front. This your sheep–shearing
Is as a meeting of the petty gods,
And you the queen on't.

PERDITA

Sir, my gracious lord,
To chide at your extremes it not becomes me:
O, pardon, that I name them! Your high self,
The gracious mark o' the land, you have obscured
With a swain's wearing, and me, poor lowly maid,
Most goddess–like prank'd up: but that our feasts
In every mess have folly and the feeders
Digest it with a custom, I should blush
To see you so attired, sworn, I think,
To show myself a glass.

FLORIZEL

I bless the time
When my good falcon made her flight across
Thy father's ground.

PERDITA

Now Jove afford you cause!
To me the difference forges dread; your greatness

Hath not been used to fear. Even now I tremble
To think your father, by some accident,
Should pass this way as you did: O, the Fates!
How would he look, to see his work so noble
Vilely bound up? What would he say? Or how
Should I, in these my borrow'd flaunts, behold
The sternness of his presence?

FLORIZEL

Apprehend
Nothing but jollity. The gods themselves,
Humbling their deities to love, have taken
The shapes of beasts upon them: Jupiter
Became a bull, and bellow'd; the green Neptune
A ram, and bleated; and the fire–robed god,
Golden Apollo, a poor humble swain,
As I seem now. Their transformations
Were never for a piece of beauty rarer,
Nor in a way so chaste, since my desires
Run not before mine honour, nor my lusts
Burn hotter than my faith.

PERDITA

O, but, sir,
Your resolution cannot hold, when 'tis
Opposed, as it must be, by the power of the king:
One of these two must be necessities,
Which then will speak, that you must
change this purpose,
Or I my life.

FLORIZEL

> Thou dearest Perdita,
> With these forced thoughts, I prithee, darken not
> The mirth o' the feast. Or I'll be thine, my fair,
> Or not my father's. For I cannot be
> Mine own, nor any thing to any, if
> I be not thine. To this I am most constant,
> Though destiny say no. Be merry, gentle;
> Strangle such thoughts as these with any thing
> That you behold the while. Your guests are coming:
> Lift up your countenance, as it were the day
> Of celebration of that nuptial which
> We two have sworn shall come.

PERDITA — daughter of ~~Polixenes~~ Leontes

> O lady Fortune,
> Stand you auspicious!

FLORIZEL — Son of Polixenes

> See, your guests approach:
> Address yourself to entertain them sprightly,
> And let's be red with mirth.

Enter Shepherd, Clown, MOPSA, DORCAS, and others, with POLIXENES and CAMILLO disguised

Shepherd

> Fie, daughter! when my old wife lived, upon
> This day she was both pantler, butler, cook,

269

Both dame and servant; welcomed all, served all;
Would sing her song and dance her turn; now here,
At upper end o' the table, now i' the middle;
On his shoulder, and his; her face o' fire
With labour and the thing she took to quench it,
She would to each one sip. You are retired,
As if you were a feasted one and not
The hostess of the meeting: pray you, bid
These unknown friends to's welcome; for it is
A way to make us better friends, more known.
Come, quench your blushes and present yourself
That which you are, mistress o' the feast: come on,
And bid us welcome to your sheep–shearing,
As your good flock shall prosper.

PERDITA

[To POLIXENES] Sir, welcome:
It is my father's will I should take on me
The hostess–ship o' the day.

To CAMILLO

You're welcome, sir.
Give me those flowers there, Dorcas. Reverend sirs,
For you there's rosemary and rue; these keep
Seeming and savour all the winter long:
Grace and remembrance be to you both,
And welcome to our shearing!

POLIXENES

Shepherdess,
A fair one are you—well you fit our ages
With flowers of winter.

PERDITA

Sir, the year growing ancient,
Not yet on summer's death, nor on the birth
Of trembling winter, the fairest
flowers o' the season
Are our carnations and streak'd gillyvors,
Which some call nature's bastards: of that kind
Our rustic garden's barren; and I care not
To get slips of them.

POLIXENES

Wherefore, gentle maiden,
Do you neglect them?

PERDITA

For I have heard it said
There is an art which in their piedness shares
With great creating nature.

POLIXENES

Say there be;
Yet nature is made better by no mean
But nature makes that mean: so, over that art
Which you say adds to nature, is an art

That nature makes. You see, sweet maid, we marry
A gentler scion to the wildest stock,
And make conceive a bark of baser kind
By bud of nobler race: this is an art
Which does mend nature, change it rather, but
The art itself is nature.

PERDITA

So it is.

POLIXENES

Then make your garden rich in gillyvors,
And do not call them bastards.

PERDITA

I'll not put
The dibble in earth to set one slip of them;
No more than were I painted I would wish
This youth should say 'twere well and only therefore
Desire to breed by me. Here's flowers for you;
Hot lavender, mints, savoury, marjoram;
The marigold, that goes to bed wi' the sun
And with him rises weeping: these are flowers
Of middle summer, and I think they are given
To men of middle age. You're very welcome.

CAMILLO

I should leave grazing, were I of your flock,
And only live by gazing.

PERDITA

Out, alas!
You'd be so lean, that blasts of January
Would blow you through and through.
Now, my fair'st friend,
I would I had some flowers o' the spring that might
Become your time of day; and yours, and yours,
That wear upon your virgin branches yet
Your maidenheads growing: O Proserpina,
For the flowers now, that frighted thou let'st fall
From Dis's waggon! daffodils,
That come before the swallow dares, and take
The winds of March with beauty; violets dim,
But sweeter than the lids of Juno's eyes
Or Cytherea's breath; pale primroses
That die unmarried, ere they can behold
Bight Phoebus in his strength—a malady
Most incident to maids; bold oxlips and
The crown imperial; lilies of all kinds,
The flower–de–luce being one! O, these I lack,
To make you garlands of, and my sweet friend,
To strew him o'er and o'er!

FLORIZEL

What, like a corse?

PERDITA

No, like a bank for love to lie and play on;
Not like a corse; or if, not to be buried,
But quick and in mine arms. Come, take your flowers:

273

Methinks I play as I have seen them do
In Whitsun pastorals: sure this robe of mine
Does change my disposition.

FLORIZEL

What you do
Still betters what is done. When you speak, sweet.
I'ld have you do it ever: when you sing,
I'ld have you buy and sell so, so give alms,
Pray so; and, for the ordering your affairs,
To sing them too: when you do dance, I wish you
A wave o' the sea, that you might ever do
Nothing but that; move still, still so,
And own no other function: each your doing,
So singular in each particular,
Crowns what you are doing in the present deed,
That all your acts are queens.

PERDITA

O Doricles,
Your praises are too large: but that your youth,
And the true blood which peepeth fairly through't,
Do plainly give you out an unstain'd shepherd,
With wisdom I might fear, my Doricles,
You woo'd me the false way.

FLORIZEL

I think you have
As little skill to fear as I have purpose
To put you to't. But come; our dance, I pray:

Your hand, my Perdita: so turtles pair,
That never mean to part.

PERDITA

I'll swear for 'em.

POLIXENES

This is the prettiest low–born lass that ever
Ran on the green–sward: nothing she does or seems
But smacks of something greater than herself,
Too noble for this place.

CAMILLO

He tells her something
That makes her blood look out: good sooth, she is
The queen of curds and cream.

Clown

Come on, strike up!

DORCAS

Mopsa must be your mistress: marry, garlic,
To mend her kissing with!

MOPSA

Now, in good time!

Clown

Not a word, a word; we stand upon our manners.
Come, strike up!

Music. Here a dance of Shepherds and Shepherdesses

POLIXENES

Pray, good shepherd, what fair swain is this
Which dances with your daughter?

Shepherd

They call him Doricles; and boasts himself
To have a worthy feeding: but I have it
Upon his own report and I believe it;
He looks like sooth. He says he loves my daughter:
I think so too; for never gazed the moon
Upon the water as he'll stand and read
As 'twere my daughter's eyes: and, to be plain.
I think there is not half a kiss to choose
Who loves another best.

POLIXENES

She dances featly.

Shepherd

So she does any thing; though I report it,
That should be silent: if young Doricles
Do light upon her, she shall bring him that

Which he not dreams of.

Enter Servant

Servant

O master, if you did but hear the pedlar at the
door, you would never dance again after a tabour and
pipe; no, the bagpipe could not move you: he sings
several tunes faster than you'll tell money; he
utters them as he had eaten ballads and all men's
ears grew to his tunes.

Clown

He could never come better; he shall come in. I
love a ballad but even too well, if it be doleful
matter merrily set down, or a very pleasant thing
indeed and sung lamentably.

Servant

He hath songs for man or woman, of all sizes; no
milliner can so fit his customers with gloves: he
has the prettiest love–songs for maids; so without
bawdry, which is strange; with such delicate
burthens of dildos and fadings, 'jump her and thump
her;' and where some stretch–mouthed rascal would,
as it were, mean mischief and break a foul gap into
the matter, he makes the maid to answer 'Whoop, do me
no harm, good man;' puts him off, slights him, with
'Whoop, do me no harm, good man.'

POLIXENES

This is a brave fellow.

Clown

Believe me, thou talkest of an admirable conceited
fellow. Has he any unbraided wares?

Servant

He hath ribbons of an the colours i' the rainbow;
points more than all the lawyers in Bohemia can
learnedly handle, though they come to him by the
gross: inkles, caddisses, cambrics, lawns: why, he
sings 'em over as they were gods or goddesses; you
would think a smock were a she–angel, he so chants
to the sleeve–hand and the work about the square on't.

Clown

Prithee bring him in; and let him approach singing.

PERDITA

Forewarn him that he use no scurrilous words in 's tunes.

Exit Servant

Clown

You have of these pedlars, that have more in them
than you'ld think, sister.

PERDITA

Ay, good brother, or go about to think.

Enter AUTOLYCUS, singing

AUTOLYCUS

Lawn as white as driven snow;
Cyprus black as e'er was crow;
Gloves as sweet as damask roses;
Masks for faces and for noses;
Bugle bracelet, necklace amber,
Perfume for a lady's chamber;
Golden quoifs and stomachers,
For my lads to give their dears:
Pins and poking–sticks of steel,
What maids lack from head to heel:
Come buy of me, come; come buy, come buy;
Buy lads, or else your lasses cry: Come buy.

Clown

If I were not in love with Mopsa, thou shouldst take
no money of me; but being enthralled as I am, it
will also be the bondage of certain ribbons and gloves.

MOPSA

I was promised them against the feast; but they come
not too late now.

DORCAS

He hath promised you more than that, or there be liars.

MOPSA

> He hath paid you all he promised you; may be, he has
> paid you more, which will shame you to give him again.

Clown

> Is there no manners left among maids? will they
> wear their plackets where they should bear their
> faces? Is there not milking–time, when you are
> going to bed, or kiln–hole, to whistle off these
> secrets, but you must be tittle–tattling before all
> our guests? 'tis well they are whispering: clamour
> your tongues, and not a word more.

MOPSA

> I have done. Come, you promised me a tawdry–lace
> and a pair of sweet gloves.

Clown

> Have I not told thee how I was cozened by the way
> and lost all my money?

AUTOLYCUS

> And indeed, sir, there are cozeners abroad;
> therefore it behoves men to be wary.

Clown

Fear not thou, man, thou shalt lose nothing here.

AUTOLYCUS

I hope so, sir; for I have about me many parcels of charge.

Clown

What hast here? ballads?

MOPSA

Pray now, buy some: I love a ballad in print o'
life, for then we are sure they are true.

AUTOLYCUS

Here's one to a very doleful tune, how a usurer's
wife was brought to bed of twenty money–bags at a
burthen and how she longed to eat adders' heads and
toads carbonadoed.

MOPSA

Is it true, think you?

AUTOLYCUS

Very true, and but a month old.

DORCAS

Bless me from marrying a usurer!

AUTOLYCUS

Here's the midwife's name to't, one Mistress
Tale–porter, and five or six honest wives that were
present. Why should I carry lies abroad?

MOPSA

Pray you now, buy it.

Clown

Come on, lay it by: and let's first see moe
ballads; we'll buy the other things anon.

AUTOLYCUS

Here's another ballad of a fish, that appeared upon
the coast on Wednesday the four–score of April,
forty thousand fathom above water, and sung this
ballad against the hard hearts of maids: it was
thought she was a woman and was turned into a cold
fish for she would not exchange flesh with one that
loved her: the ballad is very pitiful and as true.

DORCAS

Is it true too, think you?

AUTOLYCUS

Five justices' hands at it, and witnesses more than
my pack will hold.

Clown

Lay it by too: another.

AUTOLYCUS

This is a merry ballad, but a very pretty one.

MOPSA

Let's have some merry ones.

AUTOLYCUS

Why, this is a passing merry one and goes to
the tune of 'Two maids wooing a man:' there's
scarce a maid westward but she sings it; 'tis in
request, I can tell you.

MOPSA

We can both sing it: if thou'lt bear a part, thou
shalt hear; 'tis in three parts.

DORCAS

We had the tune on't a month ago.

AUTOLYCUS

I can bear my part; you must know 'tis my
occupation; have at it with you.

SONG

AUTOLYCUS

Get you hence, for I must go
Where it fits not you to know.

DORCAS

Whither?

MOPSA

O, whither?

DORCAS

Whither?

MOPSA

It becomes thy oath full well,
Thou to me thy secrets tell.

DORCAS

Me too, let me go thither.

MOPSA

Or thou goest to the orange or mill.

284

DORCAS

> If to either, thou dost ill.

AUTOLYCUS

> Neither.

DORCAS

> What, neither?

AUTOLYCUS

> Neither.

DORCAS

> Thou hast sworn my love to be.

MOPSA

> Thou hast sworn it more to me:
> Then whither goest? say, whither?

Clown

> We'll have this song out anon by ourselves: my
> father and the gentlemen are in sad talk, and we'll
> not trouble them. Come, bring away thy pack after
> me. Wenches, I'll buy for you both. Pedlar, let's
> have the first choice. Follow me, girls.

Exit with DORCAS and MOPSA

AUTOLYCUS

And you shall pay well for 'em.

Follows singing

Will you buy any tape,
Or lace for your cape,
My dainty duck, my dear–a?
Any silk, any thread,
Any toys for your head,
Of the new'st and finest, finest wear–a?
Come to the pedlar;
Money's a medler.
That doth utter all men's ware–a.

Exit

Re–enter Servant

Servant

Master, there is three carters, three shepherds,
three neat–herds, three swine–herds, that have made
themselves all men of hair, they call themselves
Saltiers, and they have a dance which the wenches
say is a gallimaufry of gambols, because they are
not in't; but they themselves are o' the mind, if it
be not too rough for some that know little but
bowling, it will please plentifully.

Shepherd

Away! we'll none on 't: here has been too much
homely foolery already. I know, sir, we weary you.

POLIXENES

You weary those that refresh us: pray, let's see
these four threes of herdsmen.

Servant

One three of them, by their own report, sir, hath
danced before the king; and not the worst of the
three but jumps twelve foot and a half by the squier.

Shepherd

Leave your prating: since these good men are
pleased, let them come in; but quickly now.

Servant

Why, they stay at door, sir.

Exit

Here a dance of twelve Satyrs

POLIXENES

O, father, you'll know more of that hereafter.

To CAMILLO

Is it not too far gone? 'Tis time to part them.
He's simple and tells much.

To FLORIZEL

How now, fair shepherd!
Your heart is full of something that does take
Your mind from feasting. Sooth, when I was young
And handed love as you do, I was wont
To load my she with knacks: I would have ransack'd
The pedlar's silken treasury and have pour'd it
To her acceptance; you have let him go
And nothing marted with him. If your lass
Interpretation should abuse and call this
Your lack of love or bounty, you were straited
For a reply, at least if you make a care
Of happy holding her.

FLORIZEL

Old sir, I know
She prizes not such trifles as these are:
The gifts she looks from me are pack'd and lock'd
Up in my heart; which I have given already,
But not deliver'd. O, hear me breathe my life
Before this ancient sir, who, it should seem,
Hath sometime loved! I take thy hand, this hand,
As soft as dove's down and as white as it,
Or Ethiopian's tooth, or the fann'd
snow that's bolted
By the northern blasts twice o'er.

POLIXENES

What follows this?
How prettily the young swain seems to wash
The hand was fair before! I have put you out:
But to your protestation; let me hear
What you profess.

FLORIZEL

Do, and be witness to 't.

POLIXENES

And this my neighbour too?

FLORIZEL

And he, and more
Than he, and men, the earth, the heavens, and all:
That, were I crown'd the most imperial monarch,
Thereof most worthy, were I the fairest youth
That ever made eye swerve, had force and knowledge
More than was ever man's, I would not prize them
Without her love; for her employ them all;
Commend them and condemn them to her service
Or to their own perdition.

POLIXENES

Fairly offer'd.

CAMILLO

This shows a sound affection.

Shepherd

> But, my daughter,
> Say you the like to him?

PERDITA

> I cannot speak
> So well, nothing so well; no, nor mean better:
> By the pattern of mine own thoughts I cut out
> The purity of his.

Shepherd

> Take hands, a bargain!
> And, friends unknown, you shall bear witness to 't:
> I give my daughter to him, and will make
> Her portion equal his.

FLORIZEL

> O, that must be
> I' the virtue of your daughter: one being dead,
> I shall have more than you can dream of yet;
> Enough then for your wonder. But, come on,
> Contract us 'fore these witnesses.

Shepherd

> Come, your hand;
> And, daughter, yours.

POLIXENES

> Soft, swain, awhile, beseech you;
> Have you a father?

FLORIZEL

> I have: but what of him?

POLIXENES

> Knows he of this?

FLORIZEL

> He neither does nor shall.

POLIXENES

> Methinks a father
> Is at the nuptial of his son a guest
> That best becomes the table. Pray you once more,
> Is not your father grown incapable
> Of reasonable affairs? is he not stupid
> With age and altering rheums? can he speak? hear?
> Know man from man? dispute his own estate?
> Lies he not bed-rid? and again does nothing
> But what he did being childish?

FLORIZEL

> No, good sir;
> He has his health and ampler strength indeed
> Than most have of his age.

POLIXENES

> By my white beard,
> You offer him, if this be so, a wrong
> Something unfilial: reason my son
> Should choose himself a wife, but as good reason
> The father, all whose joy is nothing else
> But fair posterity, should hold some counsel
> In such a business.

FLORIZEL

> I yield all this;
> But for some other reasons, my grave sir,
> Which 'tis not fit you know, I not acquaint
> My father of this business.

POLIXENES

> Let him know't.

FLORIZEL

> He shall not.

POLIXENES

> Prithee, let him.

FLORIZEL

> No, he must not.

Shepherd

> Let him, my son: he shall not need to grieve
> At knowing of thy choice.

FLORIZEL

> Come, come, he must not.
> Mark our contract.

POLIXENES

> Mark your divorce, young sir,
>
> *Discovering himself* — Florizel is Shocked and dissapointed.
>
> Whom son I dare not call; thou art too base
> To be acknowledged: thou a sceptre's heir,
> That thus affect'st a sheep–hook! Thou old traitor,
> I am sorry that by hanging thee I can
> But shorten thy life one week. And thou, fresh piece
> Of excellent witchcraft, who of force must know
> The royal fool thou copest with,—

Shepherd

> O, my heart!

POLIXENES — Forbids the wedding

> I'll have thy beauty scratch'd with briers, and made
> More homely than thy state. For thee, fond boy,
> If I may ever know thou dost but sigh

That thou no more shalt see this knack, as never
I mean thou shalt, we'll bar thee from succession;
Not hold thee of our blood, no, not our kin,
Far than Deucalion off: mark thou my words:
Follow us to the court. Thou churl, for this time,
Though full of our displeasure, yet we free thee
From the dead blow of it. And you, enchantment.—
Worthy enough a herdsman: yea, him too,
That makes himself, but for our honour therein,
Unworthy thee,—if ever henceforth thou
These rural latches to his entrance open,
Or hoop his body more with thy embraces,
I will devise a death as cruel for thee
As thou art tender to't.

Exit

PERDITA — knew he was the Prince

Even here undone!
I was not much afeard; for once or twice
I was about to speak and tell him plainly,
The selfsame sun that shines upon his court
Hides not his visage from our cottage but
Looks on alike. Will't please you, sir, be gone?
I told you what would come of this: beseech you,
Of your own state take care: this dream of mine,—
Being now awake, I'll queen it no inch farther,
But milk my ewes and weep.

CAMILLO

Why, how now, father!
Speak ere thou diest.

294

Shepherd

> I cannot speak, nor think
> Nor dare to know that which I know. O sir!
> You have undone a man of fourscore three,
> That thought to fill his grave in quiet, yea,
> To die upon the bed my father died,
> To lie close by his honest bones: but now
> Some hangman must put on my shroud and lay me
> Where no priest shovels in dust. O cursed wretch,
> That knew'st this was the prince,
> and wouldst adventure
> To mingle faith with him! Undone! undone!
> If I might die within this hour, I have lived
> To die when I desire.

Exit

FLORIZEL

> Why look you so upon me?
> I am but sorry, not afeard; delay'd,
> But nothing alter'd: what I was, I am;
> More straining on for plucking back, not following
> My leash unwillingly.

CAMILLO

> Gracious my lord,
> You know your father's temper: at this time
> He will allow no speech, which I do guess
> You do not purpose to him; and as hardly

Will he endure your sight as yet, I fear:
Then, till the fury of his highness settle,
Come not before him.

FLORIZEL

I not purpose it.
I think, Camillo?

CAMILLO

Even he, my lord.

PERDITA

How often have I told you 'twould be thus!
How often said, my dignity would last
But till 'twere known!

FLORIZEL

It cannot fail but by
The violation of my faith; and then
Let nature crush the sides o' the earth together
And mar the seeds within! Lift up thy looks:
From my succession wipe me, father; I
Am heir to my affection.

CAMILLO

Be advised.

FLORIZEL

> I am, and by my fancy: if my reason
> Will thereto be obedient, I have reason;
> If not, my senses, better pleased with madness,
> Do bid it welcome.

CAMILLO

> This is desperate, sir.

FLORIZEL

> So call it: but it does fulfil my vow;
> I needs must think it honesty. Camillo,
> Not for Bohemia, nor the pomp that may
> Be thereat glean'd, for all the sun sees or
> The close earth wombs or the profound sea hides
> In unknown fathoms, will I break my oath
> To this my fair beloved: therefore, I pray you,
> As you have ever been my father's honour'd friend,
> When he shall miss me,—as, in faith, I mean not
> To see him any more,—cast your good counsels
> Upon his passion; let myself and fortune
> Tug for the time to come. This you may know
> And so deliver, I am put to sea
> With her whom here I cannot hold on shore;
> And most opportune to our need I have
> A vessel rides fast by, but not prepared
> For this design. What course I mean to hold
> Shall nothing benefit your knowledge, nor
> Concern me the reporting.

CAMILLO

O my lord!
I would your spirit were easier for advice,
Or stronger for your need.

FLORIZEL

Hark, Perdita

Drawing her aside

I'll hear you by and by.

CAMILLO

He's irremoveable,
Resolved for flight. Now were I happy, if
His going I could frame to serve my turn,
Save him from danger, do him love and honour,
Purchase the sight again of dear Sicilia
And that unhappy king, my master, whom
I so much thirst to see.

FLORIZEL

Now, good Camillo;
I am so fraught with curious business that
I leave out ceremony.

CAMILLO

Sir, I think
You have heard of my poor services, i' the love

That I have borne your father?

FLORIZEL

> Very nobly
> Have you deserved: it is my father's music
> To speak your deeds, not little of his care
> To have them recompensed as thought on.

CAMILLO

> Well, my lord,
> If you may please to think I love the king
> And through him what is nearest to him, which is
> Your gracious self, embrace but my direction:
> If your more ponderous and settled project
> May suffer alteration, on mine honour,
> I'll point you where you shall have such receiving
> As shall become your highness; where you may
> Enjoy your mistress, from the whom, I see,
> There's no disjunction to be made, but by—
> As heavens forefend!—your ruin; marry her,
> And, with my best endeavours in your absence,
> Your discontenting father strive to qualify
> And bring him up to liking.

FLORIZEL

> How, Camillo,
> May this, almost a miracle, be done?
> That I may call thee something more than man
> And after that trust to thee.

CAMILLO

Have you thought on
A place whereto you'll go?

FLORIZEL

Not any yet:
But as the unthought–on accident is guilty
To what we wildly do, so we profess
Ourselves to be the slaves of chance and flies
Of every wind that blows.

CAMILLO

Then list to me:
This follows, if you will not change your purpose
But undergo this flight, make for Sicilia,
And there present yourself and your fair princess,
For so I see she must be, 'fore Leontes:
She shall be habited as it becomes
The partner of your bed. Methinks I see
Leontes opening his free arms and weeping
His welcomes forth; asks thee the son forgiveness,
As 'twere i' the father's person; kisses the hands
Of your fresh princess; o'er and o'er divides him
'Twixt his unkindness and his kindness; the one
He chides to hell and bids the other grow
Faster than thought or time.

FLORIZEL

Worthy Camillo,
What colour for my visitation shall I
Hold up before him?

CAMILLO

Sent by the king your father
To greet him and to give him comforts. Sir,
The manner of your bearing towards him, with
What you as from your father shall deliver,
Things known betwixt us three, I'll write you down:
The which shall point you forth at every sitting
What you must say; that he shall not perceive
But that you have your father's bosom there
And speak his very heart.

FLORIZEL

I am bound to you:
There is some sap in this.

CAMILLO

A cause more promising
Than a wild dedication of yourselves
To unpath'd waters, undream'd shores, most certain
To miseries enough; no hope to help you,
But as you shake off one to take another;
Nothing so certain as your anchors, who
Do their best office, if they can but stay you
Where you'll be loath to be: besides you know
Prosperity's the very bond of love,
Whose fresh complexion and whose heart together

Affliction alters.

PERDITA

> One of these is true:
> I think affliction may subdue the cheek,
> But not take in the mind.

CAMILLO

> Yea, say you so?
> There shall not at your father's house these
> seven years
> Be born another such.

FLORIZEL

> My good Camillo,
> She is as forward of her breeding as
> She is i' the rear our birth.

CAMILLO

> I cannot say 'tis pity
> She lacks instructions, for she seems a mistress
> To most that teach.

PERDITA

> Your pardon, sir; for this
> I'll blush you thanks.

FLORIZEL

My prettiest Perdita!
But O, the thorns we stand upon! Camillo,
Preserver of my father, now of me,
The medicine of our house, how shall we do?
We are not furnish'd like Bohemia's son,
Nor shall appear in Sicilia.

CAMILLO

My lord,
Fear none of this: I think you know my fortunes
Do all lie there: it shall be so my care
To have you royally appointed as if
The scene you play were mine. For instance, sir,
That you may know you shall not want, one word.

They talk aside

Re−enter AUTOLYCUS

AUTOLYCUS

Ha, ha! what a fool Honesty is! and Trust, his
sworn brother, a very simple gentleman! I have sold
all my trumpery; not a counterfeit stone, not a
ribbon, glass, pomander, brooch, table−book, ballad,
knife, tape, glove, shoe−tie, bracelet, horn−ring,
to keep my pack from fasting: they throng who
should buy first, as if my trinkets had been
hallowed and brought a benediction to the buyer:

by which means I saw whose purse was best in
picture; and what I saw, to my good use I
remembered. My clown, who wants but something to
be a reasonable man, grew so in love with the
wenches' song, that he would not stir his pettitoes
till he had both tune and words; which so drew the
rest of the herd to me that all their other senses
stuck in ears: you might have pinched a placket, it
was senseless; 'twas nothing to geld a codpiece of a
purse; I could have filed keys off that hung in
chains: no hearing, no feeling, but my sir's song,
and admiring the nothing of it. So that in this
time of lethargy I picked and cut most of their
festival purses; and had not the old man come in
with a whoo–bub against his daughter and the king's
son and scared my choughs from the chaff, I had not
left a purse alive in the whole army.

CAMILLO, FLORIZEL, and PERDITA come forward

CAMILLO

Nay, but my letters, by this means being there
So soon as you arrive, shall clear that doubt.

FLORIZEL

And those that you'll procure from King Leontes—

CAMILLO

Shall satisfy your father.

PERDITA

Happy be you!
All that you speak shows fair.

CAMILLO

Who have we here?

Seeing AUTOLYCUS

We'll make an instrument of this, omit
Nothing may give us aid.

AUTOLYCUS

If they have overheard me now, why, hanging.

CAMILLO

How now, good fellow! why shakest thou so? Fear
not, man; here's no harm intended to thee.

AUTOLYCUS

I am a poor fellow, sir.

CAMILLO

Why, be so still; here's nobody will steal that from
thee: yet for the outside of thy poverty we must
make an exchange; therefore discase thee instantly,
—thou must think there's a necessity in't,—and
change garments with this gentleman: though the
pennyworth on his side be the worst, yet hold thee,

305

there's some boot.

AUTOLYCUS

I am a poor fellow, sir.

Aside

I know ye well enough.

CAMILLO

Nay, prithee, dispatch: the gentleman is half flayed already.

AUTOLYCUS

Are you in earnest, sir?

Aside

I smell the trick on't.

FLORIZEL

Dispatch, I prithee.

AUTOLYCUS

Indeed, I have had earnest: but I cannot with conscience take it.

CAMILLO

Unbuckle, unbuckle.

FLORIZEL and AUTOLYCUS exchange garments

Fortunate mistress,—let my prophecy
Come home to ye!—you must retire yourself
Into some covert: take your sweetheart's hat
And pluck it o'er your brows, muffle your face,
Dismantle you, and, as you can, disliken
The truth of your own seeming; that you may—
For I do fear eyes over—to shipboard
Get undescried.

PERDITA

I see the play so lies
That I must bear a part.

CAMILLO

No remedy.
Have you done there?

FLORIZEL

Should I now meet my father,
He would not call me son.

CAMILLO

Nay, you shall have no hat.

Giving it to PERDITA

Come, lady, come. Farewell, my friend.

AUTOLYCUS

Adieu, sir.

FLORIZEL

O Perdita, what have we twain forgot!
Pray you, a word.

CAMILLO

[Aside] What I do next, shall be to tell the king
Of this escape and whither they are bound;
Wherein my hope is I shall so prevail
To force him after: in whose company
I shall review Sicilia, for whose sight
I have a woman's longing.

FLORIZEL

Fortune speed us!
Thus we set on, Camillo, to the sea−side.

CAMILLO

The swifter speed the better.

Exeunt FLORIZEL, PERDITA, and CAMILLO

AUTOLYCUS

I understand the business, I hear it: to have an
open ear, a quick eye, and a nimble hand, is
necessary for a cut–purse; a good nose is requisite
also, to smell out work for the other senses. I see
this is the time that the unjust man doth thrive.
What an exchange had this been without boot! What
a boot is here with this exchange! Sure the gods do
this year connive at us, and we may do any thing
extempore. The prince himself is about a piece of
iniquity, stealing away from his father with his
clog at his heels: if I thought it were a piece of
honesty to acquaint the king withal, I would not
do't: I hold it the more knavery to conceal it;
and therein am I constant to my profession.

Re–enter Clown and Shepherd

Aside, aside; here is more matter for a hot brain:
every lane's end, every shop, church, session,
hanging, yields a careful man work.

Clown

See, see; what a man you are now!
There is no other way but to tell the king
she's a changeling and none of your flesh and blood.

Shepherd

Nay, but hear me.

Clown

Nay, but hear me.

Shepherd

Go to, then.

Clown

She being none of your flesh and blood, your flesh
and blood has not offended the king; and so your
flesh and blood is not to be punished by him. Show
those things you found about her, those secret
things, all but what she has with her: this being
done, let the law go whistle: I warrant you.

Shepherd

I will tell the king all, every word, yea, and his
son's pranks too; who, I may say, is no honest man,
neither to his father nor to me, to go about to make
me the king's brother–in–law.

Clown

Indeed, brother–in–law was the farthest off you
could have been to him and then your blood had been
the dearer by I know how much an ounce.

AUTOLYCUS

[Aside] Very wisely, puppies!

Shepherd

Well, let us to the king: there is that in this
fardel will make him scratch his beard.

AUTOLYCUS

[Aside] I know not what impediment this complaint
may be to the flight of my master.

Clown

Pray heartily he be at palace.

AUTOLYCUS

[Aside] Though I am not naturally honest, I am so
sometimes by chance: let me pocket up my pedlar's excrement.

Takes off his false beard

How now, rustics! whither are you bound?

Shepherd

To the palace, an it like your worship.

AUTOLYCUS

311

Your affairs there, what, with whom, the condition
of that fardel, the place of your dwelling, your
names, your ages, of what having, breeding, and any
thing that is fitting to be known, discover.

Clown

We are but plain fellows, sir.

AUTOLYCUS

A lie; you are rough and hairy. Let me have no
lying: it becomes none but tradesmen, and they
often give us soldiers the lie: but we pay them for
it with stamped coin, not stabbing steel; therefore
they do not give us the lie.

Clown

Your worship had like to have given us one, if you
had not taken yourself with the manner.

Shepherd

Are you a courtier, an't like you, sir?

AUTOLYCUS

Whether it like me or no, I am a courtier. Seest
thou not the air of the court in these enfoldings?
hath not my gait in it the measure of the court?
receives not thy nose court—odor from me? reflect I
not on thy baseness court—contempt? Thinkest thou,

for that I insinuate, or toaze from thee thy
business, I am therefore no courtier? I am courtier
cap–a–pe; and one that will either push on or pluck
back thy business there: whereupon I command thee to
open thy affair.

Shepherd

My business, sir, is to the king.

AUTOLYCUS

What advocate hast thou to him?

Shepherd

I know not, an't like you.

Clown

Advocate's the court–word for a pheasant: say you
have none.

Shepherd

None, sir; I have no pheasant, cock nor hen.

AUTOLYCUS

How blessed are we that are not simple men!
Yet nature might have made me as these are,
Therefore I will not disdain.

Clown

This cannot be but a great courtier.

Shepherd

His garments are rich, but he wears
them not handsomely.

Clown

He seems to be the more noble in being fantastical:
a great man, I'll warrant; I know by the picking
on's teeth.

AUTOLYCUS

The fardel there? what's i' the fardel?
Wherefore that box?

Shepherd

Sir, there lies such secrets in this fardel and box,
which none must know but the king; and which he
shall know within this hour, if I may come to the
speech of him.

AUTOLYCUS

Age, thou hast lost thy labour.

Shepherd

Why, sir?

AUTOLYCUS

> The king is not at the palace; he is gone aboard a
> new ship to purge melancholy and air himself: for,
> if thou beest capable of things serious, thou must
> know the king is full of grief.

Shepard

> So 'tis said, sir; about his son, that should have
> married a shepherd's daughter.

AUTOLYCUS

> If that shepherd be not in hand–fast, let him fly:
> the curses he shall have, the tortures he shall
> feel, will break the back of man, the heart of monster.

Clown

> Think you so, sir?

AUTOLYCUS

> Not he alone shall suffer what wit can make heavy
> and vengeance bitter; but those that are germane to
> him, though removed fifty times, shall all come
> under the hangman: which though it be great pity,
> yet it is necessary. An old sheep–whistling rogue a
> ram–tender, to offer to have his daughter come into
> grace! Some say he shall be stoned; but that death

315

is too soft for him, say I draw our throne into a
sheep–cote! all deaths are too few, the sharpest too easy.

Clown

Has the old man e'er a son, sir, do you hear. an't
like you, sir?

AUTOLYCUS

He has a son, who shall be flayed alive; then
'nointed over with honey, set on the head of a
wasp's nest; then stand till he be three quarters
and a dram dead; then recovered again with
aqua–vitae or some other hot infusion; then, raw as
he is, and in the hottest day prognostication
proclaims, shall be be set against a brick–wall, the
sun looking with a southward eye upon him, where he
is to behold him with flies blown to death. But what
talk we of these traitorly rascals, whose miseries
are to be smiled at, their offences being so
capital? Tell me, for you seem to be honest plain
men, what you have to the king: being something
gently considered, I'll bring you where he is
aboard, tender your persons to his presence,
whisper him in your behalfs; and if it be in man
besides the king to effect your suits, here is man
shall do it.

Clown

He seems to be of great authority: close with him,
give him gold; and though authority be a stubborn

bear, yet he is oft led by the nose with gold: show
the inside of your purse to the outside of his hand,
and no more ado. Remember 'stoned,' and 'flayed alive.'

Shepherd

An't please you, sir, to undertake the business for
us, here is that gold I have: I'll make it as much
more and leave this young man in pawn till I bring it you.

AUTOLYCUS

After I have done what I promised?

Shepherd

Ay, sir.

AUTOLYCUS

Well, give me the moiety. Are you a party in this business?

Clown

In some sort, sir: but though my case be a pitiful
one, I hope I shall not be flayed out of it.

AUTOLYCUS

O, that's the case of the shepherd's son: hang him,
he'll be made an example.

Clown

Comfort, good comfort! We must to the king and show
our strange sights: he must know 'tis none of your
daughter nor my sister; we are gone else. Sir, I
will give you as much as this old man does when the
business is performed, and remain, as he says, your
pawn till it be brought you.

AUTOLYCUS

I will trust you. Walk before toward the sea−side;
go on the right hand: I will but look upon the
hedge and follow you.

Clown

We are blest in this man, as I may say, even blest.

Shepherd

Let's before as he bids us: he was provided to do us good.

Exeunt Shepherd and Clown

AUTOLYCUS

If I had a mind to be honest, I see Fortune would
not suffer me: she drops booties in my mouth. I am
courted now with a double occasion, gold and a means
to do the prince my master good; which who knows how
that may turn back to my advancement? I will bring
these two moles, these blind ones, aboard him: if he
think it fit to shore them again and that the

complaint they have to the king concerns him
nothing, let him call me rogue for being so far
officious; for I am proof against that title and
what shame else belongs to't. To him will I present
them: there may be matter in it.

Exit

Act 5, Scene 1

A room in LEONTES' palace.

Enter LEONTES, CLEOMENES, DION, PAULINA, and Servants

CLEOMENES

> Sir, you have done enough, and have perform'd
> A saint–like sorrow: no fault could you make,
> Which you have not redeem'd; indeed, paid down
> More penitence than done trespass: at the last,
> Do as the heavens have done, forget your evil;
> With them forgive yourself.

LEONTES

> Whilst I remember
> Her and her virtues, I cannot forget
> My blemishes in them, and so still think of
> The wrong I did myself; which was so much,
> That heirless it hath made my kingdom and
> Destroy'd the sweet'st companion that e'er man
> Bred his hopes out of.

319

PAULINA

True, too true, my lord:
If, one by one, you wedded all the world,
Or from the all that are took something good,
To make a perfect woman, she you kill'd
Would be unparallel'd.

LEONTES

I think so. Kill'd!
She I kill'd! I did so: but thou strikest me
Sorely, to say I did; it is as bitter
Upon thy tongue as in my thought: now, good now,
Say so but seldom.

CLEOMENES

Not at all, good lady:
You might have spoken a thousand things that would
Have done the time more benefit and graced
Your kindness better.

PAULINA

You are one of those
Would have him wed again.

DION

If you would not so,
You pity not the state, nor the remembrance

320

Of his most sovereign name; consider little
What dangers, by his highness' fail of issue,
May drop upon his kingdom and devour
Incertain lookers on. What were more holy
Than to rejoice the former queen is well?
What holier than, for royalty's repair,
For present comfort and for future good,
To bless the bed of majesty again
With a sweet fellow to't?

PAULINA

There is none worthy,
Respecting her that's gone. Besides, the gods
Will have fulfill'd their secret purposes;
For has not the divine Apollo said,
Is't not the tenor of his oracle,
That King Leontes shall not have an heir
Till his lost child be found? which that it shall,
Is all as monstrous to our human reason
As my Antigonus to break his grave
And come again to me; who, on my life,
Did perish with the infant. 'Tis your counsel
My lord should to the heavens be contrary,
Oppose against their wills.

To LEONTES

Care not for issue;
The crown will find an heir: great Alexander
Left his to the worthiest; so his successor
Was like to be the best.

LEONTES

Good Paulina,
Who hast the memory of Hermione,
I know, in honour, O, that ever I
Had squared me to thy counsel! then, even now,
I might have look'd upon my queen's full eyes,
Have taken treasure from her lips—

PAULINA

And left them
More rich for what they yielded.

LEONTES

Thou speak'st truth.
No more such wives; therefore, no wife: one worse,
And better used, would make her sainted spirit
Again possess her corpse, and on this stage,
Where we're offenders now, appear soul—vex'd,
And begin, 'Why to me?'

PAULINA

Had she such power,
She had just cause.

LEONTES

She had; and would incense me
To murder her I married.

PAULINA

I should so.
Were I the ghost that walk'd, I'ld bid you mark
Her eye, and tell me for what dull part in't
You chose her; then I'ld shriek, that even your ears
Should rift to hear me; and the words that follow'd
Should be 'Remember mine.'

LEONTES

Stars, stars,
And all eyes else dead coals! Fear thou no wife;
I'll have no wife, Paulina.

PAULINA

Will you swear
Never to marry but by my free leave?

LEONTES

Never, Paulina; so be blest my spirit!

PAULINA

Then, good my lords, bear witness to his oath.

CLEOMENES

You tempt him over–much.

PAULINA

Unless another,
As like Hermione as is her picture,
Affront his eye.

CLEOMENES

Good madam,—

PAULINA

I have done.
Yet, if my lord will marry,—if you will, sir,
No remedy, but you will,—give me the office
To choose you a queen: she shall not be so young
As was your former; but she shall be such
As, walk'd your first queen's ghost,
it should take joy
To see her in your arms.

LEONTES

My true Paulina,
We shall not marry till thou bid'st us.

PAULINA

That
Shall be when your first queen's again in breath;
Never till then.

Enter a Gentleman

Gentleman

One that gives out himself Prince Florizel,
Son of Polixenes, with his princess, she
The fairest I have yet beheld, desires access
To your high presence.

LEONTES

What with him? he comes not
Like to his father's greatness: his approach,
So out of circumstance and sudden, tells us
'Tis not a visitation framed, but forced
By need and accident. What train?

Gentleman

But few,
And those but mean.

LEONTES

His princess, say you, with him?

Gentleman

Ay, the most peerless piece of earth, I think,
That e'er the sun shone bright on.

PAULINA

O Hermione,
As every present time doth boast itself
Above a better gone, so must thy grave
Give way to what's seen now! Sir, you yourself
Have said and writ so, but your writing now
Is colder than that theme, 'She had not been,
Nor was not to be equall'd;'—thus your verse
Flow'd with her beauty once: 'tis shrewdly ebb'd,
To say you have seen a better.

Gentleman

    Pardon, madam:
The one I have almost forgot,—your pardon,—
The other, when she has obtain'd your eye,
Will have your tongue too. This is a creature,
Would she begin a sect, might quench the zeal
Of all professors else, make proselytes
Of who she but bid follow.

PAULINA

    How! not women?

Gentleman

    Women will love her, that she is a woman
More worth than any man; men, that she is
The rarest of all women.

LEONTES

Go, Cleomenes;
Yourself, assisted with your honour'd friends,
Bring them to our embracement. Still, 'tis strange

Exeunt CLEOMENES and others

He thus should steal upon us.

PAULINA

Had our prince,
Jewel of children, seen this hour, he had pair'd
Well with this lord: there was not full a month
Between their births.

LEONTES

Prithee, no more; cease; thou know'st
He dies to me again when talk'd of: sure,
When I shall see this gentleman, thy speeches
Will bring me to consider that which may
Unfurnish me of reason. They are come.

Re−enter CLEOMENES and others, with FLORIZEL and PERDITA

Your mother was most true to wedlock, prince;
For she did print your royal father off,
Conceiving you: were I but twenty−one,
Your father's image is so hit in you,
His very air, that I should call you brother,
As I did him, and speak of something wildly
By us perform'd before. Most dearly welcome!

And your fair princess,—goddess!—O, alas!
I lost a couple, that 'twixt heaven and earth
Might thus have stood begetting wonder as
You, gracious couple, do: and then I lost—
All mine own folly—the society,
Amity too, of your brave father, whom,
Though bearing misery, I desire my life
Once more to look on him.

FLORIZEL

By his command
Have I here touch'd Sicilia and from him
Give you all greetings that a king, at friend,
Can send his brother: and, but infirmity
Which waits upon worn times hath something seized
His wish'd ability, he had himself
The lands and waters 'twixt your throne and his
Measured to look upon you; whom he loves—
He bade me say so—more than all the sceptres
And those that bear them living.

LEONTES

O my brother,
Good gentleman! the wrongs I have done thee stir
Afresh within me, and these thy offices,
So rarely kind, are as interpreters
Of my behind-hand slackness. Welcome hither,
As is the spring to the earth. And hath he too
Exposed this paragon to the fearful usage,
At least ungentle, of the dreadful Neptune,
To greet a man not worth her pains, much less
The adventure of her person?

FLORIZEL

Good my lord,
She came from Libya.

LEONTES

Where the warlike Smalus,
That noble honour'd lord, is fear'd and loved?

FLORIZEL

Most royal sir, from thence; from him, whose daughter
His tears proclaim'd his, parting with her: thence,
A prosperous south–wind friendly, we have cross'd,
To execute the charge my father gave me
For visiting your highness: my best train
I have from your Sicilian shores dismiss'd;
Who for Bohemia bend, to signify
Not only my success in Libya, sir,
But my arrival and my wife's in safety
Here where we are.

LEONTES

The blessed gods
Purge all infection from our air whilst you
Do climate here! You have a holy father,
A graceful gentleman; against whose person,
So sacred as it is, I have done sin:
For which the heavens, taking angry note,

Have left me issueless; and your father's blest,
As he from heaven merits it, with you
Worthy his goodness. What might I have been,
Might I a son and daughter now have look'd on,
Such goodly things as you!

Enter a Lord

Lord

Most noble sir,
That which I shall report will bear no credit,
Were not the proof so nigh. Please you, great sir,
Bohemia greets you from himself by me;
Desires you to attach his son, who has—
His dignity and duty both cast off—
Fled from his father, from his hopes, and with
A shepherd's daughter.

LEONTES

Where's Bohemia? speak.

Lord

Here in your city; I now came from him:
I speak amazedly; and it becomes
My marvel and my message. To your court
Whiles he was hastening, in the chase, it seems,
Of this fair couple, meets he on the way
The father of this seeming lady and
Her brother, having both their country quitted
With this young prince.

330

FLORIZEL

> Camillo has betray'd me;
> Whose honour and whose honesty till now
> Endured all weathers.

Lord

> Lay't so to his charge:
> He's with the king your father.

LEONTES

> Who? Camillo?

Lord

> Camillo, sir; I spake with him; who now
> Has these poor men in question. Never saw I
> Wretches so quake: they kneel, they kiss the earth;
> Forswear themselves as often as they speak:
> Bohemia stops his ears, and threatens them
> With divers deaths in death.

PERDITA

> O my poor father!
> The heaven sets spies upon us, will not have
> Our contract celebrated.

LEONTES

You are married?

FLORIZEL

> We are not, sir, nor are we like to be;
> The stars, I see, will kiss the valleys first:
> The odds for high and low's alike.

LEONTES

> My lord,
> Is this the daughter of a king?

FLORIZEL

> She is,
> When once she is my wife.

LEONTES

> That 'once' I see by your good father's speed
> Will come on very slowly. I am sorry,
> Most sorry, you have broken from his liking
> Where you were tied in duty, and as sorry
> Your choice is not so rich in worth as beauty,
> That you might well enjoy her.

FLORIZEL

> Dear, look up:
> Though Fortune, visible an enemy,
> Should chase us with my father, power no jot

Hath she to change our loves. Beseech you, sir,
Remember since you owed no more to time
Than I do now: with thought of such affections,
Step forth mine advocate; at your request
My father will grant precious things as trifles.

LEONTES

Would he do so, I'ld beg your precious mistress,
Which he counts but a trifle.

PAULINA

Sir, my liege,
Your eye hath too much youth in't: not a month
'Fore your queen died, she was more worth such gazes
Than what you look on now.

LEONTES

I thought of her,
Even in these looks I made.

To FLORIZEL

But your petition
Is yet unanswer'd. I will to your father:
Your honour not o'erthrown by your desires,
I am friend to them and you: upon which errand
I now go toward him; therefore follow me
And mark what way I make: come, good my lord.

Exeunt

Act 5, Scene 2

Before LEONTES' palace.

Enter AUTOLYCUS and a Gentleman

AUTOLYCUS

Beseech you, sir, were you present at this relation?

First Gentleman

I was by at the opening of the fardel, heard the old
shepherd deliver the manner how he found it:
whereupon, after a little amazedness, we were all
commanded out of the chamber; only this methought I
heard the shepherd say, he found the child.

AUTOLYCUS

I would most gladly know the issue of it.

First Gentleman

I make a broken delivery of the business; but the
changes I perceived in the king and Camillo were
very notes of admiration: they seemed almost, with
staring on one another, to tear the cases of their
eyes; there was speech in their dumbness, language
in their very gesture; they looked as they had heard
of a world ransomed, or one destroyed: a notable
passion of wonder appeared in them; but the wisest

beholder, that knew no more but seeing, could not
say if the importance were joy or sorrow; but in the
extremity of the one, it must needs be.

Enter another Gentleman

Here comes a gentleman that haply knows more.
The news, Rogero?

Second Gentleman

Nothing but bonfires: the oracle is fulfilled; the
king's daughter is found: such a deal of wonder is
broken out within this hour that ballad−makers
cannot be able to express it.

Enter a third Gentleman

Here comes the Lady Paulina's steward: he can
deliver you more. How goes it now, sir? this news
which is called true is so like an old tale, that
the verity of it is in strong suspicion: has the king
found his heir?

Third Gentleman

Most true, if ever truth were pregnant by
circumstance: that which you hear you'll swear you
see, there is such unity in the proofs. The mantle
of Queen Hermione's, her jewel about the neck of it,
the letters of Antigonus found with it which they
know to be his character, the majesty of the

335

creature in resemblance of the mother, the affection
of nobleness which nature shows above her breeding,
and many other evidences proclaim her with all
certainty to be the king's daughter. Did you see
the meeting of the two kings?

Second Gentleman

No.

Third Gentleman

Then have you lost a sight, which was to be seen,
cannot be spoken of. There might you have beheld one
joy crown another, so and in such manner that it
seemed sorrow wept to take leave of them, for their
joy waded in tears. There was casting up of eyes,
holding up of hands, with countenances of such
distraction that they were to be known by garment,
not by favour. Our king, being ready to leap out of
himself for joy of his found daughter, as if that
joy were now become a loss, cries 'O, thy mother,
thy mother!' then asks Bohemia forgiveness; then
embraces his son–in–law; then again worries he his
daughter with clipping her; now he thanks the old
shepherd, which stands by like a weather–bitten
conduit of many kings' reigns. I never heard of such
another encounter, which lames report to follow it
and undoes description to do it.

Second Gentleman

What, pray you, became of Antigonus, that carried
hence the child?

336

Third Gentleman

> Like an old tale still, which will have matter to
> rehearse, though credit be asleep and not an ear
> open. He was torn to pieces with a bear: this
> avouches the shepherd's son; who has not only his
> innocence, which seems much, to justify him, but a
> handkerchief and rings of his that Paulina knows.

First Gentleman

> What became of his bark and his followers?

Third Gentleman

> Wrecked the same instant of their master's death and
> in the view of the shepherd: so that all the
> instruments which aided to expose the child were
> even then lost when it was found. But O, the noble
> combat that 'twixt joy and sorrow was fought in
> Paulina! She had one eye declined for the loss of
> her husband, another elevated that the oracle was
> fulfilled: she lifted the princess from the earth,
> and so locks her in embracing, as if she would pin
> her to her heart that she might no more be in danger
> of losing.

First Gentleman

> The dignity of this act was worth the audience of
> kings and princes; for by such was it acted.

Third Gentleman

One of the prettiest touches of all and that which
angled for mine eyes, caught the water though not
the fish, was when, at the relation of the queen's
death, with the manner how she came to't bravely
confessed and lamented by the king, how
attentiveness wounded his daughter; till, from one
sign of dolour to another, she did, with an 'Alas,'
I would fain say, bleed tears, for I am sure my
heart wept blood. Who was most marble there changed
colour; some swooned, all sorrowed: if all the world
could have seen 't, the woe had been universal.

First Gentleman

Are they returned to the court?

Third Gentleman

No: the princess hearing of her mother's statue,
which is in the keeping of Paulina,—a piece many
years in doing and now newly performed by that rare
Italian master, Julio Romano, who, had he himself
eternity and could put breath into his work, would
beguile Nature of her custom, so perfectly he is her
ape: he so near to Hermione hath done Hermione that
they say one would speak to her and stand in hope of
answer: thither with all greediness of affection
are they gone, and there they intend to sup.

Second Gentleman

I thought she had some great matter there in hand;
for she hath privately twice or thrice a day, ever
since the death of Hermione, visited that removed
house. Shall we thither and with our company piece
the rejoicing?

First Gentleman

Who would be thence that has the benefit of access?
every wink of an eye some new grace will be born:
our absence makes us unthrifty to our knowledge.
Let's along.

Exeunt Gentlemen

AUTOLYCUS

Now, had I not the dash of my former life in me,
would preferment drop on my head. I brought the old
man and his son aboard the prince: told him I heard
them talk of a fardel and I know not what: but he
at that time, overfond of the shepherd's daughter,
so he then took her to be, who began to be much
sea−sick, and himself little better, extremity of
weather continuing, this mystery remained
undiscovered. But 'tis all one to me; for had I
been the finder out of this secret, it would not
have relished among my other discredits.

Enter Shepherd and Clown

Here come those I have done good to against my will,
and already appearing in the blossoms of their fortune.

Shepherd

Come, boy; I am past moe children, but thy sons and
daughters will be all gentlemen born.

Clown

You are well met, sir. You denied to fight with me
this other day, because I was no gentleman born.
See you these clothes? say you see them not and
think me still no gentleman born: you were best say
these robes are not gentlemen born: give me the
lie, do, and try whether I am not now a gentleman born.

AUTOLYCUS

I know you are now, sir, a gentleman born.

Clown

Ay, and have been so any time these four hours.

Shepherd

And so have I, boy.

Clown

So you have: but I was a gentleman born before my
father; for the king's son took me by the hand, and
called me brother; and then the two kings called my
father brother; and then the prince my brother and

340

the princess my sister called my father father; and
so we wept, and there was the first gentleman–like
tears that ever we shed.

Shepherd

We may live, son, to shed many more.

Clown

Ay; or else 'twere hard luck, being in so
preposterous estate as we are.

AUTOLYCUS

I humbly beseech you, sir, to pardon me all the
faults I have committed to your worship and to give
me your good report to the prince my master.

Shepherd

Prithee, son, do; for we must be gentle, now we are
gentlemen.

Clown

Thou wilt amend thy life?

AUTOLYCUS

Ay, an it like your good worship.

Clown

Give me thy hand: I will swear to the prince thou
art as honest a true fellow as any is in Bohemia.

Shepherd

You may say it, but not swear it.

Clown

Not swear it, now I am a gentleman? Let boors and
franklins say it, I'll swear it.

Shepherd

How if it be false, son?

Clown

If it be ne'er so false, a true gentleman may swear
it in the behalf of his friend: and I'll swear to
the prince thou art a tall fellow of thy hands and
that thou wilt not be drunk; but I know thou art no
tall fellow of thy hands and that thou wilt be
drunk: but I'll swear it, and I would thou wouldst
be a tall fellow of thy hands.

AUTOLYCUS

I will prove so, sir, to my power.

Clown

Ay, by any means prove a tall fellow: if I do not
wonder how thou darest venture to be drunk, not
being a tall fellow, trust me not. Hark! the kings
and the princes, our kindred, are going to see the
queen's picture. Come, follow us: we'll be thy
good masters.

Exeunt

Act 5, Scene 3

A chapel in PAULINA'S house.

> *Enter LEONTES, POLIXENES, FLORIZEL, PERDITA, CAMILLO,*
> *PAULINA, Lords, and Attendants*

LEONTES

> O grave and good Paulina, the great comfort
> That I have had of thee!

PAULINA

> What, sovereign sir,
> I did not well I meant well. All my services
> You have paid home: but that you have vouchsafed,
> With your crown'd brother and these your contracted
> Heirs of your kingdoms, my poor house to visit,
> It is a surplus of your grace, which never
> My life may last to answer.

LEONTES

O Paulina,
We honour you with trouble: but we came
To see the statue of our queen: your gallery
Have we pass'd through, not without much content
In many singularities; but we saw not
That which my daughter came to look upon,
The statue of her mother.

PAULINA

As she lived peerless,
So her dead likeness, I do well believe,
Excels whatever yet you look'd upon
Or hand of man hath done; therefore I keep it
Lonely, apart. But here it is: prepare
To see the life as lively mock'd as ever
Still sleep mock'd death: behold, and say 'tis well.

PAULINA draws a curtain, and discovers HERMIONE standing like a statue

I like your silence, it the more shows off
Your wonder: but yet speak; first, you, my liege,
Comes it not something near?

LEONTES

Her natural posture!
Chide me, dear stone, that I may say indeed
Thou art Hermione; or rather, thou art she
In thy not chiding, for she was as tender
As infancy and grace. But yet, Paulina,
Hermione was not so much wrinkled, nothing

So aged as this seems.

POLIXENES

O, not by much.

PAULINA

So much the more our carver's excellence;
Which lets go by some sixteen years and makes her
As she lived now.

LEONTES

As now she might have done,
So much to my good comfort, as it is
Now piercing to my soul. O, thus she stood,
Even with such life of majesty, warm life,
As now it coldly stands, when first I woo'd her!
I am ashamed: does not the stone rebuke me
For being more stone than it? O royal piece,
There's magic in thy majesty, which has
My evils conjured to remembrance and
From thy admiring daughter took the spirits,
Standing like stone with thee.

PERDITA

And give me leave,
And do not say 'tis superstition, that
I kneel and then implore her blessing. Lady,
Dear queen, that ended when I but began,
Give me that hand of yours to kiss.

PAULINA

O, patience!
The statue is but newly fix'd, the colour's Not dry.

CAMILLO

My lord, your sorrow was too sore laid on,
Which sixteen winters cannot blow away,
So many summers dry; scarce any joy
Did ever so long live; no sorrow
But kill'd itself much sooner.

POLIXENES

Dear my brother,
Let him that was the cause of this have power
To take off so much grief from you as he
Will piece up in himself.

PAULINA

Indeed, my lord,
If I had thought the sight of my poor image
Would thus have wrought you,—for the stone is mine—
I'ld not have show'd it.

LEONTES

Do not draw the curtain.

Twelth Night, A Winter's Tale, The Tempest

PAULINA

> No longer shall you gaze on't, lest your fancy
> May think anon it moves.

LEONTES

> Let be, let be.
> Would I were dead, but that, methinks, already—
> What was he that did make it? See, my lord,
> Would you not deem it breathed? and that those veins
> Did verily bear blood?

POLIXENES

> Masterly done:
> The very life seems warm upon her lip.

LEONTES

> The fixture of her eye has motion in't,
> As we are mock'd with art.

PAULINA

> I'll draw the curtain:
> My lord's almost so far transported that
> He'll think anon it lives.

LEONTES

O sweet Paulina,
Make me to think so twenty years together!
No settled senses of the world can match
The pleasure of that madness. Let 't alone.

PAULINA

I am sorry, sir, I have thus far stirr'd you: but
I could afflict you farther.

LEONTES

Do, Paulina;
For this affliction has a taste as sweet
As any cordial comfort. Still, methinks,
There is an air comes from her: what fine chisel
Could ever yet cut breath? Let no man mock me,
For I will kiss her.

PAULINA

Good my lord, forbear:
The ruddiness upon her lip is wet;
You'll mar it if you kiss it, stain your own
With oily painting. Shall I draw the curtain?

LEONTES

No, not these twenty years.

PERDITA

So long could I
Stand by, a looker on.

PAULINA

Either forbear,
Quit presently the chapel, or resolve you
For more amazement. If you can behold it,
I'll make the statue move indeed, descend
And take you by the hand; but then you'll think—
Which I protest against—I am assisted
By wicked powers.

LEONTES

What you can make her do,
I am content to look on: what to speak,
I am content to hear; for 'tis as easy
To make her speak as move.

PAULINA

It is required
You do awake your faith. Then all stand still;
On: those that think it is unlawful business
I am about, let them depart.

LEONTES

Proceed:
No foot shall stir.

PAULINA

Music, awake her; strike!

Music

'Tis time; descend; be stone no more; approach;
Strike all that look upon with marvel. Come,
I'll fill your grave up: stir, nay, come away,
Bequeath to death your numbness, for from him
Dear life redeems you. You perceive she stirs:

HERMIONE comes down

Start not; her actions shall be holy as
You hear my spell is lawful: do not shun her
Until you see her die again; for then
You kill her double. Nay, present your hand:
When she was young you woo'd her; now in age
Is she become the suitor?

LEONTES

O, she's warm!
If this be magic, let it be an art
Lawful as eating.

POLIXENES

She embraces him.

CAMILLO

She hangs about his neck:
If she pertain to life let her speak too.

POLIXENES

Ay, and make't manifest where she has lived,
Or how stolen from the dead.

PAULINA

That she is living,
Were it but told you, should be hooted at
Like an old tale: but it appears she lives,
Though yet she speak not. Mark a little while.
Please you to interpose, fair madam: kneel
And pray your mother's blessing. Turn, good lady;
Our Perdita is found.

HERMIONE

You gods, look down
And from your sacred vials pour your graces
Upon my daughter's head! Tell me, mine own.
Where hast thou been preserved? where lived? how found
Thy father's court? for thou shalt hear that I,
Knowing by Paulina that the oracle
Gave hope thou wast in being, have preserved
Myself to see the issue.

PAULINA

There's time enough for that;
Lest they desire upon this push to trouble
Your joys with like relation. Go together,
You precious winners all; your exultation
Partake to every one. I, an old turtle,
Will wing me to some wither'd bough and there
My mate, that's never to be found again,
Lament till I am lost.

LEONTES

O, peace, Paulina!
Thou shouldst a husband take by my consent,
As I by thine a wife: this is a match,
And made between's by vows. Thou hast found mine;
But how, is to be question'd; for I saw her,
As I thought, dead, and have in vain said many
A prayer upon her grave. I'll not seek far—
For him, I partly know his mind—to find thee
An honourable husband. Come, Camillo,
And take her by the hand, whose worth and honesty
Is richly noted and here justified
By us, a pair of kings. Let's from this place.
What! look upon my brother: both your pardons,
That e'er I put between your holy looks
My ill suspicion. This is your son–in–law,
And son unto the king, who, heavens directing,
Is troth–plight to your daughter. Good Paulina,
Lead us from hence, where we may leisurely
Each one demand an answer to his part
Perform'd in this wide gap of time since first
We were dissever'd: hastily lead away.

Exeunt

352

The Tempest

Act 1, Scene 1

On a ship at sea: a tempestuous noise

of thunder and lightning heard.

Enter a Master and a Boatswain

Master

Boatswain!

Boatswain

Here, master: what cheer?

Master

Good, speak to the mariners: fall to't, yarely,
or we run ourselves aground: bestir, bestir.

Exit

Enter Mariners

Boatswain

Heigh, my hearts! cheerly, cheerly, my hearts!
yare, yare! Take in the topsail. Tend to the

master's whistle. Blow, till thou burst thy wind,
if room enough!

*Enter ALONSO, SEBASTIAN, ANTONIO, FERDINAND, GONZALO,
and others*

ALONSO

Good boatswain, have care. Where's the master?
Play the men.

Boatswain

I pray now, keep below.

ANTONIO

Where is the master, boatswain?

Boatswain

Do you not hear him? You mar our labour: keep your
cabins: you do assist the storm.

GONZALO

Nay, good, be patient.

Boatswain

When the sea is. Hence! What cares these roarers
for the name of king? To cabin: silence! trouble us not.

GONZALO

Good, yet remember whom thou hast aboard.

Boatswain

None that I more love than myself. You are a
counsellor; if you can command these elements to
silence, and work the peace of the present, we will
not hand a rope more; use your authority: if you
cannot, give thanks you have lived so long, and make
yourself ready in your cabin for the mischance of
the hour, if it so hap. Cheerly, good hearts! Out
of our way, I say.

Exit

GONZALO

I have great comfort from this fellow: methinks he
hath no drowning mark upon him; his complexion is
perfect gallows. Stand fast, good Fate, to his
hanging: make the rope of his destiny our cable,
for our own doth little advantage. If he be not
born to be hanged, our case is miserable.

Exeunt

Re-enter Boatswain

Boatswain

Down with the topmast! yare! lower, lower! Bring
her to try with main-course.

A cry within

A plague upon this howling! they are louder than
the weather or our office.

Re−enter SEBASTIAN, ANTONIO, and GONZALO

Yet again! what do you here? Shall we give o'er
and drown? Have you a mind to sink?

SEBASTIAN

A pox o' your throat, you bawling, blasphemous,
incharitable dog!

Boatswain

Work you then.

ANTONIO

Hang, cur! hang, you whoreson, insolent noisemaker!
We are less afraid to be drowned than thou art.

GONZALO

I'll warrant him for drowning; though the ship were
no stronger than a nutshell and as leaky as an
unstanched wench.

Boatswain

> Lay her a–hold, a–hold! set her two courses off to
> sea again; lay her off.

> *Enter Mariners wet*

Mariners

> All lost! to prayers, to prayers! all lost!

Boatswain

> What, must our mouths be cold?

GONZALO

> The king and prince at prayers! let's assist them,
> For our case is as theirs.

SEBASTIAN

> I'm out of patience.

ANTONIO

> We are merely cheated of our lives by drunkards:
> This wide–chapp'd rascal—would thou mightst lie drowning
> The washing of ten tides!

GONZALO

He'll be hang'd yet,
Though every drop of water swear against it
And gape at widest to glut him.

A confused noise within: 'Mercy on us!'— 'We split, we split!'—'Farewell, my wife and children!'—'Farewell, brother!'—'We split, we split, we split!'

ANTONIO

Let's all sink with the king.

SEBASTIAN

Let's take leave of him.

Exeunt ANTONIO and SEBASTIAN

GONZALO

Now would I give a thousand furlongs of sea for an acre of barren ground, long heath, brown furze, any thing. The wills above be done! but I would fain die a dry death.

Exeunt

Act 1, Scene 2

The island. Before PROSPERO'S cell.

Enter PROSPERO and MIRANDA

MIRANDA

> If by your art, my dearest father, you have
> Put the wild waters in this roar, allay them.
> The sky, it seems, would pour down stinking pitch,
> But that the sea, mounting to the welkin's cheek,
> Dashes the fire out. O, I have suffered
> With those that I saw suffer: a brave vessel,
> Who had, no doubt, some noble creature in her,
> Dash'd all to pieces. O, the cry did knock
> Against my very heart. Poor souls, they perish'd.
> Had I been any god of power, I would
> Have sunk the sea within the earth or ere
> It should the good ship so have swallow'd and
> The fraughting souls within her.

PROSPERO

> Be collected:
> No more amazement: tell your piteous heart
> There's no harm done.

MIRANDA

> O, woe the day!

PROSPERO

> No harm.
> I have done nothing but in care of thee,
> Of thee, my dear one, thee, my daughter, who
> Art ignorant of what thou art, nought knowing
> Of whence I am, nor that I am more better
> Than Prospero, master of a full poor cell,

And thy no greater father.

MIRANDA

> More to know
> Did never meddle with my thoughts.

PROSPERO

> 'Tis time
> I should inform thee farther. Lend thy hand,
> And pluck my magic garment from me. So:

> *Lays down his mantle*

> Lie there, my art. Wipe thou thine eyes; have comfort.
> The direful spectacle of the wreck, which touch'd
> The very virtue of compassion in thee,
> I have with such provision in mine art
> So safely ordered that there is no soul—
> No, not so much perdition as an hair
> Betid to any creature in the vessel
> Which thou heard'st cry, which thou saw'st sink. Sit down;
> For thou must now know farther.

MIRANDA

> You have often
> Begun to tell me what I am, but stopp'd
> And left me to a bootless inquisition,
> Concluding 'Stay: not yet.'

PROSPERO

> The hour's now come;
> The very minute bids thee ope thine ear;
> Obey and be attentive. Canst thou remember
> A time before we came unto this cell?
> I do not think thou canst, for then thou wast not
> Out three years old.

MIRANDA

> Certainly, sir, I can.

PROSPERO

> By what? by any other house or person?
> Of any thing the image tell me that
> Hath kept with thy remembrance.

MIRANDA

> 'Tis far off
> And rather like a dream than an assurance
> That my remembrance warrants. Had I not
> Four or five women once that tended me?

PROSPERO

> Thou hadst, and more, Miranda. But how is it
> That this lives in thy mind? What seest thou else
> In the dark backward and abysm of time?
> If thou remember'st aught ere thou camest here,
> How thou camest here thou mayst.

MIRANDA

But that I do not.

PROSPERO

Twelve year since, Miranda, twelve year since,
Thy father was the Duke of Milan and
A prince of power.

MIRANDA

Sir, are not you my father?

PROSPERO

Thy mother was a piece of virtue, and
She said thou wast my daughter; and thy father
Was Duke of Milan; and thou his only heir
And princess no worse issued.

MIRANDA

O the heavens!
What foul play had we, that we came from thence?
Or blessed was't we did?

PROSPERO

Both, both, my girl:
By foul play, as thou say'st, were we heaved thence,

But blessedly holp hither.

MIRANDA

O, my heart bleeds
To think o' the teen that I have turn'd you to,
Which is from my remembrance! Please you, farther.

PROSPERO

My brother and thy uncle, call'd Antonio—
I pray thee, mark me—that a brother should
Be so perfidious!—he whom next thyself
Of all the world I loved and to him put
The manage of my state; as at that time
Through all the signories it was the first
And Prospero the prime duke, being so reputed
In dignity, and for the liberal arts
Without a parallel; those being all my study,
The government I cast upon my brother
And to my state grew stranger, being transported
And rapt in secret studies. Thy false uncle—
Dost thou attend me?

MIRANDA

Sir, most heedfully.

PROSPERO

Being once perfected how to grant suits,
How to deny them, who to advance and who
To trash for over–topping, new created

The creatures that were mine, I say, or changed 'em,
Or else new form'd 'em; having both the key
Of officer and office, set all hearts i' the state
To what tune pleased his ear; that now he was
The ivy which had hid my princely trunk,
And suck'd my verdure out on't. Thou attend'st not.

MIRANDA

O, good sir, I do.

PROSPERO

I pray thee, mark me.
I, thus neglecting worldly ends, all dedicated
To closeness and the bettering of my mind
With that which, but by being so retired,
O'er–prized all popular rate, in my false brother
Awaked an evil nature; and my trust,
Like a good parent, did beget of him
A falsehood in its contrary as great
As my trust was; which had indeed no limit,
A confidence sans bound. He being thus lorded,
Not only with what my revenue yielded,
But what my power might else exact, like one
Who having into truth, by telling of it,
Made such a sinner of his memory,
To credit his own lie, he did believe
He was indeed the duke; out o' the substitution
And executing the outward face of royalty,
With all prerogative: hence his ambition growing—
Dost thou hear?

MIRANDA

Your tale, sir, would cure deafness.

PROSPERO

> To have no screen between this part he play'd
> And him he play'd it for, he needs will be
> Absolute Milan. Me, poor man, my library
> Was dukedom large enough: of temporal royalties
> He thinks me now incapable; confederates—
> So dry he was for sway—wi' the King of Naples
> To give him annual tribute, do him homage,
> Subject his coronet to his crown and bend
> The dukedom yet unbow'd—alas, poor Milan!—
> To most ignoble stooping.

MIRANDA

> O the heavens!

PROSPERO

> Mark his condition and the event; then tell me
> If this might be a brother.

MIRANDA

> I should sin
> To think but nobly of my grandmother:
> Good wombs have borne bad sons.

PROSPERO

Now the condition.
The King of Naples, being an enemy
To me inveterate, hearkens my brother's suit;
Which was, that he, in lieu o' the premises
Of homage and I know not how much tribute,
Should presently extirpate me and mine
Out of the dukedom and confer fair Milan
With all the honours on my brother: whereon,
A treacherous army levied, one midnight
Fated to the purpose did Antonio open
The gates of Milan, and, i' the dead of darkness,
The ministers for the purpose hurried thence
Me and thy crying self.

MIRANDA

Alack, for pity!
I, not remembering how I cried out then,
Will cry it o'er again: it is a hint
That wrings mine eyes to't.

PROSPERO

Hear a little further
And then I'll bring thee to the present business
Which now's upon's; without the which this story
Were most impertinent.

MIRANDA

Wherefore did they not
That hour destroy us?

PROSPERO

Well demanded, wench:
My tale provokes that question. Dear, they durst not,
So dear the love my people bore me, nor set
A mark so bloody on the business, but
With colours fairer painted their foul ends.
In few, they hurried us aboard a bark,
Bore us some leagues to sea; where they prepared
A rotten carcass of a boat, not rigg'd,
Nor tackle, sail, nor mast; the very rats
Instinctively had quit it: there they hoist us,
To cry to the sea that roar'd to us, to sigh
To the winds whose pity, sighing back again,
Did us but loving wrong.

MIRANDA

Alack, what trouble
Was I then to you!

PROSPERO

O, a cherubim
Thou wast that did preserve me. Thou didst smile.
Infused with a fortitude from heaven,
When I have deck'd the sea with drops full salt,
Under my burthen groan'd; which raised in me
An undergoing stomach, to bear up
Against what should ensue.

MIRANDA

How came we ashore?

PROSPERO

By Providence divine.
Some food we had and some fresh water that
A noble Neapolitan, Gonzalo,
Out of his charity, being then appointed
Master of this design, did give us, with
Rich garments, linens, stuffs and necessaries,
Which since have steaded much; so, of his gentleness,
Knowing I loved my books, he furnish'd me
From mine own library with volumes that
I prize above my dukedom.

MIRANDA

Would I might
But ever see that man!

PROSPERO

Now I arise:

Resumes his mantle

Sit still, and hear the last of our sea−sorrow.
Here in this island we arrived; and here
Have I, thy schoolmaster, made thee more profit
Than other princesses can that have more time
For vainer hours and tutors not so careful.

MIRANDA

Heavens thank you for't! And now, I pray you, sir,
For still 'tis beating in my mind, your reason
For raising this sea–storm?

PROSPERO

Know thus far forth.
By accident most strange, bountiful Fortune,
Now my dear lady, hath mine enemies
Brought to this shore; and by my prescience
I find my zenith doth depend upon
A most auspicious star, whose influence
If now I court not but omit, my fortunes
Will ever after droop. Here cease more questions:
Thou art inclined to sleep; 'tis a good dulness,
And give it way: I know thou canst not choose.

MIRANDA sleeps

Come away, servant, come. I am ready now.
Approach, my Ariel, come.

Enter ARIEL

ARIEL

All hail, great master! grave sir, hail! I come
To answer thy best pleasure; be't to fly,
To swim, to dive into the fire, to ride
On the curl'd clouds, to thy strong bidding task
Ariel and all his quality.

PROSPERO

Hast thou, spirit,
Perform'd to point the tempest that I bade thee?

ARIEL

To every article.
I boarded the king's ship; now on the beak,
Now in the waist, the deck, in every cabin,
I flamed amazement: sometime I'ld divide,
And burn in many places; on the topmast,
The yards and bowsprit, would I flame distinctly,
Then meet and join. Jove's lightnings, the precursors
O' the dreadful thunder–claps, more momentary
And sight–outrunning were not; the fire and cracks
Of sulphurous roaring the most mighty Neptune
Seem to besiege and make his bold waves tremble,
Yea, his dread trident shake.

PROSPERO

My brave spirit!
Who was so firm, so constant, that this coil
Would not infect his reason?

ARIEL

Not a soul
But felt a fever of the mad and play'd
Some tricks of desperation. All but mariners
Plunged in the foaming brine and quit the vessel,
Then all afire with me: the king's son, Ferdinand,

With hair up–staring,—then like reeds, not hair,—
Was the first man that leap'd; cried, 'Hell is empty
And all the devils are here.'

PROSPERO

Why that's my spirit!
But was not this nigh shore?

ARIEL

Close by, my master.

PROSPERO

But are they, Ariel, safe?

ARIEL

Not a hair perish'd;
On their sustaining garments not a blemish,
But fresher than before: and, as thou badest me,
In troops I have dispersed them 'bout the isle.
The king's son have I landed by himself;
Whom I left cooling of the air with sighs
In an odd angle of the isle and sitting,
His arms in this sad knot.

PROSPERO

Of the king's ship
The mariners say how thou hast disposed
And all the rest o' the fleet.

ARIEL

> Safely in harbour
> Is the king's ship; in the deep nook, where once
> Thou call'dst me up at midnight to fetch dew
> From the still–vex'd Bermoothes, there she's hid:
> The mariners all under hatches stow'd;
> Who, with a charm join'd to their suffer'd labour,
> I have left asleep; and for the rest o' the fleet
> Which I dispersed, they all have met again
> And are upon the Mediterranean flote,
> Bound sadly home for Naples,
> Supposing that they saw the king's ship wreck'd
> And his great person perish.

PROSPERO

> Ariel, thy charge
> Exactly is perform'd: but there's more work.
> What is the time o' the day?

ARIEL

> Past the mid season.

PROSPERO

> At least two glasses. The time 'twixt six and now
> Must by us both be spent most preciously.

ARIEL

Is there more toil? Since thou dost give me pains,
Let me remember thee what thou hast promised,
Which is not yet perform'd me.

PROSPERO

How now? moody?
What is't thou canst demand?

ARIEL

My liberty.

PROSPERO

Before the time be out? no more!

ARIEL

I prithee,
Remember I have done thee worthy service;
Told thee no lies, made thee no mistakings, served
Without or grudge or grumblings: thou didst promise
To bate me a full year.

PROSPERO

Dost thou forget
From what a torment I did free thee?

ARIEL

No.

PROSPERO

> Thou dost, and think'st it much to tread the ooze
> Of the salt deep,
> To run upon the sharp wind of the north,
> To do me business in the veins o' the earth
> When it is baked with frost.

ARIEL

> I do not, sir.

PROSPERO

> Thou liest, malignant thing! Hast thou forgot
> The foul witch Sycorax, who with age and envy
> Was grown into a hoop? hast thou forgot her?

ARIEL

> No, sir.

PROSPERO

> Thou hast. Where was she born? speak; tell me.

ARIEL

> Sir, in Argier.

PROSPERO

O, was she so? I must
Once in a month recount what thou hast been,
Which thou forget'st. This damn'd witch Sycorax,
For mischiefs manifold and sorceries terrible
To enter human hearing, from Argier,
Thou know'st, was banish'd: for one thing she did
They would not take her life. Is not this true?

ARIEL

Ay, sir.

PROSPERO

This blue–eyed hag was hither brought with child
And here was left by the sailors. Thou, my slave,
As thou report'st thyself, wast then her servant;
And, for thou wast a spirit too delicate
To act her earthy and abhorr'd commands,
Refusing her grand hests, she did confine thee,
By help of her more potent ministers
And in her most unmitigable rage,
Into a cloven pine; within which rift
Imprison'd thou didst painfully remain
A dozen years; within which space she died
And left thee there; where thou didst vent thy groans
As fast as mill–wheels strike. Then was this island—
Save for the son that she did litter here,
A freckled whelp hag–born—not honour'd with
A human shape.

ARIEL

Yes, Caliban her son.

Twelth Night, A Winter's Tale, The Tempest

PROSPERO

> Dull thing, I say so; he, that Caliban
> Whom now I keep in service. Thou best know'st
> What torment I did find thee in; thy groans
> Did make wolves howl and penetrate the breasts
> Of ever angry bears: it was a torment
> To lay upon the damn'd, which Sycorax
> Could not again undo: it was mine art,
> When I arrived and heard thee, that made gape
> The pine and let thee out.

ARIEL

> I thank thee, master.

PROSPERO

> If thou more murmur'st, I will rend an oak
> And peg thee in his knotty entrails till
> Thou hast howl'd away twelve winters.

ARIEL

> Pardon, master;
> I will be correspondent to command
> And do my spiriting gently.

PROSPERO

> Do so, and after two days
> I will discharge thee.

ARIEL

That's my noble master!
What shall I do? say what; what shall I do?

PROSPERO

Go make thyself like a nymph o' the sea: be subject
To no sight but thine and mine, invisible
To every eyeball else. Go take this shape
And hither come in't: go, hence with diligence!

Exit ARIEL

Awake, dear heart, awake! thou hast slept well; Awake!

MIRANDA

The strangeness of your story put
Heaviness in me.

PROSPERO

Shake it off. Come on;
We'll visit Caliban my slave, who never
Yields us kind answer.

MIRANDA

'Tis a villain, sir,
I do not love to look on.

377

PROSPERO

> But, as 'tis,
> We cannot miss him: he does make our fire,
> Fetch in our wood and serves in offices
> That profit us. What, ho! slave! Caliban!
> Thou earth, thou! speak.

CALIBAN

> *[Within]* There's wood enough within.

PROSPERO

> Come forth, I say! there's other business for thee:
> Come, thou tortoise! when?

> *Re−enter ARIEL like a water−nymph*

> Fine apparition! My quaint Ariel,
> Hark in thine ear.

ARIEL

> My lord it shall be done.

> *Exit*

PROSPERO

Thou poisonous slave, got by the devil himself
Upon thy wicked dam, come forth!

Enter CALIBAN

CALIBAN

As wicked dew as e'er my mother brush'd
With raven's feather from unwholesome fen
Drop on you both! a south—west blow on ye
And blister you all o'er!

PROSPERO

For this, be sure, to—night thou shalt have cramps,
Side—stitches that shall pen thy breath up; urchins
Shall, for that vast of night that they may work,
All exercise on thee; thou shalt be pinch'd
As thick as honeycomb, each pinch more stinging
Than bees that made 'em.

CALIBAN

I must eat my dinner.
This island's mine, by Sycorax my mother,
Which thou takest from me. When thou camest first,
Thou strokedst me and madest much of me, wouldst give me
Water with berries in't, and teach me how
To name the bigger light, and how the less,
That burn by day and night: and then I loved thee
And show'd thee all the qualities o' the isle,
The fresh springs, brine—pits, barren place and fertile:
Cursed be I that did so! All the charms

Of Sycorax, toads, beetles, bats, light on you!
For I am all the subjects that you have,
Which first was mine own king: and here you sty me
In this hard rock, whiles you do keep from me
The rest o' the island.

PROSPERO

Thou most lying slave,
Whom stripes may move, not kindness! I have used thee,
Filth as thou art, with human care, and lodged thee
In mine own cell, till thou didst seek to violate
The honour of my child.

CALIBAN

O ho, O ho! would't had been done!
Thou didst prevent me; I had peopled else
This isle with Calibans.

PROSPERO

Abhorred slave,
Which any print of goodness wilt not take,
Being capable of all ill! I pitied thee,
Took pains to make thee speak, taught thee each hour
One thing or other: when thou didst not, savage,
Know thine own meaning, but wouldst gabble like
A thing most brutish, I endow'd thy purposes
With words that made them known. But thy vile race,
Though thou didst learn, had that in't which
good natures
Could not abide to be with; therefore wast thou

380

Deservedly confined into this rock,
Who hadst deserved more than a prison.

CALIBAN

You taught me language; and my profit on't
Is, I know how to curse. The red plague rid you
For learning me your language!

PROSPERO

Hag–seed, hence!
Fetch us in fuel; and be quick, thou'rt best,
To answer other business. Shrug'st thou, malice?
If thou neglect'st or dost unwillingly
What I command, I'll rack thee with old cramps,
Fill all thy bones with aches, make thee roar
That beasts shall tremble at thy din.

CALIBAN

No, pray thee.

Aside

I must obey: his art is of such power,
It would control my dam's god, Setebos,
and make a vassal of him.

PROSPERO

So, slave; hence!

Exit CALIBAN

Re−enter ARIEL, invisible, playing and singing; FERDINAND following

ARIEL'S song.

Come unto these yellow sands,
And then take hands:
Courtsied when you have and kiss'd
The wild waves whist,
Foot it featly here and there;
And, sweet sprites, the burthen bear.
Hark, hark!

Burthen [dispersedly, within] Bow−wow

The watch−dogs bark!

Burthen Bow−wow

Hark, hark! I hear
The strain of strutting chanticleer
Cry, Cock−a−diddle−dow.

FERDINAND

Where should this music be? i' the air or the earth?
It sounds no more: and sure, it waits upon
Some god o' the island. Sitting on a bank,
Weeping again the king my father's wreck,
This music crept by me upon the waters,
Allaying both their fury and my passion
With its sweet air: thence I have follow'd it,

Or it hath drawn me rather. But 'tis gone.
No, it begins again.

ARIEL sings

Full fathom five thy father lies;
Of his bones are coral made;
Those are pearls that were his eyes:
Nothing of him that doth fade
But doth suffer a sea–change
Into something rich and strange.
Sea–nymphs hourly ring his knell

Burthen Ding–dong

Hark! now I hear them,—Ding–dong, bell.

FERDINAND

The ditty does remember my drown'd father.
This is no mortal business, nor no sound
That the earth owes. I hear it now above me.

PROSPERO

The fringed curtains of thine eye advance
And say what thou seest yond.

MIRANDA

What is't? a spirit?
Lord, how it looks about! Believe me, sir,
It carries a brave form. But 'tis a spirit.

PROSPERO

No, wench; it eats and sleeps and hath such senses
As we have, such. This gallant which thou seest
Was in the wreck; and, but he's something stain'd
With grief that's beauty's canker, thou mightst call him
A goodly person: he hath lost his fellows
And strays about to find 'em.

MIRANDA

I might call him
A thing divine, for nothing natural
I ever saw so noble.

PROSPERO

[Aside] It goes on, I see,
As my soul prompts it. Spirit, fine spirit! I'll free thee
Within two days for this.

FERDINAND

Most sure, the goddess
On whom these airs attend! Vouchsafe my prayer
May know if you remain upon this island;
And that you will some good instruction give
How I may bear me here: my prime request,

Which I do last pronounce, is, O you wonder!
If you be maid or no?

MIRANDA

No wonder, sir;
But certainly a maid.

FERDINAND

My language! heavens!
I am the best of them that speak this speech,
Were I but where 'tis spoken.

PROSPERO

How? the best?
What wert thou, if the King of Naples heard thee?

FERDINAND

A single thing, as I am now, that wonders
To hear thee speak of Naples. He does hear me;
And that he does I weep: myself am Naples,
Who with mine eyes, never since at ebb, beheld
The king my father wreck'd.

MIRANDA

Alack, for mercy!

FERDINAND

> Yes, faith, and all his lords; the Duke of Milan
> And his brave son being twain.

PROSPERO [Aside]

> The Duke of Milan
> And his more braver daughter could control thee,
> If now 'twere fit to do't. At the first sight
> They have changed eyes. Delicate Ariel,
> I'll set thee free for this.

> *To FERDINAND*

> A word, good sir;
> I fear you have done yourself some wrong: a word.

MIRANDA

> Why speaks my father so ungently? This
> Is the third man that e'er I saw, the first
> That e'er I sigh'd for: pity move my father
> To be inclined my way!

FERDINAND

> O, if a virgin,
> And your affection not gone forth, I'll make you
> The queen of Naples.

PROSPERO

> Soft, sir! one word more.

> *Aside*

> They are both in either's powers; but this swift business
> I must uneasy make, lest too light winning
> Make the prize light.

> *To FERDINAND*

> One word more; I charge thee
> That thou attend me: thou dost here usurp
> The name thou owest not; and hast put thyself
> Upon this island as a spy, to win it
> From me, the lord on't.

FERDINAND

> No, as I am a man.

MIRANDA

> There's nothing ill can dwell in such a temple:
> If the ill spirit have so fair a house,
> Good things will strive to dwell with't.

PROSPERO

> Follow me.
> Speak not you for him; he's a traitor. Come;
> I'll manacle thy neck and feet together:

Sea–water shalt thou drink; thy food shall be
The fresh–brook muscles, wither'd roots and husks
Wherein the acorn cradled. Follow.

FERDINAND

No;
I will resist such entertainment till
Mine enemy has more power.

Draws, and is charmed from moving

MIRANDA

O dear father,
Make not too rash a trial of him, for
He's gentle and not fearful.

PROSPERO

What? I say,
My foot my tutor? Put thy sword up, traitor;
Who makest a show but darest not strike, thy conscience
Is so possess'd with guilt: come from thy ward,
For I can here disarm thee with this stick
And make thy weapon drop.

MIRANDA

Beseech you, father.

PROSPERO

Hence! hang not on my garments.

MIRANDA

Sir, have pity;
I'll be his surety.

PROSPERO

Silence! one word more
Shall make me chide thee, if not hate thee. What!
An advocate for an imposter! hush!
Thou think'st there is no more such shapes as he,
Having seen but him and Caliban: foolish wench!
To the most of men this is a Caliban
And they to him are angels.

MIRANDA

My affections
Are then most humble; I have no ambition
To see a goodlier man.

PROSPERO

Come on; obey:
Thy nerves are in their infancy again
And have no vigour in them.

FERDINAND

So they are;
My spirits, as in a dream, are all bound up.
My father's loss, the weakness which I feel,
The wreck of all my friends, nor this man's threats,
To whom I am subdued, are but light to me,
Might I but through my prison once a day
Behold this maid: all corners else o' the earth
Let liberty make use of; space enough
Have I in such a prison.

PROSPERO

[Aside] It works.

To FERDINAND

Come on.
Thou hast done well, fine Ariel!

To FERDINAND

Follow me.

To ARIEL

Hark what thou else shalt do me.

MIRANDA

Be of comfort;
My father's of a better nature, sir,
Than he appears by speech: this is unwonted

Which now came from him.

PROSPERO

Thou shalt be free
As mountain winds: but then exactly do
All points of my command.

ARIEL

To the syllable.

PROSPERO

Come, follow. Speak not for him.

Exeunt

Act 2, Scene 1

Another part of the island.

*Enter ALONSO, SEBASTIAN, ANTONIO, GONZALO, ADRIAN,
FRANCISCO, and others*

GONZALO

Beseech you, sir, be merry; you have cause,
So have we all, of joy; for our escape
Is much beyond our loss. Our hint of woe
Is common; every day some sailor's wife,
The masters of some merchant and the merchant
Have just our theme of woe; but for the miracle,

I mean our preservation, few in millions
Can speak like us: then wisely, good sir, weigh
Our sorrow with our comfort.

ALONSO

Prithee, peace.

SEBASTIAN

He receives comfort like cold porridge.

ANTONIO

The visitor will not give him o'er so.

SEBASTIAN

Look he's winding up the watch of his wit;
by and by it will strike.

GONZALO

Sir,—

SEBASTIAN

One: tell.

GONZALO

When every grief is entertain'd that's offer'd,
Comes to the entertainer—

392

SEBASTIAN

A dollar.

GONZALO

Dolour comes to him, indeed: you
have spoken truer than you purposed.

SEBASTIAN

You have taken it wiselier than I meant you should.

GONZALO

Therefore, my lord,—

ANTONIO

Fie, what a spendthrift is he of his tongue!

ALONSO

I prithee, spare.

GONZALO

Well, I have done: but yet,—

SEBASTIAN

He will be talking.

ANTONIO

Which, of he or Adrian, for a good
wager, first begins to crow?

SEBASTIAN

The old cock.

ANTONIO

The cockerel.

SEBASTIAN

Done. The wager?

ANTONIO

A laughter.

SEBASTIAN

A match!

ADRIAN

Though this island seem to be desert,—

SEBASTIAN

Ha, ha, ha! So, you're paid.

ADRIAN

Uninhabitable and almost inaccessible,—

394

SEBASTIAN

Yet,—

ADRIAN

Yet,—

ANTONIO

He could not miss't.

ADRIAN

It must needs be of subtle, tender and delicate temperance.

ANTONIO

Temperance was a delicate wench.

SEBASTIAN

Ay, and a subtle; as he most learnedly delivered.

ADRIAN

The air breathes upon us here most sweetly.

SEBASTIAN

As if it had lungs and rotten ones.

ANTONIO

Or as 'twere perfumed by a fen.

GONZALO

Here is everything advantageous to life.

ANTONIO

True; save means to live.

SEBASTIAN

Of that there's none, or little.

GONZALO

How lush and lusty the grass looks! how green!

ANTONIO

The ground indeed is tawny.

SEBASTIAN

With an eye of green in't.

ANTONIO

He misses not much.

SEBASTIAN

No; he doth but mistake the truth totally.

GONZALO

But the rarity of it is,—which is indeed almost
beyond credit,—

SEBASTIAN

As many vouched rarities are.

GONZALO

That our garments, being, as they were, drenched in
the sea, hold notwithstanding their freshness and
glosses, being rather new–dyed than stained with
salt water.

ANTONIO

If but one of his pockets could speak, would it not
say he lies?

SEBASTIAN

Ay, or very falsely pocket up his report

GONZALO

Methinks our garments are now as fresh as when we
put them on first in Afric, at the marriage of
the king's fair daughter Claribel to the King of Tunis.

SEBASTIAN

'Twas a sweet marriage, and we prosper well in our return.

397

ADRIAN

Tunis was never graced before with such a paragon to
their queen.

GONZALO

Not since widow Dido's time.

ANTONIO

Widow! a pox o' that! How came that widow in?
widow Dido!

SEBASTIAN

What if he had said 'widower AEneas' too? Good Lord,
how you take it!

ADRIAN

'Widow Dido' said you? you make me study of that:
she was of Carthage, not of Tunis.

GONZALO

This Tunis, sir, was Carthage.

ADRIAN

Carthage?

GONZALO

I assure you, Carthage.

SEBASTIAN

His word is more than the miraculous harp; he hath raised the wall and houses too.

ANTONIO

What impossible matter will he make easy next?

SEBASTIAN

I think he will carry this island home in his pocket and give it his son for an apple.

ANTONIO

And, sowing the kernels of it in the sea, bring forth more islands.

GONZALO

Ay.

ANTONIO

Why, in good time.

GONZALO

Sir, we were talking that our garments seem now
as fresh as when we were at Tunis at the marriage
of your daughter, who is now queen.

ANTONIO

And the rarest that e'er came there.

SEBASTIAN

Bate, I beseech you, widow Dido.

ANTONIO

O, widow Dido! ay, widow Dido.

GONZALO

Is not, sir, my doublet as fresh as the first day I
wore it? I mean, in a sort.

ANTONIO

That sort was well fished for.

GONZALO

When I wore it at your daughter's marriage?

ALONSO

You cram these words into mine ears against
The stomach of my sense. Would I had never
Married my daughter there! for, coming thence,

My son is lost and, in my rate, she too,
Who is so far from Italy removed
I ne'er again shall see her. O thou mine heir
Of Naples and of Milan, what strange fish
Hath made his meal on thee?

FRANCISCO

Sir, he may live:
I saw him beat the surges under him,
And ride upon their backs; he trod the water,
Whose enmity he flung aside, and breasted
The surge most swoln that met him; his bold head
'Bove the contentious waves he kept, and oar'd
Himself with his good arms in lusty stroke
To the shore, that o'er his wave–worn basis bow'd,
As stooping to relieve him: I not doubt
He came alive to land.

ALONSO

No, no, he's gone.

SEBASTIAN

Sir, you may thank yourself for this great loss,
That would not bless our Europe with your daughter,
But rather lose her to an African;
Where she at least is banish'd from your eye,
Who hath cause to wet the grief on't.

ALONSO

Prithee, peace.

SEBASTIAN

You were kneel'd to and importuned otherwise
By all of us, and the fair soul herself
Weigh'd between loathness and obedience, at
Which end o' the beam should bow. We have lost your
son,
I fear, for ever: Milan and Naples have
More widows in them of this business' making
Than we bring men to comfort them:
The fault's your own.

ALONSO

So is the dear'st o' the loss.

GONZALO

My lord Sebastian,
The truth you speak doth lack some gentleness
And time to speak it in: you rub the sore,
When you should bring the plaster.

SEBASTIAN

Very well.

ANTONIO

And most chirurgeonly.

GONZALO

It is foul weather in us all, good sir,
When you are cloudy.

SEBASTIAN

Foul weather?

ANTONIO

Very foul.

GONZALO

Had I plantation of this isle, my lord,—

ANTONIO

He'ld sow't with nettle–seed.

SEBASTIAN

Or docks, or mallows.

GONZALO

And were the king on't, what would I do?

SEBASTIAN

'Scape being drunk for want of wine.

GONZALO

I' the commonwealth I would by contraries
Execute all things; for no kind of traffic

403

Would I admit; no name of magistrate;
Letters should not be known; riches, poverty,
And use of service, none; contract, succession,
Bourn, bound of land, tilth, vineyard, none;
No use of metal, corn, or wine, or oil;
No occupation; all men idle, all;
And women too, but innocent and pure;
No sovereignty;—

SEBASTIAN

Yet he would be king on't.

ANTONIO

The latter end of his commonwealth forgets the
beginning.

GONZALO

All things in common nature should produce
Without sweat or endeavour: treason, felony,
Sword, pike, knife, gun, or need of any engine,
Would I not have; but nature should bring forth,
Of its own kind, all foison, all abundance,
To feed my innocent people.

SEBASTIAN

No marrying 'mong his subjects?

ANTONIO

None, man; all idle: whores and knaves.

GONZALO

I would with such perfection govern, sir,
To excel the golden age.

SEBASTIAN

God save his majesty!

ANTONIO

Long live Gonzalo!

GONZALO

And,—do you mark me, sir?

ALONSO

Prithee, no more: thou dost talk nothing to me.

GONZALO

I do well believe your highness; and
did it to minister occasion to these gentlemen,
who are of such sensible and nimble lungs that
they always use to laugh at nothing.

ANTONIO

'Twas you we laughed at.

GONZALO

> Who in this kind of merry fooling am nothing
> to you: so you may continue and laugh at
> nothing still.

ANTONIO

> What a blow was there given!

SEBASTIAN

> An it had not fallen flat–long.

GONZALO

> You are gentlemen of brave metal; you would lift
> the moon out of her sphere, if she would continue
> in it five weeks without changing.

> *Enter ARIEL, invisible, playing solemn music*

SEBASTIAN

> We would so, and then go a bat–fowling.

ANTONIO

> Nay, good my lord, be not angry.

GONZALO

> No, I warrant you; I will not adventure
> my discretion so weakly. Will you laugh

me asleep, for I am very heavy?

ANTONIO

Go sleep, and hear us.

All sleep except ALONSO, SEBASTIAN, and ANTONIO

ALONSO

What, all so soon asleep! I wish mine eyes
Would, with themselves, shut up my thoughts: I find
They are inclined to do so.

SEBASTIAN

Please you, sir,
Do not omit the heavy offer of it:
It seldom visits sorrow; when it doth,
It is a comforter.

ANTONIO

We two, my lord,
Will guard your person while you take your rest,
And watch your safety.

ALONSO

Thank you. Wondrous heavy.

ALONSO sleeps. Exit ARIEL

SEBASTIAN

What a strange drowsiness possesses them!

ANTONIO

It is the quality o' the climate.

SEBASTIAN

Why
Doth it not then our eyelids sink? I find not
Myself disposed to sleep.

ANTONIO

Nor I; my spirits are nimble.
They fell together all, as by consent;
They dropp'd, as by a thunder–stroke. What might,
Worthy Sebastian? O, what might?—No more:—
And yet me thinks I see it in thy face,
What thou shouldst be: the occasion speaks thee, and
My strong imagination sees a crown
Dropping upon thy head.

SEBASTIAN

What, art thou waking?

ANTONIO

Do you not hear me speak?

SEBASTIAN

I do; and surely
It is a sleepy language and thou speak'st
Out of thy sleep. What is it thou didst say?
This is a strange repose, to be asleep
With eyes wide open; standing, speaking, moving,
And yet so fast asleep.

ANTONIO

Noble Sebastian,
Thou let'st thy fortune sleep—die, rather; wink'st
Whiles thou art waking.

SEBASTIAN

Thou dost snore distinctly;
There's meaning in thy snores.

ANTONIO

I am more serious than my custom: you
Must be so too, if heed me; which to do
Trebles thee o'er.

SEBASTIAN

Well, I am standing water.

ANTONIO

I'll teach you how to flow.

409

SEBASTIAN

> Do so: to ebb
> Hereditary sloth instructs me.

ANTONIO

> O,
> If you but knew how you the purpose cherish
> Whiles thus you mock it! how, in stripping it,
> You more invest it! Ebbing men, indeed,
> Most often do so near the bottom run
> By their own fear or sloth.

SEBASTIAN

> Prithee, say on:
> The setting of thine eye and cheek proclaim
> A matter from thee, and a birth indeed
> Which throes thee much to yield.

ANTONIO

> Thus, sir:
> Although this lord of weak remembrance, this,
> Who shall be of as little memory
> When he is earth'd, hath here almost persuade,—
> For he's a spirit of persuasion, only
> Professes to persuade,—the king his son's alive,
> 'Tis as impossible that he's undrown'd
> And he that sleeps here swims.

Twelth Night, A Winter's Tale, The Tempest

SEBASTIAN

I have no hope
That he's undrown'd.

ANTONIO

O, out of that 'no hope'
What great hope have you! no hope that way is
Another way so high a hope that even
Ambition cannot pierce a wink beyond,
But doubt discovery there. Will you grant with me
That Ferdinand is drown'd?

SEBASTIAN

He's gone.

ANTONIO

Then, tell me,
Who's the next heir of Naples?

SEBASTIAN

Claribel.

ANTONIO

She that is queen of Tunis; she that dwells
Ten leagues beyond man's life; she that from Naples
Can have no note, unless the sun were post—
The man i' the moon's too slow—till new–born chins

411

Be rough and razorable; she that—from whom?
We all were sea–swallow'd, though some cast again,
And by that destiny to perform an act
Whereof what's past is prologue, what to come
In yours and my discharge.

SEBASTIAN

What stuff is this! how say you?
'Tis true, my brother's daughter's queen of Tunis;
So is she heir of Naples; 'twixt which regions
There is some space.

ANTONIO

A space whose every cubit
Seems to cry out, 'How shall that Claribel
Measure us back to Naples? Keep in Tunis,
And let Sebastian wake.' Say, this were death
That now hath seized them; why, they were no worse
Than now they are. There be that can rule Naples
As well as he that sleeps; lords that can prate
As amply and unnecessarily
As this Gonzalo; I myself could make
A chough of as deep chat. O, that you bore
The mind that I do! what a sleep were this
For your advancement! Do you understand me?

SEBASTIAN

Methinks I do.

ANTONIO

And how does your content
Tender your own good fortune?

SEBASTIAN

I remember
You did supplant your brother Prospero.

ANTONIO

True:
And look how well my garments sit upon me;
Much feater than before: my brother's servants
Were then my fellows; now they are my men.

SEBASTIAN

But, for your conscience?

ANTONIO

Ay, sir; where lies that? if 'twere a kibe,
'Twould put me to my slipper: but I feel not
This deity in my bosom: twenty consciences,
That stand 'twixt me and Milan, candied be they
And melt ere they molest! Here lies your brother,
No better than the earth he lies upon,
If he were that which now he's like, that's dead;
Whom I, with this obedient steel, three inches of it,
Can lay to bed for ever; whiles you, doing thus,
To the perpetual wink for aye might put
This ancient morsel, this Sir Prudence, who
Should not upbraid our course. For all the rest,

They'll take suggestion as a cat laps milk;
They'll tell the clock to any business that
We say befits the hour.

SEBASTIAN

Thy case, dear friend,
Shall be my precedent; as thou got'st Milan,
I'll come by Naples. Draw thy sword: one stroke
Shall free thee from the tribute which thou payest;
And I the king shall love thee.

ANTONIO

Draw together;
And when I rear my hand, do you the like,
To fall it on Gonzalo.

SEBASTIAN

O, but one word.

They talk apart

Re−enter ARIEL, invisible

ARIEL

My master through his art foresees the danger
That you, his friend, are in; and sends me forth—
For else his project dies—to keep them living.

Sings in GONZALO's ear

While you here do snoring lie,
Open–eyed conspiracy
His time doth take.
If of life you keep a care,
Shake off slumber, and beware:
Awake, awake!

ANTONIO

Then let us both be sudden.

GONZALO

Now, good angels
Preserve the king.

They wake

ALONSO

Why, how now? ho, awake! Why are you drawn?
Wherefore this ghastly looking?

GONZALO

What's the matter?

SEBASTIAN

Whiles we stood here securing your repose,
Even now, we heard a hollow burst of bellowing

Like bulls, or rather lions: did't not wake you?
It struck mine ear most terribly.

ALONSO

I heard nothing.

ANTONIO

O, 'twas a din to fright a monster's ear,
To make an earthquake! sure, it was the roar
Of a whole herd of lions.

ALONSO

Heard you this, Gonzalo?

GONZALO

Upon mine honour, sir, I heard a humming,
And that a strange one too, which did awake me:
I shaked you, sir, and cried: as mine eyes open'd,
I saw their weapons drawn: there was a noise,
That's verily. 'Tis best we stand upon our guard,
Or that we quit this place; let's draw our weapons.

ALONSO

Lead off this ground; and let's make further search
For my poor son.

GONZALO

Heavens keep him from these beasts!
For he is, sure, i' the island.

ALONSO

Lead away.

ARIEL

Prospero my lord shall know what I have done:
So, king, go safely on to seek thy son.

Exeunt

Act 2, Scene 2

Another part of the island.

Enter CALIBAN with a burden of wood. A noise of thunder heard

CALIBAN

All the infections that the sun sucks up
From bogs, fens, flats, on Prosper fall and make him
By inch–meal a disease! His spirits hear me
And yet I needs must curse. But they'll nor pinch,
Fright me with urchin—shows, pitch me i' the mire,
Nor lead me, like a firebrand, in the dark
Out of my way, unless he bid 'em; but
For every trifle are they set upon me;
Sometime like apes that mow and chatter at me
And after bite me, then like hedgehogs which
Lie tumbling in my barefoot way and mount

Their pricks at my footfall; sometime am I
All wound with adders who with cloven tongues
Do hiss me into madness.

Enter TRINCULO

Lo, now, lo!

Here comes a spirit of his, and to torment me
For bringing wood in slowly. I'll fall flat;
Perchance he will not mind me.

TRINCULO

Here's neither bush nor shrub, to bear off
any weather at all, and another storm brewing;
I hear it sing i' the wind: yond same black
cloud, yond huge one, looks like a foul
bombard that would shed his liquor. If it
should thunder as it did before, I know not
where to hide my head: yond same cloud cannot
choose but fall by pailfuls. What have we
here? a man or a fish? dead or alive? A fish:
he smells like a fish; a very ancient and fish—
like smell; a kind of not of the newest Poor—
John. A strange fish! Were I in England now,
as once I was, and had but this fish painted,
not a holiday fool there but would give a piece
of silver: there would this monster make a
man; any strange beast there makes a man:
when they will not give a doit to relieve a lame
beggar, they will lazy out ten to see a dead
Indian. Legged like a man and his fins like
arms! Warm o' my troth! I do now let loose

my opinion; hold it no longer: this is no fish,
but an islander, that hath lately suffered by a
thunderbolt.

Thunder

Alas, the storm is come again! my best way is to
creep under his gaberdine; there is no other
shelter hereabouts: misery acquaints a man with
strange bed–fellows. I will here shroud till the
dregs of the storm be past.

Enter STEPHANO, singing: a bottle in his hand

STEPHANO

> I shall no more to sea, to sea,
> Here shall I die ashore—

This is a very scurvy tune to sing at a man's
funeral: well, here's my comfort. [Drinks]

Sings

> The master, the swabber, the boatswain and I,
> The gunner and his mate
> Loved Mall, Meg and Marian and Margery,
> But none of us cared for Kate;
> For she had a tongue with a tang,
> Would cry to a sailor, Go hang!
> She loved not the savour of tar nor of pitch,
> Yet a tailor might scratch her where'er she did itch:
> Then to sea, boys, and let her go hang!

This is a scurvy tune too: but here's my comfort.

Drinks

CALIBAN

Do not torment me: Oh!

STEPHANO

What's the matter? Have we devils here? Do you put
tricks upon's with savages and men of Ind, ha? I
have not scaped drowning to be afeard now of your
four legs; for it hath been said, As proper a man as
ever went on four legs cannot make him give ground;
and it shall be said so again while Stephano
breathes at's nostrils.

CALIBAN

The spirit torments me; Oh!

STEPHANO

This is some monster of the isle with four legs, who
hath got, as I take it, an ague. Where the devil
should he learn our language? I will give him some
relief, if it be but for that. if I can recover him
and keep him tame and get to Naples with him, he's a
present for any emperor that ever trod on neat's leather.

CALIBAN

Do not torment me, prithee; I'll bring my wood home faster.

STEPHANO

He's in his fit now and does not talk after the
wisest. He shall taste of my bottle: if he have
never drunk wine afore will go near to remove his
fit. If I can recover him and keep him tame, I will
not take too much for him; he shall pay for him that
hath him, and that soundly.

CALIBAN

Thou dost me yet but little hurt; thou wilt anon, I
know it by thy trembling: now Prosper works upon thee.

STEPHANO

Come on your ways; open your mouth; here is that
which will give language to you, cat: open your
mouth; this will shake your shaking, I can tell you,
and that soundly: you cannot tell who's your friend:
open your chaps again.

TRINCULO

I should know that voice: it should be—but he is
drowned; and these are devils: O defend me!

STEPHANO

Four legs and two voices: a most delicate monster!
His forward voice now is to speak well of his
friend; his backward voice is to utter foul speeches
and to detract. If all the wine in my bottle will
recover him, I will help his ague. Come. Amen! I
will pour some in thy other mouth.

TRINCULO

Stephano!

STEPHANO

Doth thy other mouth call me? Mercy, mercy! This is
a devil, and no monster: I will leave him; I have no
long spoon.

TRINCULO

Stephano! If thou beest Stephano, touch me and
speak to me: for I am Trinculo—be not afeard—thy
good friend Trinculo.

STEPHANO

If thou beest Trinculo, come forth: I'll pull thee
by the lesser legs: if any be Trinculo's legs,
these are they. Thou art very Trinculo indeed! How
camest thou to be the siege of this moon–calf? can
he vent Trinculos?

TRINCULO

I took him to be killed with a thunder–stroke. But
art thou not drowned, Stephano? I hope now thou art
not drowned. Is the storm overblown? I hid me
under the dead moon–calf's gaberdine for fear of
the storm. And art thou living, Stephano? O
Stephano, two Neapolitans 'scaped!

STEPHANO

Prithee, do not turn me about; my stomach is not constant.

CALIBAN

[Aside] These be fine things, an if they be
not sprites.
That's a brave god and bears celestial liquor.
I will kneel to him.

STEPHANO

How didst thou 'scape? How camest thou hither?
swear by this bottle how thou camest hither. I
escaped upon a butt of sack which the sailors
heaved o'erboard, by this bottle; which I made of
the bark of a tree with mine own hands since I was
cast ashore.

CALIBAN

I'll swear upon that bottle to be thy true subject;
for the liquor is not earthly.

STEPHANO

Here; swear then how thou escapedst.

TRINCULO

Swum ashore. man, like a duck: I can swim like a
duck, I'll be sworn.

STEPHANO

Here, kiss the book. Though thou canst swim like a
duck, thou art made like a goose.

TRINCULO

O Stephano. hast any more of this?

STEPHANO

The whole butt, man: my cellar is in a rock by the
sea–side where my wine is hid. How now, moon–calf!
how does thine ague?

CALIBAN

Hast thou not dropp'd from heaven?

STEPHANO

Out o' the moon, I do assure thee: I was the man i'
the moon when time was.

CALIBAN

I have seen thee in her and I do adore thee:
My mistress show'd me thee and thy dog and thy bush.

STEPHANO

Come, swear to that; kiss the book: I will furnish
it anon with new contents swear.

TRINCULO

By this good light, this is a very shallow monster!
I afeard of him! A very weak monster! The man i'
the moon! A most poor credulous monster! Well
drawn, monster, in good sooth!

CALIBAN

I'll show thee every fertile inch o' th' island;
And I will kiss thy foot: I prithee, be my god.

TRINCULO

By this light, a most perfidious and drunken
monster! when 's god's asleep, he'll rob his bottle.

CALIBAN

I'll kiss thy foot; I'll swear myself thy subject.

425

STEPHANO

Come on then; down, and swear.

TRINCULO

I shall laugh myself to death at this puppy–headed
monster. A most scurvy monster! I could find in my
heart to beat him,—

STEPHANO

Come, kiss.

TRINCULO

But that the poor monster's in drink: an abominable monster!

CALIBAN

I'll show thee the best springs; I'll pluck thee berries;
I'll fish for thee and get thee wood enough.
A plague upon the tyrant that I serve!
I'll bear him no more sticks, but follow thee,
Thou wondrous man.

TRINCULO

A most ridiculous monster, to make a wonder of a
Poor drunkard!

CALIBAN

I prithee, let me bring thee where crabs grow;
And I with my long nails will dig thee pignuts;
Show thee a jay's nest and instruct thee how
To snare the nimble marmoset; I'll bring thee
To clustering filberts and sometimes I'll get thee
Young scamels from the rock. Wilt thou go with me?

STEPHANO

I prithee now, lead the way without any more
talking. Trinculo, the king and all our company
else being drowned, we will inherit here: here;
bear my bottle: fellow Trinculo, we'll fill him by
and by again.

CALIBAN

[Sings drunkenly]
Farewell master; farewell, farewell!

TRINCULO

A howling monster: a drunken monster!

CALIBAN

No more dams I'll make for fish
Nor fetch in firing
At requiring;
Nor scrape trencher, nor wash dish
'Ban, 'Ban, Cacaliban
Has a new master: get a new man.

Freedom, hey–day! hey–day, freedom! freedom,
hey–day, freedom!

STEPHANO

O brave monster! Lead the way.

Exeunt

Act 3, Scene 1

Before PROSPERO'S Cell.

Enter FERDINAND, bearing a log

FERDINAND

> There be some sports are painful, and their labour
> Delight in them sets off: some kinds of baseness
> Are nobly undergone and most poor matters
> Point to rich ends. This my mean task
> Would be as heavy to me as odious, but
> The mistress which I serve quickens what's dead
> And makes my labours pleasures: O, she is
> Ten times more gentle than her father's crabbed,
> And he's composed of harshness. I must remove
> Some thousands of these logs and pile them up,
> Upon a sore injunction: my sweet mistress
> Weeps when she sees me work, and says, such baseness
> Had never like executor. I forget:
> But these sweet thoughts do even refresh my labours,
> Most busy lest, when I do it.

Twelth Night, A Winter's Tale, The Tempest

Enter MIRANDA; and PROSPERO at a distance, unseen

MIRANDA

> Alas, now, pray you,
> Work not so hard: I would the lightning had
> Burnt up those logs that you are enjoin'd to pile!
> Pray, set it down and rest you: when this burns,
> 'Twill weep for having wearied you. My father
> Is hard at study; pray now, rest yourself;
> He's safe for these three hours.

FERDINAND

> O most dear mistress,
> The sun will set before I shall discharge
> What I must strive to do.

MIRANDA

> If you'll sit down,
> I'll bear your logs the while: pray, give me that;
> I'll carry it to the pile.

FERDINAND

> No, precious creature;
> I had rather crack my sinews, break my back,
> Than you should such dishonour undergo,
> While I sit lazy by.

MIRANDA

It would become me
As well as it does you: and I should do it
With much more ease; for my good will is to it,
And yours it is against.

PROSPERO

Poor worm, thou art infected!
This visitation shows it.

MIRANDA

You look wearily.

FERDINAND

No, noble mistress;'tis fresh morning with me
When you are by at night. I do beseech you—
Chiefly that I might set it in my prayers—
What is your name?

MIRANDA

Miranda.—O my father,
I have broke your hest to say so!

FERDINAND

Admired Miranda!
Indeed the top of admiration! worth
What's dearest to the world! Full many a lady
I have eyed with best regard and many a time

The harmony of their tongues hath into bondage
Brought my too diligent ear: for several virtues
Have I liked several women; never any
With so fun soul, but some defect in her
Did quarrel with the noblest grace she owed
And put it to the foil: but you, O you,
So perfect and so peerless, are created
Of every creature's best!

MIRANDA

I do not know
One of my sex; no woman's face remember,
Save, from my glass, mine own; nor have I seen
More that I may call men than you, good friend,
And my dear father: how features are abroad,
I am skilless of; but, by my modesty,
The jewel in my dower, I would not wish
Any companion in the world but you,
Nor can imagination form a shape,
Besides yourself, to like of. But I prattle
Something too wildly and my father's precepts
I therein do forget.

FERDINAND

I am in my condition
A prince, Miranda; I do think, a king;
I would, not so!—and would no more endure
This wooden slavery than to suffer
The flesh–fly blow my mouth. Hear my soul speak:
The very instant that I saw you, did
My heart fly to your service; there resides,
To make me slave to it; and for your sake

Am I this patient log—man.

MIRANDA

Do you love me?

FERDINAND

O heaven, O earth, bear witness to this sound
And crown what I profess with kind event
If I speak true! if hollowly, invert
What best is boded me to mischief! I
Beyond all limit of what else i' the world
Do love, prize, honour you.

MIRANDA

I am a fool
To weep at what I am glad of.

PROSPERO

Fair encounter
Of two most rare affections! Heavens rain grace
On that which breeds between 'em!

FERDINAND

Wherefore weep you?

MIRANDA

At mine unworthiness that dare not offer
What I desire to give, and much less take
What I shall die to want. But this is trifling;
And all the more it seeks to hide itself,
The bigger bulk it shows. Hence, bashful cunning!
And prompt me, plain and holy innocence!
I am your wife, it you will marry me;
If not, I'll die your maid: to be your fellow
You may deny me; but I'll be your servant,
Whether you will or no.

FERDINAND

My mistress, dearest;
And I thus humble ever.

MIRANDA

My husband, then?

FERDINAND

Ay, with a heart as willing
As bondage e'er of freedom: here's my hand.

MIRANDA

And mine, with my heart in't; and now farewell
Till half an hour hence.

FERDINAND

A thousand thousand!

Exeunt FERDINAND and MIRANDA severally

PROSPERO

> So glad of this as they I cannot be,
> Who are surprised withal; but my rejoicing
> At nothing can be more. I'll to my book,
> For yet ere supper–time must I perform
> Much business appertaining.

Exit

Act 3, Scene 2

Another part of the island.

Enter CALIBAN, STEPHANO, and TRINCULO

STEPHANO

> Tell not me; when the butt is out, we will drink
> water; not a drop before: therefore bear up, and
> board 'em. Servant–monster, drink to me.

TRINCULO

> Servant–monster! the folly of this island! They
> say there's but five upon this isle: we are three
> of them; if th' other two be brained like us, the
> state totters.

STEPHANO

Drink, servant–monster, when I bid thee: thy eyes
are almost set in thy head.

TRINCULO

Where should they be set else? he were a brave
monster indeed, if they were set in his tail.

STEPHANO

My man–monster hath drown'd his tongue in sack:
for my part, the sea cannot drown me; I swam, ere I
could recover the shore, five and thirty leagues off
and on. By this light, thou shalt be my lieutenant,
monster, or my standard.

TRINCULO

Your lieutenant, if you list; he's no standard.

STEPHANO

We'll not run, Monsieur Monster.

TRINCULO

Nor go neither; but you'll lie like dogs and yet say
nothing neither.

STEPHANO

Moon–calf, speak once in thy life, if thou beest a
good moon–calf.

CALIBAN

How does thy honour? Let me lick thy shoe.
I'll not serve him; he's not valiant.

TRINCULO

Thou liest, most ignorant monster: I am in case to
justle a constable. Why, thou deboshed fish thou,
was there ever man a coward that hath drunk so much
sack as I to–day? Wilt thou tell a monstrous lie,
being but half a fish and half a monster?

CALIBAN

Lo, how he mocks me! wilt thou let him, my lord?

TRINCULO

'Lord' quoth he! That a monster should be such a natural!

CALIBAN

Lo, lo, again! bite him to death, I prithee.

STEPHANO

Trinculo, keep a good tongue in your head: if you
prove a mutineer,—the next tree! The poor monster's
my subject and he shall not suffer indignity.

436

CALIBAN

> I thank my noble lord. Wilt thou be pleased to
> hearken once again to the suit I made to thee?

STEPHANO *Marry, will I*

> kneel and repeat it; I will stand,
> and so shall Trinculo.

> *Enter ARIEL, invisible*

CALIBAN

> As I told thee before, I am subject to a tyrant, a
> sorcerer, that by his cunning hath cheated me of the island.

ARIEL

> Thou liest.

CALIBAN

> Thou liest, thou jesting monkey, thou: I would my
> valiant master would destroy thee! I do not lie.

STEPHANO

> Trinculo, if you trouble him any more in's tale, by
> this hand, I will supplant some of your teeth.

437

TRINCULO

Why, I said nothing.

STEPHANO

Mum, then, and no more. Proceed.

CALIBAN

I say, by sorcery he got this isle;
From me he got it. if thy greatness will
Revenge it on him,—for I know thou darest,
But this thing dare not,—

STEPHANO

That's most certain.

CALIBAN

Thou shalt be lord of it and I'll serve thee.

STEPHANO

How now shall this be compassed?
Canst thou bring me to the party?

CALIBAN

Yea, yea, my lord: I'll yield him thee asleep,
Where thou mayst knock a nail into his bead.

ARIEL

Thou liest; thou canst not.

CALIBAN

What a pied ninny's this! Thou scurvy patch!
I do beseech thy greatness, give him blows
And take his bottle from him: when that's gone
He shall drink nought but brine; for I'll not show him
Where the quick freshes are.

STEPHANO

Trinculo, run into no further danger:
interrupt the monster one word further, and,
by this hand, I'll turn my mercy out o' doors
and make a stock–fish of thee.

TRINCULO

Why, what did I? I did nothing. I'll go farther
off.

STEPHANO

Didst thou not say he lied?

ARIEL

Thou liest.

STEPHANO

Do I so? take thou that.

Beats TRINCULO

As you like this, give me the lie another time.

TRINCULO

I did not give the lie. Out o' your
wits and bearing too? A pox o' your bottle!
this can sack and drinking do. A murrain on
your monster, and the devil take your fingers!

CALIBAN

Ha, ha, ha!

STEPHANO

Now, forward with your tale. Prithee, stand farther
off.

CALIBAN

Beat him enough: after a little time
I'll beat him too.

STEPHANO

Stand farther. Come, proceed.

CALIBAN

Why, as I told thee, 'tis a custom with him,
I' th' afternoon to sleep: there thou mayst brain him,
Having first seized his books, or with a log
Batter his skull, or paunch him with a stake,
Or cut his wezand with thy knife. Remember
First to possess his books; for without them
He's but a sot, as I am, nor hath not
One spirit to command: they all do hate him
As rootedly as I. Burn but his books.
He has brave utensils,—for so he calls them—
Which when he has a house, he'll deck withal
And that most deeply to consider is
The beauty of his daughter; he himself
Calls her a nonpareil: I never saw a woman,
But only Sycorax my dam and she;
But she as far surpasseth Sycorax
As great'st does least.

STEPHANO

Is it so brave a lass?

CALIBAN

Ay, lord; she will become thy bed, I warrant.
And bring thee forth brave brood.

STEPHANO

Monster, I will kill this man: his daughter and I
will be king and queen—save our graces!—and
Trinculo and thyself shall be viceroys. Dost thou

441

like the plot, Trinculo?

TRINCULO

Excellent.

STEPHANO

Give me thy hand: I am sorry I beat thee; but,
while thou livest, keep a good tongue in thy head.

CALIBAN

Within this half hour will he be asleep:
Wilt thou destroy him then?

STEPHANO

Ay, on mine honour.

ARIEL

This will I tell my master.

CALIBAN

Thou makest me merry; I am full of pleasure:
Let us be jocund: will you troll the catch
You taught me but while–ere?

STEPHANO

At thy request, monster, I will do reason, any
reason. Come on, Trinculo, let us sing.

Sings

Flout 'em and scout 'em
And scout 'em and flout 'em
Thought is free.

CALIBAN

That's not the tune.

Ariel plays the tune on a tabour and pipe

STEPHANO

What is this same?

TRINCULO

This is the tune of our catch, played by the picture
of Nobody.

STEPHANO

If thou beest a man, show thyself in thy likeness:
if thou beest a devil, take't as thou list.

TRINCULO

O, forgive me my sins!

STEPHANO

He that dies pays all debts: I defy thee. Mercy upon us!

CALIBAN

Art thou afeard?

STEPHANO

No, monster, not I.

CALIBAN

Be not afeard; the isle is full of noises,
Sounds and sweet airs, that give delight and hurt not.
Sometimes a thousand twangling instruments
Will hum about mine ears, and sometime voices
That, if I then had waked after long sleep,
Will make me sleep again: and then, in dreaming,
The clouds methought would open and show riches
Ready to drop upon me that, when I waked,
I cried to dream again.

STEPHANO

This will prove a brave kingdom to me, where I shall
have my music for nothing.

CALIBAN

When Prospero is destroyed.

STEPHANO

That shall be by and by: I remember the story.

TRINCULO

The sound is going away; let's follow it, and
after do our work.

STEPHANO

Lead, monster; we'll follow. I would I could see
this tabourer; he lays it on.

TRINCULO

Wilt come? I'll follow, Stephano.

Exeunt

Act 3, Scene 3

Another part of the island.

*Enter ALONSO, SEBASTIAN, ANTONIO, GONZALO, ADRIAN,
FRANCISCO, and others*

GONZALO

By'r lakin, I can go no further, sir;
My old bones ache: here's a maze trod indeed
Through forth–rights and meanders! By your patience,
I needs must rest me.

ALONSO

Old lord, I cannot blame thee,
Who am myself attach'd with weariness,
To the dulling of my spirits: sit down, and rest.
Even here I will put off my hope and keep it
No longer for my flatterer: he is drown'd
Whom thus we stray to find, and the sea mocks
Our frustrate search on land. Well, let him go.

ANTONIO

[Aside to SEBASTIAN] I am right glad that he's so
out of hope.
Do not, for one repulse, forego the purpose
That you resolved to effect.

SEBASTIAN

[Aside to ANTONIO] The next advantage
Will we take throughly.

ANTONIO

[Aside to SEBASTIAN] Let it be to–night;
For, now they are oppress'd with travel, they
Will not, nor cannot, use such vigilance
As when they are fresh.

SEBASTIAN

[Aside to ANTONIO] I say, to–night: no more.

Solemn and strange music

ALONSO

What harmony is this? My good friends, hark!

GONZALO

Marvellous sweet music!

Enter PROSPERO above, invisible. Enter several strange Shapes, bringing in a banquet; they dance about it with gentle actions of salutation; and, inviting the King, to eat, they depart

ALONSO

Give us kind keepers, heavens! What were these?

SEBASTIAN

A living drollery. Now I will believe
That there are unicorns, that in Arabia
There is one tree, the phoenix' throne, one phoenix
At this hour reigning there.

ANTONIO

I'll believe both;
And what does else want credit, come to me,
And I'll be sworn 'tis true: travellers ne'er did
lie,
Though fools at home condemn 'em.

GONZALO

If in Naples
I should report this now, would they believe me?
If I should say, I saw such islanders—
For, certes, these are people of the island—
Who, though they are of monstrous shape, yet, note,
Their manners are more gentle–kind than of
Our human generation you shall find
Many, nay, almost any.

PROSPERO

[Aside] Honest lord,
Thou hast said well; for some of you there present
Are worse than devils.

ALONSO

I cannot too much muse
Such shapes, such gesture and such sound, expressing,
Although they want the use of tongue, a kind
Of excellent dumb discourse.

PROSPERO *[Aside]*

Praise in departing.

FRANCISCO

They vanish'd strangely.

SEBASTIAN

No matter, since
They have left their viands behind; for we have stomachs.
Will't please you taste of what is here?

ALONSO

    Not I.

GONZALO

    Faith, sir, you need not fear. When we were boys,
    Who would believe that there were mountaineers
    Dew–lapp'd like bulls, whose throats had hanging at 'em
    Wallets of flesh? or that there were such men
    Whose heads stood in their breasts? which now we find
    Each putter–out of five for one will bring us
    Good warrant of.

ALONSO

    I will stand to and feed,
    Although my last: no matter, since I feel
    The best is past. Brother, my lord the duke,
    Stand to and do as we.

    Thunder and lightning. Enter ARIEL, like a harpy; claps his wings upon
    the table; and, with a quaint device, the banquet vanishes

ARIEL

    You are three men of sin, whom Destiny,
    That hath to instrument this lower world
    And what is in't, the never–surfeited sea

449

Hath caused to belch up you; and on this island
Where man doth not inhabit; you 'mongst men
Being most unfit to live. I have made you mad;
And even with such–like valour men hang and drown
Their proper selves.

ALONSO, SEBASTIAN draw their swords

You fools! I and my fellows
Are ministers of Fate: the elements,
Of whom your swords are temper'd, may as well
Wound the loud winds, or with bemock'd–at stabs
Kill the still–closing waters, as diminish
One dowle that's in my plume: my fellow–ministers
Are like invulnerable. If you could hurt,
Your swords are now too massy for your strengths
And will not be uplifted. But remember—
For that's my business to you—that you three
From Milan did supplant good Prospero;
Exposed unto the sea, which hath requit it,
Him and his innocent child: for which foul deed
The powers, delaying, not forgetting, have
Incensed the seas and shores, yea, all the creatures,
Against your peace. Thee of thy son, Alonso,
They have bereft; and do pronounce by me:
Lingering perdition, worse than any death
Can be at once, shall step by step attend
You and your ways; whose wraths to guard you from—
Which here, in this most desolate isle, else falls
Upon your heads—is nothing but heart–sorrow
And a clear life ensuing.

*He vanishes in thunder; then, to soft music enter the Shapes again, and
dance, with mocks and mows, and carrying out the table*

PROSPERO

>Bravely the figure of this harpy hast thou
>Perform'd, my Ariel; a grace it had, devouring:
>Of my instruction hast thou nothing bated
>In what thou hadst to say: so, with good life
>And observation strange, my meaner ministers
>Their several kinds have done. My high charms work
>And these mine enemies are all knit up
>In their distractions; they now are in my power;
>And in these fits I leave them, while I visit
>Young Ferdinand, whom they suppose is drown'd,
>And his and mine loved darling.

Exit above

GONZALO

>I' the name of something holy, sir, why stand you
>In this strange stare?

ALONSO

>O, it is monstrous, monstrous:
>Methought the billows spoke and told me of it;
>The winds did sing it to me, and the thunder,
>That deep and dreadful organ–pipe, pronounced
>The name of Prosper: it did bass my trespass.
>Therefore my son i' the ooze is bedded, and
>I'll seek him deeper than e'er plummet sounded
>And with him there lie mudded.

Exit

SEBASTIAN

> But one fiend at a time,
> I'll fight their legions o'er.

ANTONIO

> I'll be thy second.

> *Exeunt SEBASTIAN, and ANTONIO*

GONZALO

> All three of them are desperate: their great guilt,
> Like poison given to work a great time after,
> Now 'gins to bite the spirits. I do beseech you
> That are of suppler joints, follow them swiftly
> And hinder them from what this ecstasy
> May now provoke them to.

ADRIAN

> Follow, I pray you.

> *Exeunt*

Act 4, Scene 1

Before PROSPERO'S cell.

> *Enter PROSPERO, FERDINAND, and MIRANDA*

PROSPERO

If I have too austerely punish'd you,
Your compensation makes amends, for I
Have given you here a third of mine own life,
Or that for which I live; who once again
I tender to thy hand: all thy vexations
Were but my trials of thy love and thou
Hast strangely stood the test here, afore Heaven,
I ratify this my rich gift. O Ferdinand,
Do not smile at me that I boast her off,
For thou shalt find she will outstrip all praise
And make it halt behind her.

FERDINAND

I do believe it
Against an oracle.

PROSPERO

Then, as my gift and thine own acquisition
Worthily purchased take my daughter: but
If thou dost break her virgin–knot before
All sanctimonious ceremonies may
With full and holy rite be minister'd,
No sweet aspersion shall the heavens let fall
To make this contract grow: but barren hate,
Sour–eyed disdain and discord shall bestrew
The union of your bed with weeds so loathly
That you shall hate it both: therefore take heed,
As Hymen's lamps shall light you.

FERDINAND

As I hope
For quiet days, fair issue and long life,
With such love as 'tis now, the murkiest den,
The most opportune place, the strong'st suggestion.
Our worser genius can, shall never melt
Mine honour into lust, to take away
The edge of that day's celebration
When I shall think: or Phoebus' steeds are founder'd,
Or Night kept chain'd below.

PROSPERO

Fairly spoke.
Sit then and talk with her; she is thine own.
What, Ariel! my industrious servant, Ariel!

Enter ARIEL

ARIEL

What would my potent master? here I am.

PROSPERO

Thou and thy meaner fellows your last service
Did worthily perform; and I must use you
In such another trick. Go bring the rabble,
O'er whom I give thee power, here to this place:
Incite them to quick motion; for I must
Bestow upon the eyes of this young couple
Some vanity of mine art: it is my promise,
And they expect it from me.

ARIEL

Presently?

PROSPERO

Ay, with a twink.

ARIEL

Before you can say 'come' and 'go,'
And breathe twice and cry 'so, so,'
Each one, tripping on his toe,
Will be here with mop and mow.
Do you love me, master? no?

PROSPERO

Dearly my delicate Ariel. Do not approach
Till thou dost hear me call.

ARIEL

Well, I conceive.

Exit

PROSPERO

Look thou be true; do not give dalliance
Too much the rein: the strongest oaths are straw
To the fire i' the blood: be more abstemious,
Or else, good night your vow!

455

FERDINAND

> I warrant you sir;
> The white cold virgin snow upon my heart
> Abates the ardour of my liver.

PROSPERO

> Well.
> Now come, my Ariel! bring a corollary,
> Rather than want a spirit: appear and pertly!
> No tongue! all eyes! be silent.

Soft music

Enter IRIS

IRIS

> Ceres, most bounteous lady, thy rich leas
> Of wheat, rye, barley, vetches, oats and pease;
> Thy turfy mountains, where live nibbling sheep,
> And flat meads thatch'd with stover, them to keep;
> Thy banks with pioned and twilled brims,
> Which spongy April at thy hest betrims,
> To make cold nymphs chaste crowns; and thy broom –groves,
> Whose shadow the dismissed bachelor loves,
> Being lass–lorn: thy pole–clipt vineyard;
> And thy sea–marge, sterile and rocky–hard,
> Where thou thyself dost air;—the queen o' the sky,
> Whose watery arch and messenger am I,
> Bids thee leave these, and with her sovereign grace,
> Here on this grass–plot, in this very place,
> To come and sport: her peacocks fly amain:

Approach, rich Ceres, her to entertain.

Enter CERES

CERES

     Hail, many–colour'd messenger, that ne'er
     Dost disobey the wife of Jupiter;
     Who with thy saffron wings upon my flowers
     Diffusest honey–drops, refreshing showers,
     And with each end of thy blue bow dost crown
     My bosky acres and my unshrubb'd down,
     Rich scarf to my proud earth; why hath thy queen
     Summon'd me hither, to this short–grass'd green?

IRIS

     A contract of true love to celebrate;
     And some donation freely to estate
     On the blest lovers.

CERES

     Tell me, heavenly bow,
     If Venus or her son, as thou dost know,
     Do now attend the queen? Since they did plot
     The means that dusky Dis my daughter got,
     Her and her blind boy's scandal'd company
     I have forsworn.

IRIS

Of her society
Be not afraid: I met her deity
Cutting the clouds towards Paphos and her son
Dove–drawn with her. Here thought they to have done
Some wanton charm upon this man and maid,
Whose vows are, that no bed–right shall be paid
Till Hymen's torch be lighted: but vain;
Mars's hot minion is returned again;
Her waspish–headed son has broke his arrows,
Swears he will shoot no more but play with sparrows
And be a boy right out.

CERES

High'st queen of state,
Great Juno, comes; I know her by her gait.

Enter JUNO

JUNO

How does my bounteous sister? Go with me
To bless this twain, that they may prosperous be
And honour'd in their issue.

They sing:

JUNO

Honour, riches, marriage–blessing,
Long continuance, and increasing,
Hourly joys be still upon you!
Juno sings her blessings upon you.

CERES

> Earth's increase, foison plenty,
> Barns and garners never empty,
> Vines and clustering bunches growing,
> Plants with goodly burthen bowing;
> Spring come to you at the farthest
> In the very end of harvest!
> Scarcity and want shall shun you;
> Ceres' blessing so is on you.

FERDINAND

> This is a most majestic vision, and
> Harmoniously charmingly. May I be bold
> To think these spirits?

PROSPERO

> Spirits, which by mine art
> I have from their confines call'd to enact
> My present fancies.

FERDINAND

> Let me live here ever;
> So rare a wonder'd father and a wife
> Makes this place Paradise.

Juno and Ceres whisper, and send Iris on employment

459

Twelth Night, A Winter's Tale, The Tempest

PROSPERO

> Sweet, now, silence!
> Juno and Ceres whisper seriously;
> There's something else to do: hush, and be mute,
> Or else our spell is marr'd.

IRIS

> You nymphs, call'd Naiads, of the windring brooks,
> With your sedged crowns and ever–harmless looks,
> Leave your crisp channels and on this green land
> Answer your summons; Juno does command:
> Come, temperate nymphs, and help to celebrate
> A contract of true love; be not too late.

> *Enter certain Nymphs*

> You sunburnt sicklemen, of August weary,
> Come hither from the furrow and be merry:
> Make holiday; your rye–straw hats put on
> And these fresh nymphs encounter every one
> In country footing.

> *Enter certain Reapers, properly habited: they join with the Nymphs in a graceful dance; towards the end whereof PROSPERO starts suddenly, and speaks; after which, to a strange, hollow, and confused noise, they heavily vanish*

PROSPERO

> *[Aside]* I had forgot that foul conspiracy
> Of the beast Caliban and his confederates

Against my life: the minute of their plot
Is almost come.

To the Spirits

Well done! avoid; no more!

FERDINAND

This is strange: your father's in some passion
That works him strongly.

MIRANDA

Never till this day
Saw I him touch'd with anger so distemper'd.

PROSPERO

You do look, my son, in a moved sort,
As if you were dismay'd: be cheerful, sir.
Our revels now are ended. These our actors,
As I foretold you, were all spirits and
Are melted into air, into thin air:
And, like the baseless fabric of this vision,
The cloud–capp'd towers, the gorgeous palaces,
The solemn temples, the great globe itself,
Ye all which it inherit, shall dissolve
And, like this insubstantial pageant faded,
Leave not a rack behind. We are such stuff
As dreams are made on, and our little life
Is rounded with a sleep. Sir, I am vex'd;

Bear with my weakness; my, brain is troubled:
Be not disturb'd with my infirmity:
If you be pleased, retire into my cell
And there repose: a turn or two I'll walk,
To still my beating mind.

FERDINAND

|
| We wish your peace.

MIRANDA

|

Exeunt

PROSPERO

Come with a thought I thank thee, Ariel: come.

Enter ARIEL

ARIEL

Thy thoughts I cleave to. What's thy pleasure?

PROSPERO

Spirit,
We must prepare to meet with Caliban.

ARIEL

Ay, my commander: when I presented Ceres,
I thought to have told thee of it, but I fear'd
Lest I might anger thee.

PROSPERO

Say again, where didst thou leave these varlets?

ARIEL

I told you, sir, they were red–hot with drinking;
So fun of valour that they smote the air
For breathing in their faces; beat the ground
For kissing of their feet; yet always bending
Towards their project. Then I beat my tabour;
At which, like unback'd colts, they prick'd
their ears,
Advanced their eyelids, lifted up their noses
As they smelt music: so I charm'd their ears
That calf–like they my lowing follow'd through
Tooth'd briers, sharp furzes, pricking goss and thorns,
Which entered their frail shins: at last I left them
I' the filthy–mantled pool beyond your cell,
There dancing up to the chins, that the foul lake
O'erstunk their feet.

PROSPERO

This was well done, my bird.
Thy shape invisible retain thou still:
The trumpery in my house, go bring it hither,
For stale to catch these thieves.

ARIEL

I go, I go.

Exit

PROSPERO

A devil, a born devil, on whose nature
Nurture can never stick; on whom my pains,
Humanely taken, all, all lost, quite lost;
And as with age his body uglier grows,
So his mind cankers. I will plague them all,
Even to roaring.

Re—enter ARIEL, loaden with glistering apparel, TE>

Come, hang them on this line.

*PROSPERO and ARIEL remain invisible. Enter
CALIBAN, STEPHANO, and TRINCULO, all wet*

CALIBAN

Pray you, tread softly, that the blind mole may not
Hear a foot fall: we now are near his cell.

STEPHANO

Monster, your fairy, which you say is
a harmless fairy, has done little better than
played the Jack with us.

TRINCULO

> Monster, I do smell all horse–piss; at
> which my nose is in great indignation.

STEPHANO

> So is mine. Do you hear, monster? If I should take
> a displeasure against you, look you,—

TRINCULO

> Thou wert but a lost monster.

CALIBAN

> Good my lord, give me thy favour still.
> Be patient, for the prize I'll bring thee to
> Shall hoodwink this mischance: therefore speak softly.
> All's hush'd as midnight yet.

TRINCULO

> Ay, but to lose our bottles in the pool,—

STEPHANO

> There is not only disgrace and dishonour in that,
> monster, but an infinite loss.

TRINCULO

That's more to me than my wetting: yet this is your
harmless fairy, monster.

STEPHANO

I will fetch off my bottle, though I be o'er ears
for my labour.

CALIBAN

Prithee, my king, be quiet. Seest thou here,
This is the mouth o' the cell: no noise, and enter.
Do that good mischief which may make this island
Thine own for ever, and I, thy Caliban,
For aye thy foot–licker.

STEPHANO

Give me thy hand. I do begin to have bloody thoughts.

TRINCULO

O king Stephano! O peer! O worthy Stephano! look
what a wardrobe here is for thee!

CALIBAN

Let it alone, thou fool; it is but trash.

TRINCULO

O, ho, monster! we know what belongs to a frippery.
O king Stephano!

STEPHANO

Put off that gown, Trinculo; by this hand, I'll have
that gown.

TRINCULO

Thy grace shall have it.

CALIBAN

The dropsy drown this fool I what do you mean
To dote thus on such luggage? Let's alone
And do the murder first: if he awake,
From toe to crown he'll fill our skins with pinches,
Make us strange stuff.

STEPHANO

Be you quiet, monster. Mistress line,
is not this my jerkin? Now is the jerkin under
the line: now, jerkin, you are like to lose your
hair and prove a bald jerkin.

TRINCULO

Do, do: we steal by line and level, an't like your grace.

STEPHANO

I thank thee for that jest; here's a garment for't:
wit shall not go unrewarded while I am king of this
country. 'Steal by line and level' is an excellent
pass of pate; there's another garment for't.

TRINCULO

Monster, come, put some lime upon your fingers, and
away with the rest.

CALIBAN

I will have none on't: we shall lose our time,
And all be turn'd to barnacles, or to apes
With foreheads villanous low.

STEPHANO

Monster, lay–to your fingers: help to bear this
away where my hogshead of wine is, or I'll turn you
out of my kingdom: go to, carry this.

TRINCULO

And this.

STEPHANO

Ay, and this.

*A noise of hunters heard. Enter divers Spirits, in shape
of dogs and hounds, and hunt them about, PROSPERO*

and ARIEL setting them on

PROSPERO

Hey, Mountain, hey!

ARIEL

Silver I there it goes, Silver!

PROSPERO

Fury, Fury! there, Tyrant, there! hark! hark!

CALIBAN, STEPHANO, and TRINCULO, are driven out

Go charge my goblins that they grind their joints
With dry convulsions, shorten up their sinews
With aged cramps, and more pinch−spotted make them
Than pard or cat o' mountain.

ARIEL

Hark, they roar!

PROSPERO

Let them be hunted soundly. At this hour
Lie at my mercy all mine enemies:
Shortly shall all my labours end, and thou
Shalt have the air at freedom: for a little
Follow, and do me service.

Exeunt

Act 5, Scene 1

Before PROSPERO'S cell.

Enter PROSPERO in his magic robes, and ARIEL

PROSPERO

> Now does my project gather to a head:
> My charms crack not; my spirits obey; and time
> Goes upright with his carriage. How's the day?

ARIEL

> On the sixth hour; at which time, my lord,
> You said our work should cease.

PROSPERO

> I did say so,
> When first I raised the tempest. Say, my spirit,
> How fares the king and's followers?

ARIEL

> Confined together
> In the same fashion as you gave in charge,
> Just as you left them; all prisoners, sir,
> In the line–grove which weather–fends your cell;
> They cannot budge till your release. The king,
> His brother and yours, abide all three distracted
> And the remainder mourning over them,

Brimful of sorrow and dismay; but chiefly
Him that you term'd, sir, 'The good old lord Gonzalo;'
His tears run down his beard, like winter's drops
From eaves of reeds. Your charm so strongly works 'em
That if you now beheld them, your affections
Would become tender.

PROSPERO

Dost thou think so, spirit?

ARIEL

Mine would, sir, were I human.

PROSPERO

And mine shall.
Hast thou, which art but air, a touch, a feeling
Of their afflictions, and shall not myself,
One of their kind, that relish all as sharply,
Passion as they, be kindlier moved than thou art?
Though with their high wrongs I am struck to the quick,
Yet with my nobler reason 'gaitist my fury
Do I take part: the rarer action is
In virtue than in vengeance: they being penitent,
The sole drift of my purpose doth extend
Not a frown further. Go release them, Ariel:
My charms I'll break, their senses I'll restore,
And they shall be themselves.

ARIEL

I'll fetch them, sir.

471

Exit

PROSPERO

> Ye elves of hills, brooks, standing lakes and groves,
> And ye that on the sands with printless foot
> Do chase the ebbing Neptune and do fly him
> When he comes back; you demi–puppets that
> By moonshine do the green sour ringlets make,
> Whereof the ewe not bites, and you whose pastime
> Is to make midnight mushrooms, that rejoice
> To hear the solemn curfew; by whose aid,
> Weak masters though ye be, I have bedimm'd
> The noontide sun, call'd forth the mutinous winds,
> And 'twixt the green sea and the azured vault
> Set roaring war: to the dread rattling thunder
> Have I given fire and rifted Jove's stout oak
> With his own bolt; the strong–based promontory
> Have I made shake and by the spurs pluck'd up
> The pine and cedar: graves at my command
> Have waked their sleepers, oped, and let 'em forth
> By my so potent art. But this rough magic
> I here abjure, and, when I have required
> Some heavenly music, which even now I do,
> To work mine end upon their senses that
> This airy charm is for, I'll break my staff,
> Bury it certain fathoms in the earth,
> And deeper than did ever plummet sound
> I'll drown my book.

Solemn music

Re–enter ARIEL before: then ALONSO, with a frantic gesture, attended by GONZALO; SEBASTIAN and ANTONIO in like manner, attended by ADRIAN and FRANCISCO they all enter the circle which PROSPERO

472

had made, and there stand charmed; which PROSPERO observing,
speaks:

A solemn air and the best comforter
To an unsettled fancy cure thy brains,
Now useless, boil'd within thy skull! There stand,
For you are spell–stopp'd.
Holy Gonzalo, honourable man,
Mine eyes, even sociable to the show of thine,
Fall fellowly drops. The charm dissolves apace,
And as the morning steals upon the night,
Melting the darkness, so their rising senses
Begin to chase the ignorant fumes that mantle
Their clearer reason. O good Gonzalo,
My true preserver, and a loyal sir
To him you follow'st! I will pay thy graces
Home both in word and deed. Most cruelly
Didst thou, Alonso, use me and my daughter:
Thy brother was a furtherer in the act.
Thou art pinch'd fort now, Sebastian. Flesh and blood,
You, brother mine, that entertain'd ambition,
Expell'd remorse and nature; who, with Sebastian,
Whose inward pinches therefore are most strong,
Would here have kill'd your king; I do forgive thee,
Unnatural though thou art. Their understanding
Begins to swell, and the approaching tide
Will shortly fill the reasonable shore
That now lies foul and muddy. Not one of them
That yet looks on me, or would know me Ariel,
Fetch me the hat and rapier in my cell:
I will discase me, and myself present
As I was sometime Milan: quickly, spirit;
Thou shalt ere long be free.

ARIEL sings and helps to attire him

Where the bee sucks. there suck I:
In a cowslip's bell I lie;
There I couch when owls do cry.
On the bat's back I do fly
After summer merrily.
Merrily, merrily shall I live now
Under the blossom that hangs on the bough.

PROSPERO

Why, that's my dainty Ariel! I shall miss thee:
But yet thou shalt have freedom: so, so, so.
To the king's ship, invisible as thou art:
There shalt thou find the mariners asleep
Under the hatches; the master and the boatswain
Being awake, enforce them to this place,
And presently, I prithee.

ARIEL

I drink the air before me, and return
Or ere your pulse twice beat.

Exit

GONZALO

All torment, trouble, wonder and amazement
Inhabits here: some heavenly power guide us
Out of this fearful country!

PROSPERO

Behold, sir king,
The wronged Duke of Milan, Prospero:
For more assurance that a living prince
Does now speak to thee, I embrace thy body;
And to thee and thy company I bid
A hearty welcome.

ALONSO

Whether thou best he or no,
Or some enchanted trifle to abuse me,
As late I have been, I not know: thy pulse
Beats as of flesh and blood; and, since I saw thee,
The affliction of my mind amends, with which,
I fear, a madness held me: this must crave,
An if this be at all, a most strange story.
Thy dukedom I resign and do entreat
Thou pardon me my wrongs. But how should Prospero
Be living and be here?

PROSPERO

First, noble friend,
Let me embrace thine age, whose honour cannot
Be measured or confined.

GONZALO

Whether this be
Or be not, I'll not swear.

PROSPERO

You do yet taste
Some subtilties o' the isle, that will not let you
Believe things certain. Welcome, my friends all!

Aside to SEBASTIAN and ANTONIO

But you, my brace of lords, were I so minded,
I here could pluck his highness' frown upon you
And justify you traitors: at this time
I will tell no tales.

SEBASTIAN

[Aside] The devil speaks in him.

PROSPERO

No.
For you, most wicked sir, whom to call brother
Would even infect my mouth, I do forgive
Thy rankest fault; all of them; and require
My dukedom of thee, which perforce, I know,
Thou must restore.

ALONSO

If thou be'st Prospero,
Give us particulars of thy preservation;
How thou hast met us here, who three hours since
Were wreck'd upon this shore; where I have lost—
How sharp the point of this remembrance is!—
My dear son Ferdinand.

PROSPERO

I am woe for't, sir.

ALONSO

Irreparable is the loss, and patience
Says it is past her cure.

PROSPERO

I rather think
You have not sought her help, of whose soft grace
For the like loss I have her sovereign aid
And rest myself content.

ALONSO

You the like loss!

PROSPERO

As great to me as late; and, supportable
To make the dear loss, have I means much weaker
Than you may call to comfort you, for I
Have lost my daughter.

ALONSO

A daughter?
O heavens, that they were living both in Naples,
The king and queen there! that they were, I wish
Myself were mudded in that oozy bed

Where my son lies. When did you lose your daughter?

PROSPERO

In this last tempest. I perceive these lords
At this encounter do so much admire
That they devour their reason and scarce think
Their eyes do offices of truth, their words
Are natural breath: but, howsoe'er you have
Been justled from your senses, know for certain
That I am Prospero and that very duke
Which was thrust forth of Milan, who most strangely
Upon this shore, where you were wreck'd, was landed,
To be the lord on't. No more yet of this;
For 'tis a chronicle of day by day,
Not a relation for a breakfast nor
Befitting this first meeting. Welcome, sir;
This cell's my court: here have I few attendants
And subjects none abroad: pray you, look in.
My dukedom since you have given me again,
I will requite you with as good a thing;
At least bring forth a wonder, to content ye
As much as me my dukedom.

Here PROSPERO discovers FERDINAND and MIRANDA playing at chess

MIRANDA

Sweet lord, you play me false.

FERDINAND

No, my dear'st love,
I would not for the world.

MIRANDA

Yes, for a score of kingdoms you should wrangle,
And I would call it, fair play.

ALONSO

If this prove
A vision of the Island, one dear son
Shall I twice lose.

SEBASTIAN

A most high miracle!

FERDINAND

Though the seas threaten, they are merciful;
I have cursed them without cause.

Kneels

ALONSO

Now all the blessings
Of a glad father compass thee about!
Arise, and say how thou camest here.

MIRANDA

O, wonder!
How many goodly creatures are there here!
How beauteous mankind is! O brave new world,
That has such people in't!

PROSPERO

'Tis new to thee.

ALONSO

What is this maid with whom thou wast at play?
Your eld'st acquaintance cannot be three hours:
Is she the goddess that hath sever'd us,
And brought us thus together?

FERDINAND

Sir, she is mortal;
But by immortal Providence she's mine:
I chose her when I could not ask my father
For his advice, nor thought I had one. She
Is daughter to this famous Duke of Milan,
Of whom so often I have heard renown,
But never saw before; of whom I have
Received a second life; and second father
This lady makes him to me.

ALONSO

I am hers:
But, O, how oddly will it sound that I
Must ask my child forgiveness!

PROSPERO

There, sir, stop:
Let us not burthen our remembrance with
A heaviness that's gone.

GONZALO

I have inly wept,
Or should have spoke ere this. Look down, you god,
And on this couple drop a blessed crown!
For it is you that have chalk'd forth the way
Which brought us hither.

ALONSO

I say, Amen, Gonzalo!

GONZALO

Was Milan thrust from Milan, that his issue
Should become kings of Naples? O, rejoice
Beyond a common joy, and set it down
With gold on lasting pillars: In one voyage
Did Claribel her husband find at Tunis,
And Ferdinand, her brother, found a wife
Where he himself was lost, Prospero his dukedom
In a poor isle and all of us ourselves
When no man was his own.

ALONSO

[To FERDINAND and MIRANDA] Give me your hands:
Let grief and sorrow still embrace his heart
That doth not wish you joy!

GONZALO

Be it so! Amen!

Re-enter ARIEL, with the Master and Boatswain amazedly following

O, look, sir, look, sir! here is more of us:
I prophesied, if a gallows were on land,
This fellow could not drown. Now, blasphemy,
That swear'st grace o'erboard, not an oath on shore?
Hast thou no mouth by land? What is the news?

Boatswain

The best news is, that we have safely found
Our king and company; the next, our ship—
Which, but three glasses since, we gave out split—
Is tight and yare and bravely rigg'd as when
We first put out to sea.

ARIEL

[Aside to PROSPERO] Sir, all this service
Have I done since I went.

PROSPERO

[Aside to ARIEL] My tricksy spirit!

ALONSO

These are not natural events; they strengthen
From strange to stranger. Say, how came you hither?

Boatswain

If I did think, sir, I were well awake,
I'ld strive to tell you. We were dead of sleep,
And—how we know not—all clapp'd under hatches;
Where but even now with strange and several noises
Of roaring, shrieking, howling, jingling chains,
And more diversity of sounds, all horrible,
We were awaked; straightway, at liberty;
Where we, in all her trim, freshly beheld
Our royal, good and gallant ship, our master
Capering to eye her: on a trice, so please you,
Even in a dream, were we divided from them
And were brought moping hither.

ARIEL

[Aside to PROSPERO] Was't well done?

PROSPERO

[Aside to ARIEL] Bravely, my diligence. Thou shalt be free.

ALONSO

This is as strange a maze as e'er men trod
And there is in this business more than nature
Was ever conduct of: some oracle
Must rectify our knowledge.

PROSPERO

Sir, my liege,
Do not infest your mind with beating on
The strangeness of this business; at pick'd leisure
Which shall be shortly, single I'll resolve you,
Which to you shall seem probable, of every
These happen'd accidents; till when, be cheerful
And think of each thing well.

Aside to ARIEL

Come hither, spirit:
Set Caliban and his companions free;
Untie the spell.

Exit ARIEL

How fares my gracious sir?
There are yet missing of your company
Some few odd lads that you remember not.

*Re−enter ARIEL, driving in CALIBAN, STEPHANO and TRINCULO, in
their stolen apparel*

STEPHANO

Every man shift for all the rest, and
let no man take care for himself; for all is
but fortune. Coragio, bully–monster, coragio!

TRINCULO

If these be true spies which I wear in my head,
here's a goodly sight.

CALIBAN

O Setebos, these be brave spirits indeed!
How fine my master is! I am afraid
He will chastise me.

SEBASTIAN

Ha, ha!
What things are these, my lord Antonio?
Will money buy 'em?

ANTONIO

Very like; one of them
Is a plain fish, and, no doubt, marketable.

PROSPERO

Mark but the badges of these men, my lords,
Then say if they be true. This mis–shapen knave,
His mother was a witch, and one so strong

That could control the moon, make flows and ebbs,
And deal in her command without her power.
These three have robb'd me; and this demi—devil—
For he's a bastard one—had plotted with them
To take my life. Two of these fellows you
Must know and own; this thing of darkness!
Acknowledge mine.

CALIBAN

I shall be pinch'd to death.

ALONSO

Is not this Stephano, my drunken butler?

SEBASTIAN

He is drunk now: where had he wine?

ALONSO

And Trinculo is reeling ripe: where should they
Find this grand liquor that hath gilded 'em?
How camest thou in this pickle?

TRINCULO

I have been in such a pickle since I
saw you last that, I fear me, will never out of
my bones: I shall not fear fly—blowing.

SEBASTIAN

Why, how now, Stephano!

STEPHANO

O, touch me not; I am not Stephano, but a cramp.

PROSPERO

You'ld be king o' the isle, sirrah?

STEPHANO

I should have been a sore one then.

ALONSO

This is a strange thing as e'er I look'd on.

Pointing to Caliban

PROSPERO

He is as disproportion'd in his manners
As in his shape. Go, sirrah, to my cell;
Take with you your companions; as you look
To have my pardon, trim it handsomely.

CALIBAN

Ay, that I will; and I'll be wise hereafter
And seek for grace. What a thrice–double ass
Was I, to take this drunkard for a god
And worship this dull fool!

PROSPERO

Go to; away!

ALONSO

Hence, and bestow your luggage where you found it.

SEBASTIAN

Or stole it, rather.

Exeunt CALIBAN, STEPHANO, and TRINCULO

PROSPERO

Sir, I invite your highness and your train
To my poor cell, where you shall take your rest
For this one night; which, part of it, I'll waste
With such discourse as, I not doubt, shall make it
Go quick away; the story of my life
And the particular accidents gone by
Since I came to this isle: and in the morn
I'll bring you to your ship and so to Naples,
Where I have hope to see the nuptial
Of these our dear–beloved solemnized;
And thence retire me to my Milan, where
Every third thought shall be my grave.

ALONSO

I long
To hear the story of your life, which must
Take the ear strangely.

488

PROSPERO

I'll deliver all;
And promise you calm seas, auspicious gales
And sail so expeditious that shall catch
Your royal fleet far off.

Aside to ARIEL

My Ariel, chick,
That is thy charge: then to the elements
Be free, and fare thou well! Please you, draw near.

Exeunt

EPILOGUE

SPOKEN BY PROSPERO

Now my charms are all o'erthrown,
And what strength I have's mine own,
Which is most faint: now, 'tis true,
I must be here confined by you,
Or sent to Naples. Let me not,
Since I have my dukedom got
And pardon'd the deceiver, dwell
In this bare island by your spell;
But release me from my bands
With the help of your good hands:
Gentle breath of yours my sails
Must fill, or else my project fails,
Which was to please. Now I want
Spirits to enforce, art to enchant,

Twelth Night, A Winter's Tale, The Tempest

And my ending is despair,
Unless I be relieved by prayer,
Which pierces so that it assaults
Mercy itself and frees all faults.
As you from crimes would pardon'd be,
Let your indulgence set me free.

Printed in the United Kingdom
by Lightning Source UK Ltd.
102473UKS00001B/59-60